JACKPOT!

*Nurturing **Student Investment***
*Through **Assessment***

NICOLE
DIMICH

CASSANDRA
ERKENS

TOM
SCHIMMER

Solution Tree | Press
a division of
Solution Tree

the **Solution Tree**
Assessment Center

555 North Morton Street
Bloomington, IN 47404
800.733.6786 (toll free) / 812.336.7700
FAX: 812.336.7790

email: info@SolutionTree.com
SolutionTree.com

Visit **go.SolutionTree.com/assessment** to download the free reproducibles in this book.

Printed in the United States of America

Library of Congress Cataloging-in-Publication Data

Names: Erkens, Cassandra, author. | Schimmer, Tom, author. | Dimich,
    Nicole, author.
Title: Jackpot! : nurturing student investment through assessment /
    Cassandra Erkens, Tom Schimmer, Nicole Dimich.
Description: Bloomington, IN : Solution Tree Press, [2022] | Includes
    bibliographical references and index.
Identifiers: LCCN 2022007901 (print) | LCCN 2022007902 (ebook) | ISBN
    9781943874804 (paperback) | ISBN 9781943874811 (ebook)
Subjects: LCSH: Motivation in education. | Educational tests and
    measurements. | Effective teaching.
Classification: LCC LB1065 .E75 2022 (print) | LCC LB1065 (ebook) | DDC
    370.15/4--dc23
LC record available at https://lccn.loc.gov/2022007901
LC ebook record available at https://lccn.loc.gov/2022007902

Solution Tree
Jeffrey C. Jones, CEO
Edmund M. Ackerman, President

Solution Tree Press
President and Publisher: Douglas M. Rife
Associate Publisher: Sarah Payne-Mills
Managing Production Editor: Kendra Slayton
Editorial Director: Todd Brakke
Art Director: Rian Anderson
Copy Chief: Jessi Finn
Production Editor: Alissa Voss
Content Development Specialist: Amy Rubenstein
Copy Editor: Jessi Finn
Proofreader: Elijah Oates
Text and Cover Designer: Abigail Bowen
Associate Editor: Sarah Ludwig
Editorial Assistants: Charlotte Jones and Elijah Oates

ACKNOWLEDGMENTS

This book is dedicated to *you*. If you are reading it, then it's safe to assume you are intentionally striving to engage learners in the most profound work of their lifetimes: learning to learn so they can become jackpots on their own.

Thank you for embracing this work!

With gratitude,
Nicole, Cassie, and Tom

Solution Tree Press would like to thank the following reviewers:

John D. Ewald
Education Consultant
Former Superintendent, Principal, Teacher
Frederick, Maryland

Thomas Krawczewicz
Director of Educational Resources
DeMatha Catholic High School
Hyattsville, Maryland

Johanna Josaphat
Social Studies Teacher
The Urban Assembly Unison School
Brooklyn, New York

Karen Matteson
District Instructional Coach and
 Math Specialist
Cortland Enlarged City School District
Cortland, New York

Brian Kenney
Principal
Whittier Elementary School
Clinton, Iowa

Visit **go.SolutionTree.com/assessment** to download the free reproducibles in this book.

TABLE OF CONTENTS

Reproducibles are in italics.

3 | *Assessment Architecture* *59*

4 | *Interpretation of Results* *85*

5 | *Communication* *109*

6   *Instructional Agility* *139*

Epilogue *179*

References and Resources *185*

Index *195*

ABOUT THE AUTHORS

Nicole Dimich has a passion for education and lifelong learning, which has led her to extensively explore, facilitate, and implement innovative practices in school transformation. She works with elementary and secondary educators in presentations, trainings, and consultations that address today's most critical issues, all in the spirit of facilitating increased student learning and confidence.

Nicole was a school transformation specialist, where she coached individual teachers and teams of teachers in assessment, literacy, and high expectations for all students. Nicole was also a program evaluator and trainer at the Princeton Center for Leadership Training in New Jersey. A former middle and high school English teacher, she is committed to making schools into places where all students feel invested and successful.

A featured presenter at conferences internationally, Nicole empowers educators to build their capacity for and implement engaging assessment design, formative assessment practices, common assessment design and analysis, response to intervention (RTI) systems, data-driven decisions, student work protocols, and motivational strategies.

Nicole is the executive director of Thrive Ed, a nonprofit working to fundamentally transform education by empowering students, teachers, and leadership teams to innovate and thrive. Nicole earned a master of arts degree in human development from Saint Mary's University and a bachelor of arts degree in English and psychology from Concordia College.

Nicole is the author of *Design in Five: Essential Phases to Create Engaging Assessment Practice* and the coauthor of multiple books, including *Motivating Students: 25 Strategies to Light the Fire of Engagement*, *Growing Tomorrow's Citizens in Today's Classrooms: Assessing Seven Critical Competencies*, *Instructional Agility: Responding to Assessment With Real-Time Decisions*, and *Essential Assessment: Six Tenets for Bringing Hope, Efficacy, and*

Achievement to the Classroom. She has also contributed to the best-selling *The Teacher as Assessment Leader* and *The Principal as Assessment Leader* series.

To learn more about Nicole's work, visit http://allthingsassessment.info or follow @NicoleDimich on Twitter.

Cassandra Erkens is a presenter, facilitator, coach, trainer of trainers, keynote speaker, author, and above all, teacher. She presents nationally and internationally on assessment, instruction, school improvement, and Professional Learning Communities at Work® (PLCs at Work).

Cassandra has served as an adjunct faculty member at Hamline and Cardinal Stritch universities, where she took teachers through graduate education courses. She has authored and coauthored a wide array of published trainings, and she has designed and delivered the training-of-trainers programs for two major education-based companies.

As an educator and recognized leader, Cassandra has served as a senior high school English teacher, director of staff development at the district level, regional school improvement facilitator, and director of staff and organization development in the private sector.

Cassandra is the author of *Collaborative Common Assessments: Teamwork. Instruction. Results.*, *The Handbook for Collaborative Common Assessments: Tools for Design, Delivery, and Data Analysis*, and *Making Homework Matter*, and the coauthor of *Leading by Design: An Action Framework for PLC at Work Leaders*, *Growing Tomorrow's Citizens in Today's Classrooms: Assessing Seven Critical Competencies*, *Instructional Agility: Responding to Assessment With Real-Time Decisions*, and *Essential Assessment: Six Tenets for Bringing Hope, Efficacy, and Achievement to the Classroom*. She has also contributed to *The Teacher as Assessment Leader* and *The Principal as Assessment Leader* as well as *The Collaborative Teacher: Working Together as a Professional Learning Community* and *The Collaborative Administrator: Working Together as a Professional Learning Community*.

To learn more about Cassandra's work, visit http://allthingsassessment.info or follow @cerkens on Twitter.

Tom Schimmer is an author and a speaker with expertise in assessment, grading, leadership, and behavioral support. Tom is a former district-level leader, school administrator, and teacher. As a district-level leader, he was a member of the senior management team responsible for overseeing the efforts to support and build the instructional and assessment capacities of teachers and administrators.

Tom is a sought-after speaker who presents internationally for schools and districts. He has worked extensively throughout North America, as well as nineteen other countries. He earned a teaching degree from Boise State University and a master's degree in curriculum and instruction from the University of British Columbia.

Tom is the author and coauthor of multiple books, including *Growing Tomorrow's Citizens in Today's Classrooms: Assessing Seven Critical Competencies, Standards-Based Learning in Action: Moving From Theory to Practice, Instructional Agility: Responding to Assessment With Real-Time Decisions, Essential Assessment: Six Tenets for Bringing Hope, Efficacy, and Achievement to the Classroom*, and *Grading From the Inside Out: Bringing Accuracy to Student Assessment Through a Standards-Based Mindset*.

To learn more about Tom's work, visit http://allthingsassessment.info or follow @TomSchimmer on Twitter.

To book Nicole Dimich, Cassandra Erkens, or Tom Schimmer for professional development, contact pd@SolutionTree.com.

INTRODUCTION

It's a common complaint among educators that schools are places students go to watch teachers work very hard. Earnest but frustrated teachers often bemoan students as increasingly less motivated, less willing, less interested, and all around less concerned about what it takes to learn in deep and meaningful ways. Though a blanket categorization can never apply to all students, the perceived population of disengaged learners or intentional non-learners seems large enough to warrant the common lament that "today's students just don't seem to care" throughout the K–12, and even postsecondary, system. That perception is supported in the research, as numerous studies show that secondary and college students, for example, are increasingly apathetic and disengaged from their schooling and that student disengagement is not restricted to any finite demographic or underrepresented group (Yacek & Jonas, 2019). Even before the COVID-19 pandemic, a 2017 report by FutureEd at Georgetown University noted the following about American students:

> More than 7 million students nationwide miss three weeks or more of school, a level of absenteeism linked to significantly diminished academic performance. A fifth of the nation's schools report that 20 percent or more of their students are chronically absent. No state is untouched by the problem. (Jordan & Miller, 2017, p. 1)

What happened? Are students lazier? Did captivating, dynamic media displays lure them away from boring, stagnant texts? Did digital tools pamper them into listless detachment? Is it a teacher issue? A student issue? Or did the systems that schools traditionally employ to require learning gradually become less effective as generations changed?

Student investment is the jackpot of education, prized yet elusive. Educators and even noneducators consider student investment *the* precursor to profound and life-long learning. Teaching would be so much easier if all students were invested in their own learning. Learners would be interested, motivated, self-driven, reflective, and goal oriented. More than that, students would become keen decision makers in service of increasing their own academic achievement.

Assessment practices "must build hope, efficacy, and achievement for learners and teachers" (Erkens, Schimmer, & Dimich, 2017, p. 5). In this learning environment, the following six tenets ground all assessment policies and practices (Erkens et al., 2017).

1. **Student investment** occurs when assessment and self-regulation have a symbiotic relationship.

2. The **communication of assessment results** must generate productive responses from learners and all the stakeholders who support them.

3. **Assessment architecture** is most effective when it is planned, purposeful, and intentionally sequenced in advance of instruction by all of those responsible for the delivery.

4. **Assessment purposes** (formative and summative) must be interdependent to maximize learning and verify achievement.

5. **Instructional agility** occurs when emerging evidence informs real-time modifications within the context of the expected learning.

6. The **interpretation of assessment results** must be accurate, accessible, and reliable.

A learning-rich culture provides opportunities for taking risks, failing productively, and celebrating successes.

Student investment is critically important to teaching and assessment processes if teachers are to excite, elicit, nurture, and challenge the very best in each student. It is a broad category that incorporates all the ideal traits (passion, persistence, commitment), behaviors (focus, energy, effort), and discrete self-regulation skills (self-assessing, self-reflecting, setting goals, soliciting feedback) students would need to commit to learning until they attain proficiency, or at best, mastery.

Without the ability to access or inspire a learner's personal investment, a teacher cannot partner with the student, rendering the teacher's best instructional efforts insufficient to the task at hand. Of the six interrelated tenets in the assessment framework (Erkens et al., 2017; see figure I.1), student investment is the only tenet for which the ultimate control source lies within the student, not the teacher. So, teachers can strategically design for student investment to occur, but they can never completely control for it as they can for the other tenets of the framework.

Fortunately, when teachers implement the other five tenets, they can generally inspire student investment. Without student investment, it would be nearly impossible for any educational system to meet its primary goal of increasing hope, efficacy,

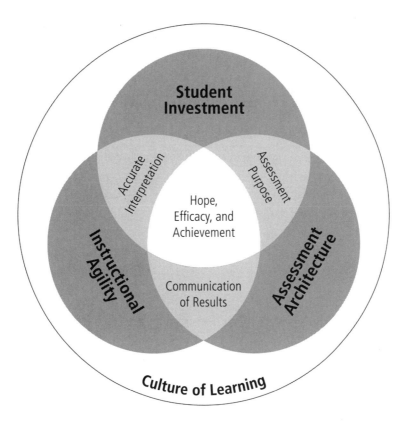

Source: Erkens et al., 2017, p. 6.

Figure I.1: *The six assessment tenets framework.*

and achievement for all learners. While it can feel as if the onus for investing rests solely in the hands of each learner, the truth is that it's up to educators to create the conditions and implement the practices necessary to build hope, efficacy, and achievement, consistently noticing and adjusting their strategies as they relentlessly pursue options for students to invest in their learning. The following sections examine why student investment is so elusive, discuss common practices that undermine student investment, and outline how this book will support your efforts to invest students in their own learning.

Why Student Investment Is Elusive

Everyday conversations in a school can quickly reveal that educators place a premium on perseverance, attention to precision, risk taking, and mistake making. These core components serve deep learning and a commitment to academic achievement and lead to students investing in learning. In short, teachers strive to make the right stuff—namely, investing in personal learning—happen.

So why, then, does student investment seem so elusive for teachers? To be clear, the 21st century teaching force is the best it has ever been, accomplishing improved academic gains with dwindling resources and within increasingly challenging circumstances (DuFour, 2015). So, if teachers are doing their very best *and* achieving more, why is it that students seem to not be investing in their learning?

To be certain, 21st century students are no worse at learning than previous generations of students. In fact, rising technological knowledge, skill, and access among students has clearly illustrated the modern student population is highly engaged in real-world issues and learning about the things that interest them, which aren't always the things educators are striving to teach. A report by the Pew Research Center (Anderson & Jiang, 2018) notes that "YouTube, Instagram and Snapchat are the most popular online platforms among teens. Fully 95% of teens have access to a smartphone, and 45% say they are online 'almost constantly.'" Learners are not only *consuming* information but also *producing* content on readily accessible platforms.

Learners are organizing their arguments, mobilizing their efforts, and initiating— if not demanding—calls for change in all the present social crises: climate change, gun laws, pandemics, politics, economics, hunger, housing, and social justice issues, to name just a few. Similar to the teaching force, the modern student population might just be the most creative, thoughtful, energetic, passionate, and brilliant young people to date. In any case, swapping out current students for ones teachers perceive to be more invested simply isn't an option. Public and private educational systems alike must reach and teach *all* who come through their doors.

So, if it's not the students and it's not the teachers, then what is impeding students from investing in their own learning in school? When the people operating within the system aren't the problem, it's time to check the system itself (Deming, 1986; Jenkins, 2011; Senge et al., 2012). Educational consultant Lee Jenkins (2011) notes, "When students have their intrinsic motivation removed, system problems are dominating" (p. 12). Do the assessment practices most commonly employed in a traditional education system align with the values educators hold most dear? Might the practices themselves be undermining the tenet of student investment?

How Practices Can Undermine Student Investment

The self-regulation of learning occurs when students set goals and then carry out the necessary cognitive, affective, and behavioral processes designed to help them reach those goals (Zimmerman & Schunk, 2011). Whether organized into three phases (Zimmerman, 2011) or four (Pintrich & Zusho, 2002), self-regulation is most often presented as a cyclical model of phases or sequences that occur as students progress toward proficiency. While these phases are not separate silos that students mechanically move through, assessment and grading expert Susan M. Brookhart (2013a) says conceptualizing self-regulation as a series of steps is helpful in order to cross self-regulation with classroom assessment. Thus, teachers can use the process of classroom assessment to teach students to be more self-regulatory—in other words, more *invested*—in their learning.

Professor D. Royce Sadler (1989) theorizes formative assessment as being a model for how students could monitor their own learning. Sadler's (1989) three conditions for students are "(a) an understanding of their performance goals; (b) an opportunity to compare performance goals with actual performance; and (c) an opportunity to close the gap between their desired performance and actual performance" (p. 121). These three conditions perfectly align with educational researcher Barry J. Zimmerman's (2011) three phases of self-regulation: (1) forethought, (2) performance, and (3) reflection. This laid the foundation for how formative assessment can be operationalized in classrooms: teachers can use the cycle of formative assessment to teach students to be more self-regulatory—more invested—in their learning.

Sometimes, schools start the process by teaching students self-regulation strategies in the hope that such work will activate the intrinsic motivation and intentional agency required for learning. However, the underpinnings of a student's willingness and ability to self-regulate are interdependent, so if even one belief or practice (a policy, procedure, tradition, and so on) misaligns, the desired result can fall miserably short. A strategy out of alignment with policies, such as grading practices, or offered in isolation from a greater context of other conditions only leads to *self-regulation lite*.

There are four common assumptions that gird self-regulation lite efforts.

1. Learners' understanding of a growth mindset motivates them to develop one.

2. Providing feedback on learners' effort encourages them to continue trying.

3. Providing self-assessment and reflection tools triggers students' ability and interest in naturally continuing the processes.

4. Providing data notebooks inspires learners to assess themselves, set goals, monitor their own progress, and increase their own achievement.

Though well-intended desires underpin each assumption, the desires alone will not suffice. And while it's true that people can *behave* their way into believing, consistent practice opportunities for self-talking, goal setting, or data tracking will be equally insufficient if the bigger system does not allow for the mastery of standards born of productive failure and intellectual risk taking.

Collectively, systems components such as imbalanced assessment systems, unreliable scoring protocols, conflicting interpretations of proficiency or mastery, unproductive feedback, heavy evaluation efforts, inconsistent grading practices, ineffective grading and reporting policies, clunky reassessment protocols, and a competitive culture can undermine a single teacher's or even a grade level's or department's best efforts to maximize student success. The first step toward transforming individuals or a team will be disingenuous if not embedded in a large-scale, whole-system change (Deming, 1993; Jenkins, 2011; Senge et al., 2012).

As far back as 1986, author, consultant, and systems thinker W. Edwards Deming noted that rampant large-scale concerns are more often systems issues than people issues—from the provider to the consumer, or in education, from the teacher to the student. Attaining true and consistent student achievement requires deep, systematic change. It requires every educator in the system to examine the school's culture, attend to the educators' mindsets, and then analyze, dismantle, edit, or generate the practices and policies that will be essential for students to truly and permanently invest in their individual learning.

About This Book

This book is patterned on the illuminating framework for professional learning communities (PLCs) offered in *Learning by Doing: A Handbook for Professional Learning Communities at Work* (DuFour, DuFour, Eaker, Many, & Mattos, 2016). Its six chapters explore the five assessment framework tenets that support the sixth tenet of student investment, and the overarching framework of focusing on hope, efficacy, and achievement while creating a culture that supports intellectual risk taking and productive failure. This book isolates each feature to explore the interdependent features that inhibit or facilitate students' ability to invest. Each chapter includes seven parts.

- **Part 1: Case Study.** Each chapter begins with a glimpse into a real-life teacher's well-intended efforts to increase student investment that went astray, along with a follow-up analysis of what went wrong.

- **Part 2: Celebrations and Considerations.** Although the case studies presented ultimately fail in their aims, each one contains strategies to celebrate. This section analyzes the strengths of the case studies, presenting research to support why such strategies are effective.

- **Part 3: Action to Take.** This section considers the research underpinning the components missing from the case study strategies and provides suggestions for more thoughtful implementation.

- **Part 4: A Learning Continuum for Implementation.** When applying new interventions, educators often need a continuum of implementation so they can monitor both their own and their students' progress. This section contains tools to help educators scaffold their strategy implementation as they move forward or, occasionally, backward in their implementation journey.

- **Part 5: Tips for Moving Forward.** These lists of tips can help educators avoid the most common pitfalls when generating student investment.

- **Part 6: Questions to Guide Your Conversations With Students.** This section provides key questions to facilitate conversations with students while monitoring for effectiveness on student investment.

- **Part 7: Dangerous Detours and Seductive Shortcuts.** Finally, this section outlines common pitfalls and easily made errors that have the potential to derail even the best-laid plans for implementation. By avoiding these shortcomings, educators will be as prepared as possible to ensure their student investment strategies have the best possible chances of success.

Before students can deeply invest, educators must equally invest in revamping the system. As Deming (1986) often explained, the issue is not *who* but rather *what* when it comes to systems failures. Increasing student investment can happen only with educator investment. *Everyone* must think and act differently if educators are to capture and hit the jackpot of education.

CHAPTER 1

HOPE, EFFICACY, AND ACHIEVEMENT IN A LEARNING CULTURE

Setting learning goals helps us to be independent.

—Consensus statement from high school students with individualized education plans

Learning is always risky. A lack of certainty or even clarity on learners' behalf can catapult them into a fear of exposing their perceived naivete and, worse, the threat of failure. In *Essential Assessment*, Erkens, Schimmer, and Dimich (2017) state, "Deep learning requires a posture of vulnerability. In the classroom, learners are always at risk because they must reveal misconceptions and navigate errors while engaging in new ways of thinking or acting" (p. 133). Rick Stiggins (2008), founder of the Assessment Training Institute in Portland, Oregon, says:

> [Students] decide whether the learning is worth the effort it will take to attain it, or whether trying is worth the risk of public failure. If they come down on the wrong side of these decisions, it doesn't matter what the adults decide. There will be no learning. (p. 232)

For students to invest in their learning, they must be willing to take intellectual risks. This means they understand the cognitive challenges before them, they anticipate and accept the plausibility of errors on the journey, and they maintain a sense of optimism about their potential to succeed. Students' ability to self-regulate is directly proportional to their willingness to engage in intellectual risk taking. To encourage students to take the risks required for deep learning, teachers would be wise to first establish a culture of learning within their classrooms. Teachers can enhance student investment and its associated constructs of hope, efficacy, and achievement by creating a learning culture that supports intellectual risk taking, productive failure, and a growth mindset (Dweck, 2016).

Part 1: Case Study

As a second-grade teacher, Ms. Merrie knew how important it was to create a culture of learning in her classroom. She wanted her learners to take risks, make mistakes, and learn deeply, and she believed that culture mattered, so she was careful to create a cheerful and nurturing environment. She wanted to make sure her students maintained a sense of hope and efficacy while they worked to increase their personal achievement levels. Because her students were in second grade, Ms. Merrie knew she'd already have to retrain them to learn to be learners.

She set about creating brightly colored posters that highlighted important things to know about learning. For example, one of her posters offered students eight different things they could say when she called on them instead of saying, "I don't know." Another poster gave her students growth mindset thoughts to consider when faced with a challenge instead of the fixed mindset thoughts they were likely experiencing. For example, if a student felt she was failing at mathematics, she should avoid saying, "I quit," and instead say, "I should try something different." Likewise, if a student felt overwhelmed, he should say, "My first attempt did not work, but my second attempt is sure to be better." Ms. Merrie loved the encouraging messages she found all over her walls.

Ms. Merrie was also careful to model trying to talk the right way in the right moments. She created catchphrases she could use when she saw students struggle. The three statements she loved and repeated the most were as follows.

1. "It's OK to make mistakes in my classroom as long as you work harder to improve."

2. "If you don't understand what you're supposed to be doing, be sure to ask a friend."

3. "Why don't you take a minute and have a little think about that so you can make a better choice."

She believed these statements would help her students continue to feel empowered so they could solve some of their own questions and concerns. If she redirected their thoughts and spoke to them as if they were capable, then her students would become invested and capable of self-regulating by the end of the year.

In addition to setting the right tone, Ms. Merrie knew she'd have to teach reflection and self-assessment strategies to ensure the activities were meaningful. Goal setting would naturally incorporate both reflection and self-assessment, so Ms. Merrie started there. And, to make it manageable as she got started, she decided to begin in just one course—mathematics. It was a great fit because in her experience, second graders most often needed to improve their mathematics scores.

She went through the textbook and found the daily learning goal and the assessment that the students would use to do the work. She wrote both the goal and the assessment page numbers on the whiteboard so students could easily transfer the information to their goal sheets. Every day, when the students entered the mathematics lesson, they saw the new learning goal for the day on the board (for example, "I can skip-count" or "I can compare numbers up to 100"). Their first activity was to write the goal at the top of a fresh page for their goal folder. Underneath the goal they transcribed, they wrote the page number for their practice work, and next to that assessment page number, they would put their score after the assessment was corrected.

Once the unit was complete, the students added up how many questions they answered correctly during the unit, but they often needed help when the numbers got big. When they determined their total, Ms. Merrie would show them what their number equated to as a grade. After Ms. Merrie assigned their final grade for a unit, the students emptied their goal folders to start the process all over again with new goal sheets for the next unit.

Once the goal sheets were in place, Ms. Merrie decided students should be able to talk about how they were doing in mathematics with their parents. She began adding a line for parent signatures at the bottom of a few goal sheets and would periodically have the students ask their parents or guardians to sign off on them to indicate that these conversations had occurred.

It was a good plan—in theory. It should have helped students personalize and track what was happening in their mathematics textbook, but Ms. Merrie immediately noticed that many students were not good at understanding, much less discussing, the mathematics goals. The goal-transcription process became stressful for students and teacher alike. Ms. Merrie found herself checking everyone's goals before they even began. Worse, parents began to complain through phone calls and emails that mathematics lessons were turning into transcribing lessons, and they didn't understand what they were supposed to be doing with the goal sheets the students brought home.

After three units of using the new mathematics goal sheets, Ms. Merrie was ready to throw in the towel. The final straw for the goal sheets came when she realized that having the students record their scores on the mathematics pages did nothing to improve the students' achievement by the time the summative assessment took place. To her great surprise and even greater dismay, Ms. Merrie worried that her positive posters and reinforcement statements were not working. Her students still seemed worried about making mistakes in mathematics, and a few of them would consistently cast their eyes to the ground when she would advise them to seek counsel from a friend if they felt lost. Maybe, she reasoned, this work was just too hard for second graders.

Reflection

As a well-intentioned and well-informed teacher, Ms. Merrie understood that she must use the assessment process to monitor and increase her students' achievement levels. She grasped the purpose of assessment as a vehicle to "build hope, efficacy, and achievement for learners and teachers" (Erkens et al., 2017, p. 5). Because two-thirds of that equation (hope and efficacy) live in the affective realm, Ms. Merrie recognized the need to create a positive learning culture so her students could invest deeply in their own learning. She was careful to address that first before implementing goal sheets. But even with her attention to that detail, her efforts clearly weren't working. Her students did not seem to believe her empowering words, her encouragement of developing a growth mindset, and her goal orientation. What went wrong? Why weren't students investing?

Part 2: Celebrations and Considerations

Like many teachers, Ms. Merrie desired to create a highly engaged classroom in which students invested in their own well-being and ultimate success. It's worth noting and celebrating that Ms. Merrie tried to put in place *many* features she knew were part of the robust, comprehensive system required to support self-regulation among students. Likewise, she understood she would need to teach new processes and ways of thinking, so she created and integrated scaffolds like goal templates and future-oriented growth mindset stems to inform and guide her students through the processes she was expecting of them.

Because culture matters, Ms. Merrie was careful to address that first, telling students that making mistakes was an important part of the learning journey. She knew creating the groundwork for intellectual risk taking was an important precursor to engaging students in self-regulation activities like setting and monitoring learning goals. She would need to begin with a positive culture that fostered growth so her students could invest deeply in their own learning. She also realized that she would require direct instruction to lead all her students in the right direction. Self-regulation activities involve certain skills that are not magically preprogrammed into all learners. If she didn't teach these skills explicitly, especially in a traditionally evaluative environment, only a few students would grasp the significance of their errors, independently correct their thinking, and then commit to continued learning.

So, Ms. Merrie paid attention to the language both she and her students used when they came upon challenges that would involve intellectual risk. In concrete ways, Ms. Merrie tried to get her students to behave their way into thinking differently. Moreover, she tried to reinforce her words with age-appropriate scaffolds such as brightly colored anchor charts with key prompts for goal setting as well as verbal modeling of the appropriate types of thinking when one encounters a complex problem or mistake. All these efforts were intended to lead students closer to understanding the importance of and the process for setting goals and tracking progress. In her attention to culture, Ms. Merrie successfully included many key features that teachers often overlook on the journey to increasing student investment.

Ms. Merrie was also correct that all students would require direct instruction on the self-regulation behaviors of goal setting, self-assessment, and self-reflection. Her laser-like focus on isolating and teaching the self-regulation processes within the discipline of mathematics as a starting point made the work more manageable for both herself and her learners.

Ms. Merrie was clear that without a growth mindset, her students' self-regulation behaviors would be limited to monitoring what existed rather than exploring the unbounded possibilities of what could be. She knew that, more than just a general willingness to re-engage, a true growth orientation could lead to a genuine compulsion to take intellectual risks and learn from potential failure. Growth-oriented learners don't just tolerate failure; rather, they embrace it as an opportunity to deepen their learning (Dweck, 2016; Schumpeter, 2011).

In fact, it seems as if Ms. Merrie thought of everything and cleared a pathway to success with aligned structures and tools to support her students along the way. So why wasn't it working? Why weren't her second-grade students investing as she'd hoped they would?

To begin, true investment involves both focus *and* commitment. Employing strategies like growth mindset thinking stems, learning goals, or self-assessment and reflection activities are fantastic beginnings with the *potential* for deep investment, but they remain hollow activities in any classroom where students do not feel truly empowered to achieve mastery.

In a November 2018 report published by the Education Trust, experts highlight the significance of student-owned, intrinsic features behind genuine commitment such as motivation, focus, and desire in classroom assignments:

> For students to thrive and achieve at high levels, they must be interested
> and emotionally invested in their learning. Why? Because motivation, or

the desire that propels one to do something, leads to engagement, where students are being attentive to their tasks, putting forth positive effort, persisting through challenges, and advancing their ideas and understandings with a sense of intention. (Dabrowski & Marshall, 2018, p. 1)

So, while Ms. Merrie was striving to create a strategic pathway to success, key components were not yet in place in her classroom. Ms. Merrie had created the aesthetics of student investment; she identified and activated some motivational beliefs associated with intellectual risk taking. However, the process itself requires high levels of confidence, efficacy, and hopefulness on the individual student's part, as well as the space for learners to engage in self-determined adaptive learning behaviors. In Ms. Merrie's classroom, students used forms to generate function rather than the other way around. If Ms. Merrie had begun with the ultimate purpose of generating empowered learners, then she would have needed to attend to increasing student interest, empowering student choice, generating student ownership in shared learning expectations, and maintaining a hope-filled environment. As they stood, Ms. Merrie's tools might have been able to teach the cognitive, metacognitive, and behavioral domains for student investment, but they had yet to address the affective domain.

Part 3: Action to Take

To establish a learning culture, educators must build trust and always maintain a stance of empathy, whether they are highlighting student learning gaps with teacher-assigned scores and feedback or asking students to reveal their own gaps through a self-assessment. Even if the imperfect sample of student work is kept private or shared anonymously, the *gap* is exposed for the student. There is an undeniable emotional dynamic in the process of learning.

While a culture can be friendly and inviting through aesthetics, tone, and kind words, the truth is found in the systems of procedures, policies, and expectations, and though the results may not be immediately palpable or visible, such systems can eventually threaten intellectual risk taking if they disadvantage or penalize learners when their initial risks are unsuccessful. In that case, students will disengage altogether, and simply teaching them how to self-regulate within those challenging conditions will not suffice to re-engage them. Teachers wanting to deeply engage learners in the process of self-regulation must maintain the instructional goal of building confidence through identifying winning streaks, highlighting student assets, navigating productive failure with a learning stance, and ultimately, celebrating achievement.

For students to regulate their own way through the potential minefield of intellectual risk taking, teachers must attend to the cognitive, affective, and behavioral domains involved. When exploring the features of self-regulation, Heidi L. Andrade (2013), professor of educational psychology, cites research noting that "every theory of learning includes a mechanism of regulation of learners' thinking, affect, and behavior" (p. 21). *Investing* in one's own learning requires a truly broad spectrum of beliefs and behaviors.

Many of the interdependent skills and self-theories straddle the affective, cognitive, and behavioral domains. Figure 1.1 provides a general outline of the critical competencies required for students to self-regulate. This figure indicates why each competency is critical by outlining how its absence deters a student's ability for self-regulation.

	Domain Explanation	Feature	Definition	Impact on Self-Regulation If Competency Is Missing
Affective Domain	How a learner feels during the experience of learning (This determines how far a learner is willing to continue engaging.)	Hope	The expectation and desire for success	Without hope, self-regulation involves the documentation of minutiae for compliance.
		Efficacy	A personal belief in one's ability and skills to achieve success	Without efficacy, students feel out of control, so efforts to learn feel hit-or-miss—like the lottery.
Cognitive Domain	How a learner thinks about what is happening relative to what needs to be happening	Cognition	The act of thinking and comprehending	Without cognition, students cannot master concepts and skills, so there is little to regulate relative to learning.
		Metacognition	The skill of reflection about one's own thinking or processes	Without metacognition, students are unable to discover, appreciate, and refine who they are as learners and how they learn.
Behavioral Domain	A learner's drive and personal tools or resources employed to engage and adjust along the way so as to ensure mastery	Effort	The exertion of mental or physical power toward a desired outcome	Without effort, learners take a passive stance; they are *led to* rather than *leading toward* their desired outcome.
		Adaptive learning strategies	A self-identified set of preferred skills, strategies, and processes used to overcome the challenges a learner faces	Without intervention strategies, learners cannot reduce the discrepancy between where they are and where they need to be.

Figure 1.1: Critical domains for self-regulation.

To master the competencies of self-regulation, learners must not only acquire a host of skills and beliefs but also learn these in the context of hope and efficacy as it relates to ultimate achievement. The mechanics of self-regulation skills are insufficient to achieve true investment on behalf of students. True investment cannot happen if educators do not first attend to the affective domain; from there, educators can then attend to the cognitive and behavioral domains.

Affective Domain

Each learner enters school with a set of personal aspirations, hopes, dreams, and curiosities. Each also comes preloaded with emotions, attitudes, perceptions, beliefs, and feelings. When attending to the affective domain, teachers must tap into the emotions, interests, values, and motivations that will excite continued learning while simultaneously avoiding the emotions or experiences that will inhibit learning for their students.

Formative assessment expert Dylan Wiliam (2013) notes that students who are fully engaged in learning are always "*both* metacognitively governed *and* affectively charged" (p. 212). The affective domain is tied to how a student feels during the learning process, and it is as important as the cognitive domain when learning. If a student does not *feel* efficacious, hopeful, or competent, the student will often make the decision to opt out.

Wiliam (2013) acknowledges the ultimate decision making always sits with the learner when he states, "As a result of the appraisal, the student activates energy and attention along one of two pathways: (1) the *growth* pathway or the (2) *well-being* pathway" (p. 212). Students on the growth pathway are open to any information, including that which is internally sourced, that grows their competence; students on the well-being pathway seek to avoid any negative feelings of intellectual inadequacy. If growth does not seem feasible, students will opt to protect themselves on the pathway to well-being. Students might deem the long-range goal of academic achievement to be either out of reach or insignificant enough that they can overcome it later. The affective domain governs personal choices, so addressing this domain cannot be an afterthought for teachers. It's so powerful they should simultaneously consider it while mapping out the intellectual challenges (cognitive domain) that lie ahead.

The following sections describe actions teachers can take to help their students feel hopeful and efficacious and develop a growth mindset.

Hope

Researchers affirm that the role hope plays in a student's motivation or willingness to invest has not received the attention it deserves (Lopez, 2013; Usher & Kober, 2012). Psychologist Shane J. Lopez (2013) states:

> Hope is not simply an attitude or belief that benefits us in some mysterious way. Hope can lift our spirits, buoy our energy, and make life seem worth living. But it also changes our day-to-day behavior. How we think about the future has a direct influence on what we do today. (p. 20)

Hope is the light at the end of the tunnel; it's about expectations. When students are hopeful, they persist in the pursuit of success, even when that success is not immediate. Lopez (2014) notes that not only does hope drive personal choices, it also strongly predicts a student's potential to be successful in college or career experiences—likely an even stronger predictor than ACT test scores.

There are many day-to-day systems in schools that quash hope too quickly. Many of these features are alive and well in the very classrooms where teachers are striving to inspire student investment. Their efforts are noble but fall flat as students still refuse to invest. Some of these less-than-favorable features include the following.

- Teachers score all formative practice work.
- Teachers use all formative and summative scores—even if they are weighted differently—to determine the final grade.
- Teachers do not empower students to revise projects after receiving feedback.
- Students receive reduced scores for second-chance submissions or revised products.
- Teachers use grading algorithms that reward total point accumulation.

Each of the aforementioned practices has the potential to prohibit learners from taking an intellectual risk, leading them to instead opt for the path of well-being. In other words, teachers can instruct students to say "not yet" in the face of challenge, but if the option for achieving the highest marks dissipates with early mistakes, then the true answer is actually "not possible." Students can invest only if hope remains viable.

Efficacy

It would be hard to feel efficacious in the absence of hope; hence, the two affective features of learning often move forward in tandem and frame a student's sense of expectancy and aspiration. Efficacy is born of a belief in one's personal capacity to achieve a desired state or a level of effectiveness. The overarching concept of efficacy comprises many features: confidence, self-esteem, self-assessment, and self-affirmation, to name a few (Hattie & Yates, 2014). It incorporates how a student *feels* about their potential to succeed, so it is critical in a student's capacity to invest repeatedly in the throes of intellectual challenge. It's only when a student feels they *can* be successful that the willingness to re-engage emerges. A student without efficacy struggles to invest in learning unless a teacher constructs a sense of confidence. For example, a teacher might put the student on a winning streak by showcasing the student's strengths and then engaging them in metacognitive processes regarding their existing or developing skills to support intellectual risk taking.

Winning streaks, phenomena coined by professor Rosabeth Moss Kanter (2004), emphasize that students' prior successes, especially after overcoming failure, create the opportunity for the students to reinvest because of the promise of potential future success (Donohoo, 2017; Dweck, 2000, 2016; Kanter, 2004). In her seminal work *Confidence: How Winning Streaks and Losing Streaks Begin and End*, Kanter (2004) states, "Confidence influences the willingness to invest—to commit money, time, reputation, emotional energy, or other resources—or to withhold or hedge investment. This investment, or its absence, shapes the ability to perform" (p. 7). In other words, students truly invest when they can identify personal strengths or options to develop such strengths, and their confidence and efficacy continue to strengthen with each accomplishment.

Helping students identify their capacities increases confidence, thereby building efficacy. When teachers further develop students' sense that they can and will be successful—by increasing the students' belief in self and faith in their potential to develop skills that ensure the belief is realistic—they set both themselves and their students up for successful learning experiences.

Like confidence and efficacy, efficacy and self-esteem are intricately linked, though not synonymous. Both are internal, incremental systems that develop based on positive or growth-oriented experiences and the resulting evidence of success. The author of *Mindset*, Carol S. Dweck (2000), states:

> [Self-esteem] is not an internal quality that is fed by easy successes and diminished by failures. It is a positive way of experiencing yourself when you are fully engaged and are using your abilities to the utmost in pursuit of something you value. (p. 4)

Self-esteem (n.d.), defined as "a confidence and satisfaction in oneself: self-respect," is not built through compliments; rather, it is established through evidence of prior successes in challenging circumstances.

It is a mistake to assume that complimenting a student based on observed talents or skills will build efficacy or self-esteem. Contrary to typical understandings, compliments lead to fixed mindsets—for example, "The teacher already thinks I'm great, so if I can't live up to their expectations, then I will be a failure." Compliments do not increase efficacy, confidence, or self-esteem. But it is possible to engage students in *discovering* their natural or developing talents, skills, or abilities through identifying their own strengths and being metacognitive about their discoveries.

Efficacy is born from within—through self-discovery while on winning streaks—rather than painted on externally. A far better approach to enhancing student efficacy is to avoid compliments altogether and instead provide feedback that notices the facts and then invites personal awareness of what took place through pointed queries. For example, instead of hearing, "You're such a great problem solver!" a student would most benefit from hearing, "I noticed that you generated more than one possible solution to the problem, selected your preferred option, and then confirmed your choice actually solved the problem. How does that strategy set you up for future success in problem solving?" Of course, a myriad of different reflective questions could follow that description of the valued skill, but the ultimate point is to invite the student into drawing personal affirmations that lead to increased efficacy.

Growth Mindset

Following the release of Dweck's 2006 book about mindset, teachers placed a plethora of growth mindset posters on their classroom walls to help learners reframe their growth-oriented perspective. No matter students' age group, popular growth mindset anchor charts tried to highlight the differences between fixed and growth mindset thinking. For example, one such chart might have shown two columns outlining a right and a wrong way to approach a learning challenge (for example, instead of thinking, "This is too hard, and I want to give up," think, "This is a challenge, so I'll try lots of strategies"). Unfortunately, merely teaching students about what a growth mindset is and why it is important, or altering their verbal responses to a challenging situation, does not guarantee a growth mindset will follow, even if those positive affirmations are repeated with regularity. In fact, in an interview with *The Atlantic* reporter Christine Gross-Loh (2016), Dweck expresses concern about the oversimplification of her research, which she claims has led to an alarming, growing trend of a "false growth mindset."

Instead, Dweck notes the long and persistent journey to developing learners' growth mindset includes helping them develop an accurate picture of where they are in the process, teaching them to recognize their triggers to challenges, engaging them in goal setting and self-monitoring, coaching them through navigating cognitive dissonance and instructional hurdles, adding to their reserve of intervention strategies, and guiding their reflective processes (as cited in Gross-Loh, 2016). This way, they *can* develop a growth mindset that empowers them to take intellectual risks and appreciate mistakes as opportunities to learn. In fact, a growth mindset is not a state of being; rather, it is a coping strategy that learners engage when faced with challenges (Frey, Hattie, & Fisher, 2018).

Growth mindsets develop over time and after personally successful experiences with tackling and overcoming hurdles. In their book *Developing Assessment-Capable Visible*

Learners, Grades K–12, Nancy Frey, John Hattie, and Douglas Fisher (2018) state, "[This means] we must regularly create tasks that challenge students, equip them with problem-solving strategies, and assist them in making decisions about what they might do next. Under those conditions, a growth mindset can be developed" (p. 17). When such work is done with consistency and comprehensiveness, with depth and sustained practice, then students can activate a growth mindset without even knowing what it's called and without mentally checklisting alternative things to think in the face of challenge.

Cognitive Domain

When designing classroom instruction, teachers always attend to how students are thinking and what they should be thinking about—in other words, student cognition. *Cognition* involves thinking, information processing, and reasoning. Educators cannot teach if they do not first consider how students think while learning.

Metacognition involves thinking about thinking. In other words, students notice how they are mentally processing information and draw conclusions about their strengths and weaknesses, areas of interest and disinterest, and strategies for deepening their understanding and skills. Both cognitive and metacognitive processes impact student investment.

Cognition

Cognitive challenge is a necessary condition to engage students in learning. A teacher's very first opportunity to guide students to invest cognitively is to figure out the just-right stretch for the students—instruction or tasks with no challenge will disengage learning, while instruction or tasks with too much challenge will disinvite learning (Frey et al., 2018). Because challenge involves risk and effort, it's important to create a high degree of relevance so students will *choose* to enter the conversation. So, once teachers have established a just-right level of challenge, they must design ways to establish relevance for the expected learning (for example, generating cognitive dissonance, piquing curiosity, exposing dichotomies, or inspiring creativity, to name a few).

Student investment requires cognitive challenge. If teachers over-scaffold instruction or assessment tasks (for example, "Select the letter with the appropriate piece of evidence from options A–E that best supports the author's claim," or "Fill in the graphic organizer, and then write a paper following the order and using the ideas in the organized graphic") to lighten the cognitive load, they only succeed in underwhelming and underempowering the students. Unempowered students are uninvested students. To be clear, scaffolds are not inherently wrong, but teachers should not overuse them because of a perception that students can't do the work without them. The goal is to gradually remove scaffolds so that students become independent thinkers and knowledge producers.

The best way to help students become invested learners and independent, growth-oriented thinkers is to provide them with learning-capable strategies (for example, questioning, researching, seeking feedback, receiving feedback, revising and refining, setting goals, and monitoring progress) with which to triumph over challenge and then to reinforce their learning successes and independence by engaging them in metacognition.

Metacognition

Simply defined, metacognition involves thinking about thinking. It involves selecting knowledge or skills to apply in a new situation and then taking a bird's-eye view to monitor the application's effectiveness, thereby taking active control of the cognitive processes being engaged (Hattie, 2012). As Hattie (2009) states, "Meta-cognitive activities can include planning how to approach a given learning task, evaluating progress, and monitoring comprehension" (p. 188). They can also include self-questioning, self-assessing, and reflecting. Basically, metacognitive strategies can help students invest by engaging them in answering the questions that will anchor their personal learning. In her book *Seven Strategies of Assessment for Learning*, Jan Chappuis (2015) puts the questions in student-friendly terms:

- "Where am I going?"
- "Where am I now?" and,
- "How can I close the gap?" (p. 10)

In order to be lifelong learners, students need to become masters of their own best ways to gather, store, and retrieve information. Citing the early works of Robert J. Marzano (1998), John Hattie (2009) states:

> [Marzano] regarded the meta-cognitive system as the "engine" or primary vehicle for enhancement of the mental processes within the cognitive system and recommended providing students with clear targets of knowledge and skills, and strategies for the processes involved with what they are learning. (p. 14)

It might seem as if students should engage in metacognitive processes only *after* they have attained a high degree of content or procedural fluency because students could then free up their cognitive resources to explore their internal terrain. However, "when tasks are very complex for the student, the quality of meta-cognitive skills rather than intellectual ability is the main determinant of learning outcomes" (Hattie, 2009, p. 30). In such situations, learners must call on their mental shortcuts, intuition, and improvisations to address the challenge at hand "rather than call upon knowledge and skill components that are associated with intellectual ability" (Hattie, 2009, p. 30). In his meta-analysis of the most influential factors to support learning, Hattie (2012) finds when teachers engage students in activating metacognitive strategies, it generates an impressive effect size of 0.69 in achievement gains. This, in essence, bolsters the argument that one of the most powerful things teachers can do is teach students how to self-regulate through metacognitive processes *while they are learning*.

Metacognition happens before, during, and after the learning—through both instruction- and assessment-based activities. The goal is not merely to increase intellectual capital but also to introduce students to themselves as learners. The assessment processes should "help students take greater control over what they learn and how they learn it, and . . . provide personal insight into who they are as learners and people, and what they might want to do with their lives" (Conley, 2018, pp. 69–70). When assessment processes incorporate metacognitive moments of reflection, students can look in the mirror of self-discovery and *meet* themselves. When those reflective questions are strength based, the image reflected back is one of hope and efficacy.

Behavioral Domain

School is a place students go to learn, but rarely do schools stop to teach students *how* to learn. This is not to say that teachers should stop addressing curriculum for any period just to teach the learning process in isolation. Rather, it is to note that learning habits should not be assumed, so schools must formally incorporate teaching students how to learn into instruction and assessment processes. Educators must use content to teach skills, and teaching self-regulation—a next-generation skill—is a must for any teacher who wants students to invest in their learning (Erkens, Schimmer, & Dimich, 2019).

To be actively involved in learning is to apply effort and employ a series of strategies that helps the learner adapt to and address the situations at hand. The work of developing both effort and adaptive learning strategies requires instruction, rehearsal, feedback, and ongoing refinement for students to become mastery-oriented learners who can truly invest in their educational journey.

Effort

Effort is defined as the exertion of mental or physical power toward a desired outcome. It is the gusto, or the *oomph*, a learner applies to conquer a hurdle. Of course, educators want students to apply effort, but in her book *Mindset*, Dweck (2016) notes that many people—including students and teachers—think brilliance should be effort*less*. She notes that "as a society we value natural, effortless accomplishment over achievement through effort" (Dweck, 2006, p. 41). The same can be said for schools. Somehow, it became widely accepted that the only people who must work hard to learn are those who struggle with learning. In fact, Dweck (2006) goes on to say, "No matter what your ability is, effort is what ignites that ability and turns it into accomplishment" (p. 41). Even geniuses must engage in effort. Often, the literature on self-regulation boils down to motivation and effort because they seem to provide the palatable difference between accomplishing something and not achieving it.

Teachers can help students focus on effort by teaching them the value of it. Stories of geniuses who experienced breakthrough moments and of underdogs who overcame significant hurdles help students understand the power of effort. Teachers can also engage the class in studying the impact of their own efforts. To do this, ask students to answer two questions at the bottom of any formal assessment: (1) "Estimate how much time you put into preparing for this assessment," and (2) "Describe the strategy or strategies you used to prepare for the assessment." After scoring the exams, aggregate the data, quantifying and incorporating the qualitative effort data, to study the difference effort can make. A data chart might look like figure 1.2.

Grade Earned	Percentage of Class Earning the Grade	Average Amount of Time Spent Preparing	Average Number of Prep Strategies	Types of Strategies
A	23 percent	65 minutes	4	Reread key passages from the text. Review and reorganize notes with highlighters, and add notations as needed. Engage someone else in practice quizzing. Craft rehearsal answers.
B	31 percent	53 minutes	2	Review practice problems. Rewatch or listen to online supplements (Khan Academy lectures or recorded teacher lectures).
C	44 percent	35 minutes	1	Self-quiz with flash cards.
And so on . . .				

Figure 1.2: *Sample data from assessment survey results to study the effectiveness of effort.*

Before returning the individual students' assessments, share the results from the class findings, and ask students to guess their grade just based on how much effort they believe they put into the prep work. After students see their results, offer a reflection question through which the students establish a stretch goal for themselves regarding applying effort in future ventures.

Another way teachers can help students focus on effort is by guiding students to explore their own levels and style of applying effort. Teachers can do this by having students gather in groups to explore all the various strategies or activities they used to study for a test or prepare for a project and then having the students create an anchor chart labeled "Effort-Based Activities." Once the anchor chart is completed, refer to it often, asking students to identify from the list one tried-and-true strategy they prefer and one they have not tried yet as they prepare for an upcoming experience. Follow up after the designated experience, asking students to reflect on their overall results, the effectiveness of their preparation strategies that led to their results, and any insights or discoveries they have about their personal style or preferences. Discussing what effort looks like when learning in the classroom, modeling, and reflecting on examples from emerging evidence can help teachers nurture effort as students simultaneously explore their levels of effort and effective strategies for increasing effort.

Feedback on Effort

Unfortunately, in the learning experience, effort is hard to see. Mental exertion is internal and therefore invisible, and physical effort (such as taking notes, confirming sources, and checking and rechecking solutions) often takes place beyond the teacher's purview. Evaluating whether a student has applied *enough* effort, visible or not, is impossible and dangerous to do because effort is personal and loaded with individualized variables that fluctuate conditionally for each student. Great harm is done when teachers encourage or even demand more effort at a time when students are applying their very best effort; likewise, teachers do equal damage if they praise effort they assume must have been involved when, in fact, natural talent won the day. Unwarranted praise for nonexistent effort may inadvertently reinforce the wrong thing; however, experts agree that authentically praising effort reinforces perseverance (Dweck, 2006; Frey et al., 2018).

It is a mistake to assume that simply providing feedback on effort will encourage learners to continue trying. Dweck's (2016) revised edition of *Mindset* includes a common mantra that effort makes a difference, so teachers should praise effort and not the student. But such praise, Dweck now fears, has become the hollow consolation prize for students who weren't naturally succeeding (as cited in Gross-Loh, 2016). Students may struggle to grasp challenging concepts, but they will almost always know when a teacher's praise is unwarranted. Such a practice has now created what Dweck calls a "false growth mindset" (as cited in Gross-Loh, 2016).

Praising effort when students do not meet the learning target is akin to inviting the learners to redouble their efforts with the same ineffective strategies that likely caused the gap in the first place. Instead, educators should use effort-based feedback to "focus on the learning process," Dweck advises, "and show how hard work, good strategies, and good use of resources lead to better learning" (as cited in Gross-Loh, 2016). The best way to offer feedback on a student's effort is to first invite the student into a reflection on what effort they employed (for example, "Why did you decide to approach the problem the way you did?") and how effective they found the effort to be (for example, "Was the strategy successful? Would you change anything next time?"). Then provide descriptive reinforcement of specific tasks that were either described by the student or directly observed by the teacher. When effort-based feedback restates the specifics of the effort applied and highlights the valued attributes of those activities, students can better examine their effort's impact and then identify the strategies to replicate or replace moving forward. Effort feedback must feed forward.

Adaptive Learning Strategies

Experts in the field of formative assessment agree that the primary instructional decision maker in every classroom is the student (Brookhart, 2011; Chappuis, 2015; Stiggins, 2018; Wiliam, 2011, 2018a). A student's instructional decision making can happen in a snap. Wiliam (2013) notes that the student sometimes engages or disengages based on a single data point, whether erroneous or accurate. He states, "Attention to the growth pathway leads the student to attempt to increase competence, while attention to the well-being pathway is designed to prevent threat, harm, or loss" (Wiliam, 2013, p. 212). Hence, students can best engage and re-engage in their learning experiences if their teachers give them continual exposure to various learning strategies, invite them to explore their effectiveness with those strategies, and empower them to make instructional decisions that support their personal next steps. Students need their own toolkit of instructional correctives so they can adjust before they even require a formal intervention.

Because no two students are exactly alike, and because a single strategy or skill can often be adapted to meet a variety of needs, it's important to help students understand *adaptive* learning strategies. In other words, there is no one-size-fits-all approach when teaching students the strategies that support their learning. Instead, it's best to provide a wide array of strategies over time. This way, teachers allow students to vary the strategies as needed and to discover what works best in what circumstances so that they truly have a toolkit of resources. Offering students a single strategy, template, or tool to use repeatedly and in the same way with each application never empowers them.

Students find it helpful to see their teachers practice metacognition in front of them, offering think-alouds as they model important strategies that will support learning. Beginning to develop their customized toolkit of preferred and successful strategies also helps students. It's beneficial to isolate target areas to develop over time, to avoid creating a random and seemingly infinite list of strategies. Figure 1.3 (page 26) offers a list of categories to consider when building a student's strategy toolkit.

Category of Strategies for Student Use	Specific Skills or Strategies to Teach and Employ
Self-Regulation Strategies	Goal setting Self-assessment Self-reflection Self-monitoring Feedback seeking and interpretation Self-advocacy
Information-Gathering Strategies	Research Note taking Source credibility Evaluation of evidence Validation of evidence Debate and challenge
Peer-to-Peer Strategies	Peer feedback Error analysis Collaborative scoring Asking and answering of questions Paraphrasing Selection of think-alike partners and think-different partners
Memorization Strategies	Mnemonics Rhythms and music Rhymes and alliterations Acronyms Metaphors and analogies Charts and diagrams Visualizations
Note-Taking Strategies	T-charts Diagrams Imagery Annotation
Study Strategies	Note cards Self- or peer quizzes Annotation

Figure 1.3: Adaptive learning strategies to teach students.

Teaching students to learn involves building their toolkit and their metacognition so they can become mastery oriented. As Dweck (2013) notes about her studies in growth mindset, "Almost all of the students in the mastery-oriented group engaged in some form of self-instruction or self-monitoring designed to aid their performance. So, in response to obstacles the mastery-oriented group just dug in more vigorously" (p. 9). To dig in and self-correct, students need a battery of customizable options.

When teachers activate their learners as instructional resources to themselves, they can empower these learners to become instructional resources to one another. In this way, an entire classroom of students builds a learning community that develops what Andy Hargreaves and Michael Fullan (2012) call *intellectual and social capital*. When that happens, students take over the learning in amazing ways.

- Learners collaboratively increase understanding by engaging in rich dialogue and active debate. In doing so, they challenge each other's thinking, extend current thinking, and create new possibilities.

- Learners provide peer feedback based on inter-rater reliability with the teacher. With practiced consistency scoring strong and weak examples, teachers can exponentially increase the quantity and quality of feedback each learner receives from peers.

- Learners establish a social norm of *excellence for all*, relying on positive social pressure and collective support to motivate and encourage all learners to achieve mastery.

- Learners expand their collective insights and repertoire of skills and strategies to address errors and gaps in understanding.

- Learners engage in productive group work as they prepare for a work world full of collaboration-rich opportunities.

Part 4: A Learning Continuum for Implementation

Cultivating assessment practices that accomplish hope, efficacy, and achievement requires significant change in mindset and practice. Incremental changes in teacher and student action can lead to new mindsets and a rich culture of learning. When learners and educators alike have agency, hope, efficacy, and achievement follow.

Educators and students can use the continuum in figure 1.4 (page 28) to understand critical steps on the journey toward embracing assessment practices that build hope, efficacy, and achievement. The journey will often begin with a *teacher-directed* practice and move to *teacher-centered* actions. As teachers develop a clear vision of student investment, practices move to more *learner-centered* approaches and then

	Teacher Directed	Teacher Centered	Learner Centered	Learner Directed

Our school, team, or classroom employs assessment practices that build hope, efficacy, and achievement and establish a strong learning culture.	Growth Mindset
	• Teachers, the school, or both have identified common language to encourage students to learn from mistakes. Encouraging messages are posted in classrooms to signal reinforcing the power of persistence and effort. Their effort will pay off in terms of more learning and increased success.
	
	Self-Regulation and Efficacy
	• Teachers share with students what they notice about students' learning and effort and what seems to help or hinder learning in general.
		Growth Mindset
		• Teachers and the school use common language and help students reframe their thinking when they notice students are disengaging or giving up and not seeing success as possible.
		
		Self-Regulation and Efficacy
		• Teachers guide students in reflecting on what helps them learn and what gets in the way, reflecting in general on how things are going.
		• Teachers identify students' strengths and weaknesses and direct their next steps.
		• Teachers provide lessons on the areas of need and require
			Growth Mindset, Self-Regulation, and Efficacy
			• Growth mindset is fostered along with a sense of efficacy and self-regulation as teachers guide students in reflecting on:
			  • Their strengths and weaknesses, using concrete evidence from their work
			  • What helps them learn and understand
			  • What gets in the way of their learning
			
			Teachers use this assessment information to design instruction to meet the needs and next steps of students.
				Growth Mindset, Self-Regulation, and Efficacy
				• Growth mindset is fostered along with a sense of efficacy and self-regulation as students reflect on:
				  • Their strengths and weaknesses, using concrete evidence from their work
				  • What helps them learn and understand
				  • What gets in the way of their learning
				
				These actions inform students' decisions about what to learn next, how to learn, and how to demonstrate their evidence of learning.

• Teachers encourage students to try harder and often reward compliant behaviors with additional points or enticing extrinsic rewards such as parties or food. Choice and Relevance • Teachers determine how students demonstrate their proficiency and learning. • Teachers identify what might interest students by using an inventory and then making connections to activities, events, or issues that relate to their current context.	students to engage in their designed instruction. Students may or may not know why they are experiencing that instruction. Choice and Relevance • Teachers determine how students demonstrate their proficiency and learning. • Teachers identify what might interest students by using an inventory and then making connections to activities, events, or issues that relate to their current context. • Teachers collect feedback and may use that feedback to determine choices and topics of learning and assessment evidence.	• Teachers engage students in thinking about different assessments that are relevant, interesting, and at grade level or beyond. Choice and Relevance • Teachers center student needs and ideas by reworking choices and relevant options in what students are learning, how they are learning, and how they will be assessed. • Student feedback guides instructional choices and assessment evidence. Teachers are still mostly leading the decisions that students can make about how they show their learning.	• Students and teachers co-create learning experiences and next steps to achieve essential standards and critical competencies. • Students are able to clearly articulate what they are learning, where they are in their learning, and where they need to go next to learn more. Choice and Relevance • Teachers and students co-create the process for reflecting and making choices to achieve the intended learning leading to choices that are meaningful, of high quality, and at grade level and beyond. • Students make choices about (a) the evidence they use to show mastery and (b) the topics they explore because they have a deep interest or want to make a difference or impact the issues they explore.

Figure 1.4: Continuum for nurturing student investment through hope, efficacy, and achievement.

learner-directed ones while students unlearn relying on the teacher for understanding their learning. Each step on the continuum provides teacher actions that signify where one is on the journey. It is important to note that while this figure is offered as a continuum leading to student investment (learner-directed action), there will be times when teachers and students move back and forth on this continuum as they notice the impact a given move or practice has on student achievement and confidence.

Part 5: Tips for Moving Forward

As teachers might quickly discover when launching efforts to invest students in their own learning, the best of intentions can easily go awry when striving to increase hope, efficacy, and achievement. Much time and consideration can be put into designing tools and protocols (and even creating the appropriate climate for intellectual risk taking) with little indication that the educators' best-laid intentions are making a dent in student investment. Teachers interested in truly investing students in their own learning must design for the psychology behind motivation, the factors related to relevance for each individual student, and the symbiotic relationship that assessment has with the learning, before, during, and even after the learning process. *How* teachers interact with the students and their results along the journey is just as important as—if not more important than—the forms students fill in to reflect on or monitor their results. The following tips can help educators avoid the most common pitfalls when generating student investment.

- **Ensure *some* proficiency:** In most cases, familiarity with what they are learning will influence the depth to which students can invest in their own learning. For meaningful goal setting to occur, learners must be able to identify the discrepancy between where they are now and where they want to be. Without a foundation of knowledge or skills, this discrepancy will remain, at best, opaque, which is likely to result in goals that are vague and too generic. Not all students are simultaneously ready to invest and take ownership; some need longer to learn. This means teachers will need to ensure readiness for the students to have a productive experience. There is still a place for direct instruction, which may be most beneficial in the beginning to establish a baseline of understanding; front-loading can often pay off on the back end.

- **Initiate ownership *before* the learning:** While this might feel like a contradiction to the previous point, think of it as a complementary one. Most teachers find the reflection aspect of student investment a little easier to implement. Before the learning—during the forethought phase (Zimmerman, 2011)—learners can begin to set goals based on their understanding of the learning expectations and their own self-motivation beliefs. Asking students to consider their interest level, their expected results, their anticipated hurdles or roadblocks (and how they might proactively plan to avoid or resolve them), and their level of confidence they will reach their goals immediately positions learners as active participants in their learning. Student investment is a *before*, *during*, and *after* exercise that expects learners to make real decisions about what they need to maximize their success.

- **Focus learners' attention on the immediate:** While there is nothing wrong with long-term goal setting, short-term goals will provide learners with a more immediate sense of success. Remaining efficacious about eventual success can be challenging if initial goals are set too far into the future or involve too many steps. If students set more immediate initial goals, over time, this could lead to a compound-interest phenomenon whereby students invest in their learning longer since their efficacy is less fragile. When it comes to goal setting, the cliché, "Think big, but start small," is applicable and appropriate. The habit of goal reaching is the foundation on which learners believe they will reach future goals; this is the primary source of hope and efficacy going forward.

- **Focus learners' attention inward:** A key aspect of student investment and goal reaching is *causal attribution*—to what do learners attribute their successes? It is critical that learners attribute their successes to an internal causation so they see their successes as outcomes of their doing. If learners attribute their successes to an external causation (which might be unstable and uncontrollable), they might see their successes as lucky things they cannot forecast with any assurance. Have learners build the habit of looking inward to place success at the center of their sphere of control. Questions focused on the efficient use of time, effective access to resources, and ways in which initial obstacles were overcome (to name only a few) will send the not-so-subtle message that success is not a function of good fortune, but rather an output of what a learner puts in (Brookhart, 2013a; Weiner, 1979).

- **Emphasize quality over counting:** To help learners position themselves as active decision makers and users of assessment results, focus their attention on the quality of what they have produced or how far they have come. Counting how many aspects were correct does little to identify what's next and how learners can continue to grow throughout their trajectory. Bring learners back to the success criteria to pinpoint what aspects were strong and what aspects need strengthening. Counting correct responses or evidence reveals *what was* but does nothing to indicate how a learner might improve the quality. In that sense, reflective questions that ask learners to describe the specific elements of their learning would be most helpful. Rather than asking yes-or-no questions like, *Did you grab the readers' attention in the opening paragraph?* teachers might prompt, *Describe the ways in which you grabbed the readers' attention in your opening paragraph and how you might build on that to maintain the readers' attention throughout your piece.* Blending criteria with reflection questions can be an easy way to initiate this focus on quality.

- **Teach learners to set their own just-right goals:** Ms. Merrie (case study, page 10) faced the challenge of setting the goals. While there is a place for teacher-centric goal setting, learners will never truly invest if they are passive recipients of the whole experience. Also, setting specific just-right goals ensures the goals are neither too sophisticated nor pedestrian. Goals need to be self-energizing and appropriately challenging (Hattie, 2009) to prevent students from just settling for doing their best, given that what is best for any learner on any given day can fluctuate. Goal reaching is about rising to challenges, not lowering the bar to reach a goal by default. Preassessments can help teachers and students understand each learner's level of readiness and what *just right* actually means.

Part 6: Questions to Guide Your Conversations With Students

At the core of student investment is intentionally bringing students in as partners in designing their school experience. Some students have the knowledge and skills to do this without much guidance while others need modeling, instruction, encouragement, multiple opportunities, and feedback. When students are invested in their learning, they have embraced a growth mindset and can recognize when they are engaging and disengaging with that mindset. They are learning to self-regulate and make choices to deepen their learning and to describe their learning and motivation.

The following sets of prompts are designed to facilitate conversations with students. (Visit **go.SolutionTree.com/assessment** for reproducible versions of these questions.)

These conversations should lead the teacher to understand how to best foster student investment and the students to begin recognizing their own investment and changes they can make to invest. This requires intentional moves, listening, and openness by both student and educator. While these questions are designed for a classroom teacher, other people can use them at various levels of the school experience. These questions can be used to engage students in thinking about recreating a culture that allows for this student voice and influence.

Questions to elicit conversation on growth mindset include the following.

- What does it mean to have a growth mindset?

- Describe a time when you worked hard and saw improvement. What did you do? What happened that led you to improve? How did you know you had improved?

- When you get really overwhelmed, what are the ways you cope? How do teachers encourage you when you are overwhelmed?

- What actions shut you down or get in the way of your learning?

Questions to elicit conversation on self-regulation and efficacy include the following.

- When you have a lot to do in your classes or in school, what kind of planning do you do?

- How do you know what you are learning? How do you reflect on what you are learning, what you are strong at, and what you need to improve?

- Do you believe that if you engage with school, you will learn more? Do you believe you will be more prepared for the future? Do you believe you will learn things that will help you as you get older, take more classes, or enter the next grade?

Questions to elicit conversation on choice and relevance include the following.

- How would you describe the different times you have choice in school?

- What are some of your interests? How would you like to learn about them in school?

- What kind of instruction helps you learn? What kind of instruction or kinds of things get in the way of your learning?

- Where do you think the school, teachers, and classrooms could offer more choice? What might happen if students got more choices?

- Are there times when too many choices overwhelm you? When?

Part 7: Dangerous Detours and Seductive Shortcuts

In addition to strategically putting certain components in place to ensure students are genuinely empowered to self-regulate, educators must attend to the often-overlooked nuances that can easily run interference on a teacher's best-laid plans. Though the following detours and shortcuts might seem obvious, they offer glimpses into how small details could derail a comprehensive plan. As the saying goes, the devil is in the details.

- **Reciting platitudes:** Parroting catchphrases, popular expressions, posters, and slogans is simply not enough. Any efforts to build hope and efficacy must be substantive and teach learners transferable practices, skills, and habits. Reciting inauthentic mantras or forcing oneself to complete every *can't* sentence with the word *yet* can feel disingenuous. Maybe these platitudes can help at the beginning, but learners must go much deeper if investment is to become their default disposition.

- **Focusing on only procedures:** The clinical exercise of following a protocol or process might produce the illusion of investment, but in the long term, it will likely fall short of expectations. Investment that leads to hope and efficacy is as much an *emotional* investment as a procedural one. While following protocols can be a great way to introduce learners to how they can become more invested, it is important to include a focus on efficacy ahead of the learning, perseverance during the learning, and levels of satisfaction after the learning to nudge learners to see the affective side of investment.

- **Being too teacher-centric:** At first, teachers will need to create the culture, processes, and opportunities for investment; however, real investment happens when teachers are able to step aside and allow learners to drive their own investment. Stepping aside does not mean teachers lose control or step back; it's not a zero-sum game. Stepping aside means students—where most natural and applicable—can authentically become key decision makers in their learning. Teachers will always guide and be at the center of the classroom experience, but they have ways to enable learners to fully invest instead of remaining passive recipients of what their teacher has decided.

- **Doing too much, too soon:** Authentic investment takes time, and some learners will need to learn new habits that run counter to their typical school experience. Ease them in. Obviously, classrooms are unique, and learners are at different levels of readiness to invest in their own learning, but teachers would be wise to start small as they attempt to unravel passive habits that may have formed over the previous years. Too much too soon may overwhelm learners.

CHAPTER 2
ASSESSMENT PURPOSE

Take a chance. Do your best. Don't rush.
Don't just think that something is acceptable—make it great!
—Fourth-grade student

With any assessment, the most critical question for teachers to answer is *why*—specifically, why they want to gather evidence. Once teachers establish their purpose, they will know what subsequent action to take. This principle holds true for students as well, since the purpose of any self-assessment exercise defines how granular (formative) or holistic (summative) their examination will be and help them identify how to respond once they recognize their current standing. While it's easy and alluring to jump straight to designing the assessment itself (namely, assessment architecture), students and teachers alike must know why the evidence is necessary to make efficient and effective instructional responses more likely.

Teachers can enhance student investment by utilizing classroom assessments according to their correct purposes—to improve and prove learning—within a balanced formative–summative assessment system. With assessment, *balance* means the strategic (not equal) use of assessment within a learning continuum so that the established purpose matches the subsequent actions.

Part 1: Case Study

Mr. Stroelle, a teaching veteran with fifteen years of experience teaching high school science, wanted to increase his students' motivation and achievement for the upcoming year. Many of his teaching colleagues had been expanding their use of formative assessments and finding increased student achievement by the time the summative assessment occurred, and he wished to achieve similar results in his classes. Some colleagues, however, expressed concern, fatigue, and even frustration over the amount of time and energy it took to implement the process. So, Mr. Stroelle decided to limit his effort to his biology class for the first year and, if successful, expand that effort to his other classes.

For Mr. Stroelle, implementing more formative assessments meant using two things: (1) pre- and post-tests and (2) more quizzes. To begin, Mr. Stroelle created the summative test in advance and then used that same test as the pretest. In that way, he reasoned, students could see what they needed to work on during the unit of study, and he could prove whether growth happened by comparing the pretest results to the post-test results. Having students understand their learning gaps early in the process—even if they couldn't hold on to the pretest in their folders—should dramatically increase their attention and effort during the unit. Next, Mr. Stroelle tried to increase the number of quizzes he gave. It helped that Mr. Stroelle knew the district curriculum and pacing guide so well and had organized his curricular resources sequentially. His background knowledge and experience would likely make his efforts go more smoothly than some of his peers'. He could foresee using one formative assessment for each major concept in the unit of study. He'd document the students' results and return the quizzes so students could each see what they needed to improve in time for the summative assessment.

The difficulty, he anticipated, would come with scoring everything. Not only were the number of data to record going to increase, but students were supposed to reflect on their performance so they could improve over time. Did he need to score their self-reflections, too? That seemed a bit overwhelming so early in the change process. If he wasn't careful, he *and* his students might quickly become overwhelmed while they tried the new system. He decided to have students keep track of their own results. They could keep their quizzes in their unit folders after he returned them, monitor their scores for improvements over time, and use their quizzes as study guides for the summative assessment. In fact, they could even keep their homework in those same folders, so they'd have everything in one location. It might be problematic that everything would have different point values and some topics would have more assessment data than others, but at least students would be able to get the gist of how they were performing, which had never happened in his classroom prior to this year.

Mr. Stroelle planned to award points for the students' folder work. That way, he could guarantee students took the evidence-gathering process seriously. He would include the evidence folder scores with all the other formative and summative scores, tallying them up at the end and reporting the final grade based on the average of the students' combined examples in each unit of study.

Mr. Stroelle noticed that his students did not appreciate the new system. They groaned each time he requested they pull out their evidence folders and reflect on their progress. At first, he thought it was just because they did not like change and being held accountable. But the more they advanced in the school year, the more he felt himself inwardly groan when they had to pull out the evidence folders. It all seemed like many extra steps for no reason. Mr. Stroelle was not seeing his students improve or their motivation increase, but he sure was doing a lot of extra work for very little reward.

Reflection

Mr. Stroelle attended to the research to guide his instructional choices. He was clear that employing quality formative assessment practices could greatly improve his students' learning. He began giving serious thought to the purposes of the various assessments within his classroom, though he did not yet make those purposes interdependent. Erkens, Schimmer, and Dimich (2017) state, "The formative and summative purposes of assessment must be interdependent to maximize learning and to verify achievement" (p. 29). Still, Mr. Stroelle attempted to increase his use of formative assessments to improve learning, which was supposed to make a dramatic difference. Yet neither he nor his students found value in his efforts. Why? What went wrong with Mr. Stroelle's well-intended effort to use formative assessments to increase achievement?

Part 2: Celebrations and Considerations

Mr. Stroelle not only attended to the research but also tapped into his peers' expertise and experiences before he launched a major effort to improve the quality of and increase the amount of formative assessment within his classroom. He began small, with a single course, and used a laser-like focus to align his efforts with the curriculum. He knew he needed to formatively assess the major concepts and skills on his tests so learners would be successful by the time they got to the summative assessment. He also understood he would be more successful if he created a summative assessment first so he understood the formative components he would need along the way. Backward design truly helped Mr. Stroelle begin to make the process more transparent and manageable for his overall system.

A major area of concern for Mr. Stroelle was the misunderstanding that formative assessment is just preassessments and quizzes. His formative assessment did not empower his students to make substantive changes between formative moments. Their preassessment data might have helped them target initial areas of concern; however, they had no way of monitoring progress in between, especially when they could not hold on to their first results. His system was akin to weighing oneself on the first day of a diet, following the expected routines and caloric intake for a given time period without any measurements in the middle, and then hoping the diet worked by the second and final trip to the scale. So, while the measurements in the middle could potentially have utility for students, without their initial preassessments, they had no baseline with which to determine progress.

Worse, Mr. Stroelle himself made no attempt to use the students' formative data to inform and redirect his core instructional maneuvers. The entire purpose of formative assessment is to gather information that helps inform the instructional maneuvers both the teacher and the students must perform to improve achievement between assessments (Erkens et al., 2017). The changes that are needed to improve achievement cannot rest solely on the students' shoulders.

While the research on the impact of preassessments is limited (Guskey, 2018), experts disagree on the best way to navigate the pre- or post-test protocol. Some recommend the exact system that Mr. Stroelle was using—the preassessment is a direct match to the postassessment. Some would argue that pre- and postassessments need to match to clearly reveal the exact improvements between assessment one and assessment two and accurately measure growth. On the other hand, others would suggest the results derived from an identical postassessment could more likely indicate a high degree of recall capacity than a deep level of learning (Guskey, 2018; Guskey & McTighe, 2016). They would argue the best way to measure true learning is to have students address the exact same skills or content but with different questions so simple recall is not a factor in determining growth. It is fortunate that Mr. Stroelle opted to include quizzes around significant skills throughout the unit of study. In this manner, he built a viable alternative for ensuring true growth on the summative assessment or postassessment, should he have chosen to triangulate his evidence.

His efforts to assign points to student reflection defeated the purpose of the overall activity. The use of a point system creates a compliance orientation that puts a premium on completion and distracts from the intent to focus on learning. If students were completing the reflective questions, then it was time for Mr. Stroelle to engage in reflection regarding his own process. He could have asked himself: What could I do to make my reflective protocol so invaluable that students couldn't stand to miss it? How could their reflective insights qualify them for or disqualify them from having to engage in practice activities during the formative phases? and How could they tap into their reflections to improve their overall learning throughout the unit of study? It's only when educators can find answers to those types of questions that students will find reflective practices to be invaluable resources.

To succeed in using a data-tracking system, a student must both understand what each data point means and be able to generate comparative inferences between data points. The student's age and relative proficiency factor into how sophisticated the comparative inferences will be. Older students will be able to make more sophisticated connections and think longer term about what's next. This simple feature does not work when students are recording the number of items they got right on an assessment, whether it's formative or summative in nature. First, for data points to have comparable value, they must have equal weight. Imagine a student has four correct out of ten possible on one assignment and ten correct out of forty possible on the next. On a simple bar graph that tracks correct answers, the ten looks like the better score, and if charted in the same graph, it will look like a gain of six points (from four to ten)! However, for the first assessment, the score would be 40 percent correct, and for the second, the score would be 25 percent correct.

Second, proficiency should never be determined by total point accumulation. Two students, for example, can each earn a score of 80 percent on an assessment, but if they got different items wrong in receiving the same point total, do they truly match in proficiency level? What if all the items wrong for student A are within a single learning target, whereas the items wrong for student B spread across the various learning targets but only require strategic-thinking responses? Further, there is the issue of quality or *type* of error; simple mistakes and egregious omissions are considered the same in a points and percentages system. Earning equal numbers of points or even common percentages does not equate to having the same degree of proficiency (Erkens, 2019). Students are misled when they record point totals that reveal they correctly answered many questions, yet significant gaps in their understanding remain.

A far better option is for teachers to employ common language around metrics that define proficiency, such as proficiency scales or holistic or analytic rubrics. Students can develop accurate, accessible, and reliable interpretations of their own proficiency levels by developing inter-rater reliability with their teacher when scoring student work. In assessment, reliability is about consistency, such that *inter-rater reliability* refers to consistency among the *raters* (assessors). The most desirable outcome is that the students' interpretations of evidence align with those of the teacher. Framing ongoing teacher-to-teacher, teacher-to-student, and student-to-student conversations around what proficiency looks like can help all stakeholders deeply understand and own shared, clear expectations. It also facilitates the exploration of mastery, breaking the perception that *perfection* and *mastery* are synonymous. Experts themselves are imperfect, but that doesn't make them less masterful. Clarifying that notion for students offers them hope and opens the opportunity for them to engage in intellectual risk taking while developing a growth mindset.

Part 3: Action to Take

To emphasize overall levels of proficiency (such as grades) when the purpose is next steps would be a mismatch. Having purpose drive the design of assessment experiences can avoid this emphasis. Classroom assessment should be the primary source of information that guides instructional decisions on behalf of students and teachers. Professor of education James H. McMillan (2013) states, "Our collective assertion is that [classroom assessment] is the most powerful type of measurement in education that influences student learning" (p. 4).

Other measures, while powerful, can offer validating data, but they are less frequent, less responsive, and often less trusted by the classroom teacher, who remains closest to individual learners and can better identify their emerging needs. Educational researcher Paul Black (2013) validates teacher concerns about external assessments, stating, "Even the best external tests are bound to be of limited validity" (p. 171). Classroom assessments have two primary purposes—(1) formative and (2) summative— and as a result must build on a focused yet fluid pathway that results in student learning. When students feel that learning is possible and doable, they have a much higher likelihood of investing and engaging in that step.

Research is expansive and consistent in its conclusion that formative assessment is a high-yield strategy, generating some of the largest gains in student achievement when implemented well (Andrade, 2013; Black, 2013; Chappuis, 2015; Chappuis & Stiggins, 2020; Heritage, 2013; Stiggins, 2014; Wiliam, 2011, 2018a). Despite that clear finding dating back to Paul Black and Dylan Wiliam's 1998 groundbreaking study, the *use* of formative assessment has generated lingering confusion and continues to upend school policies and procedures. Noting that the research on the value and purpose of summative assessment has not matched the accelerated studies in formative assessment, Black (2013) adds:

> The net effect has been that the changes have not improved the state of discord between these two functions of assessment; however, they may have highlighted more clearly the awareness of this discord and of its harmful effects on teaching and learning. (p. 167)

Grading policies, processes, and recording software will continue to fluctuate if a deep dive into the various assessment types' purposes, processes, and impacts on student motivation does not occur.

Though the terms *formative* and *summative* are easily defined, putting them into practice can be more challenging. *Formative assessment* is readily understood to happen during learning, as learning is forming. But how it is used is less clear. Is it an event? A type of quiz? Should it be graded? Is it a process? Though educators understand formative assessment is a process that includes a multitude of ways to gather evidence of and then respond to student learning, the most popular references to its application still identify it as an event—for example, "I gave a formative assessment," or "I only count my formative assessments as 10 percent of the overall grade." It's hard to record process evidence, especially as it's either *moving* data (recording the most recent evidence) or qualitative data (descriptive in nature). Traditional gradebooks often have no space for either feature.

Equally, there are questions and misconceptions about *summative assessment*, even though it is easily defined as summary data to determine where students ended up in the final phases of their learning (Black, 2013). Such questions include: Should it include everything I taught? Does it have to be a lengthy, traditional test? Should it be really challenging for students? and Shouldn't it mirror the types of assessments students will see as large-scale assessments? It's challenging to consider a single data point—as many unit designs have one summative assessment and the next unit moves to completely different standards—a sufficient and accurate representation of where a student landed on the proficiency expectations for that unit.

Clearly, definitions are insufficient mechanisms to answer the abounding questions and concerns. The purposes are understood: formative assessments are used to improve learning while summative assessments prove learning. But the work remains nuanced. Experts caution that the title does not define the assessment; rather, it's how the resulting evidence is *used* that defines the assessment (Black, 2013; Chappuis & Stiggins, 2020; Wiliam, 2011, 2018a). That notion allows the purpose of the assessment to morph over time, permitting formatives to become summative and summatives to become formative as learning advances. Moreover, the assessment purposes are interdependent, meaning educators must use formative and summative assessments in streamlined, connected, iterative, and synergistic ways to capitalize on student investment and maximize student learning (Andrade, 2013; Black, 2013). Educators must embrace assessment purposes as positive opportunities to elicit insight regarding student learning (Andrade, 2013; Black, 2013; Heritage, 2013).

The manifestation of student investment begins with intentionality at the forethought and planning stage. As teachers identify the intended learning, the specific learning targets that represent the steps toward achieving that learning, and the success criteria that allow for accurate inferences and judgments of quality, the path to proficiency becomes clear, making the opportunity for investing at the outset more likely. Of course, as students become well versed in this process, teachers will also have the opportunity to transfer the primary responsibility to the students. Teachers would not back away entirely; rather, they would guide and facilitate this process of student-led determinations at all stages.

Assessment Maps

A first step in creating a pathway that could be interdependent involves mapping out the standards involved. Erkens (2016) offers a simplified image of what such a pathway might look like (see figure 2.1).

Common Core State Standards, Reading Informational Texts

Target 1: RI.3.1 Ask and answer questions to demonstrate understanding of a text, referring explicitly to the text as the basis for the answers.

Target 2: RI.3.2 Determine the main idea of a text.

Target 3: RI.3.2 Recount the key details and explain how they support the main idea.

Target 4: RI.3.3 Describe the relationship between a series of historical events, scientific ideas or concepts, or steps in technical procedures in a text, using language that pertains to time, sequence, and cause/effect.

Assessments: (H) homework, (CP) checkpoint, (Project) projects, and (Final) final assessments

	H1	H2	H3	CP1	H4	H5	CP2	H6	H7	Project	Final
Target 1	X	X		X					X	X	X
Target 2		X	X	X		X	X			X	X
Target 3			X		X	X	X	X	X	X	X
Target 4					X		X	X	X	X	X

Source for standards: National Governors Association Center for Best Practices & Council of Chief State School Officers, 2010.

Source: Erkens, 2016, p. 66.

Figure 2.1: *Elementary assessment map example.*

Once the assessment pathway is built, teachers have more clarity on the purpose of each assessment as well as more freedom to adjust instruction while still keeping an eye on the big picture.

Assessment maps are directive yet malleable. They are directive in that the end goal remains clear and stationary, but they are malleable in that teachers add, modify, remove, or replace planned formative assessments based on the emerging evidence. This malleability allows students inside the process to become primary decision makers based on that emerging evidence. For students to be fully invested, they must see the pathway—the map—that leads to that end goal. If the map becomes a set of lockstep requirements—a set of immovable checkboxes to be ticked—it becomes weaponized as it is nonresponsive and thus insensitive. In their report for the Education Trust titled *Motivation and Engagement in Student Assignments: The Role of Choice and Relevancy*, Joan Dabrowski and Tanji Reed Marshall (2018) note:

> An opposite approach [to student choice] plays out when teachers control all aspects of the assignment or guide students in lockstep fashion through each step. In these scenarios, students are made to relinquish all power and decision making, and teachers revert to using power to control bodies and minds instead of using their autonomy to invite learning. (p. 1)

If teachers desire to involve and invest students in their own learning, they can do so by allowing students to *see* the learning intentions as well as the planned practice opportunities; this way, students can take an active role in decision making regarding instructional maneuvers. When students can use sufficient quality evidence of a mastered learning expectation to opt out of future practice work for that same expectation, they often do more work than originally assigned so teachers cannot assign them more work. A significant feature of forethought and planning, then, includes advanced consideration of how students will be invited into monitoring the instructional decision making required during the learning process (Dimich, 2015).

Learning Intentions

Experts agree that one of the very best ways to engage students in monitoring their own learning is to make the learning intentions visible and available from the beginning to the end of the learning experience (Black, 2013; Chappuis, 2015; Chappuis & Stiggins, 2020; Heritage, 2013; Wiliam, 2011, 2013, 2018a). *Learning intentions* include both the learning targets (what students must learn) and the criteria for success (how students will be evaluated). Dylan Wiliam (2018a) suggests that teachers not only share the learning intentions but also spend time clarifying and building shared knowledge throughout the formative processes so specific strengths and aspects that need strengthening become clearer and hopefully more aligned between the teacher and the student.

Learning Targets

Learning targets are statements that refer to what students must know and be able to do after successful instruction (Chappuis, 2015). They are pulled directly from the standards and serve many purposes. Chappuis (2015) states, "Clear learning targets guide instruction, assignments, formative assessments, and summative assessments. Learning targets determine how we track achievement and, ultimately, how we figure grades. Classifying them prior to instruction offers several benefits" (p. 36). When it comes to investing students in the learning, clear targets also serve as the scaffolding to success by guiding the instructional decisions that students must make if they are to accomplish standard proficiency. For example, if the learning intention were to determine the theme of a story, one learning target might be "knowing the difference between theme and plot" because, of course, students must know what theme is before they can find it. If the learning outcome were to add and subtract fractions, then the learning targets would include the ability to find the lowest common multiple of two numbers, since that is how students would find common denominators.

Getting the right learning targets isn't as easy as simply turning lengthy standards into a multitude of target-specific statements. If teachers don't begin by considering how the number-one consumer of the information—the student—will interact with the targets, then the identified targets become challenges rather than supports on the learning pathway. According to Erkens (2015b), common errors include the following.

- **There are too many learning targets:** It's an overwhelming list to consider, much less work through.

- **There is a target (or more) per day:** Inevitably, even one target per day will move too fast for learners to grasp and fully integrate the learning required. Learners will have no way to fix a missed target because it is behind them after a single day of exposure or practice.

- **The identified targets are too discrete:** Many times, the targets link to recall-level work and right-or-wrong answers rather than the deep learning and reasoning required for learners to monitor and ultimately celebrate growth over time.

- **The learning targets are too granular:** When targets are too granular, they are also disconnected from the big picture and the supporting rationale. For example, teachers use reading strategies like chunking words or looking at pictures to help learners access bigger concepts like word recognition or inference and comprehension. When targets are written about strategies (for example, "I can chunk words"), they distract the learners from the more significant purpose and blur the final goal. So, when strategies need to be the focus of the learning, it's best to write the rationale or end goal directly into the target (such as, "I am learning to chunk parts of words I already know so I can recognize words quickly").

Developing learning targets can be challenging. In truth, beyond the notion of putting targets in student-friendly terms, experts don't always agree on the best way to develop learning targets. But if student investment is to be a factor in the design equation, then it's important to create a manageable number of targets through which students can deepen the learning by monitoring progress over time, refine the learning by implementing feedback between attempts at mastery, and accurately predict their results based on prior evidence during the journey.

There are six criteria for creating and activating the learning targets within the standards: learning targets must be (1) aligned, (2) focused, (3) visible, (4) available, (5) measurable, and (6) extendable (Erkens, 2015b).

Aligned

No matter what, learning targets must derive from and specifically remain aligned with the standards. This is not always as easy as it sounds. First, the curricular resources that teachers are required to use can include competing expectations. Second, some standards are large and may have multiple features embedded, making it difficult to tease out a single statement. Finally, as teachers create meaning regarding the complex standards, it's a fair and common practice to alter the language to understandable terms. When this happens, however, a teacher's prior schema could potentially hijack the standard's true intent, the synonyms applied might not be direct correlations, or the rigor of the expectation could accidentally be reduced. It's always important to use revisionary processes, including potential peer review, to examine the final teacher-generated targets in relation to the initial standards.

Focused

Learning targets should focus the students on the larger *end goal* and drive instructional efforts in that direction. As such, they embed a rationale that can create meaning or purpose for each assessment that encounters the target. A target that says, "I am learning reading strategies," misses the ultimate point of learning to read. Or a target that says, "I can diagram sentences," misses the mark of striving to improve sentence fluency. There is no doubt that learning to diagram sentences or understand sentence parts is important, but creating that as an end goal directs the learners' attention away from the purpose and becomes a ready place for students to disinvest. "Sure," they might utter with an eye roll, "like I'm going to sit around and diagram sentences after high school!" However, they will need to fluently write as productive citizens who will have to file forms, applications, or letters at some point. Yes, discrete skills are necessary, and yes, it's important to make those expectations visible, but work to keep the most important end goals in the learners' sight lines.

Questions to ensure learning targets are aligned and focused include the following:

- Are the targets we've identified specifically tied to standards?
- Are the targets stated in ways that appropriately aim toward the end goal (for example, learning to read versus learning reading strategies) and add purpose to the learning? (Erkens, 2015b)

Visible

Students cannot hit a learning expectation if they cannot see it or if it doesn't hold still for them (Chappuis, 2015; Chappuis & Stiggins, 2020). Making learning targets visible involves so much more than writing them on the board or on anchor charts around the room. To help facilitate ready tracking of learning expectations, teachers can create assessment blueprints that reveal where the targets are embedded within the assessment for both their preplanning purposes and any reflective assessment forms they might develop for postassessment efforts. Students will be able to conduct a more accurate reflection when they can see where the targets are during the formative phases and where the targets were embedded in the summative assessment during the reflection phases. When the targets are revealed with enough consistency throughout the formative phases, teachers should be able to conduct a lesson near the end of a unit of study and then ask the students to identify which learning targets were being addressed during the lesson. When learning targets remain visible, students are better able to revisit and understand them.

Available

Standards are written in educational language, making them challenging for students to understand. Simply transferring them to a bulleted list will not make them readily available for student understanding. Likewise, putting *I can* in front of any learning-oriented expectation will not suffice. Experts agree a better approach is to put targets in student-friendly terms (Chappuis, 2015; Chappuis & Stiggins, 2020; Wiliam, 2011, 2018a). However, in the process, academic language must be maintained. Chappuis (2015) recommends writing the target in student-friendly terms and then adding a *this means I can* clarifier, like so: "I can infer. This means when reading, I make a good guess and back it with my schema and text clues."

Even that, however, is insufficient for developing shared knowledge. So, it's important to revisit the targets showing examples and non-examples and revealing common misunderstandings or errors with the target to further clarify the meaning during the learning phases.

Questions to ensure learning targets are visible and available include the following:

- Do the learners know the targets and are they visible throughout the learning process?
- Are the targets stated in student-friendly terms so learners can clearly understand the expectations? (Erkens, 2015b)

Measurable

If students are to track their learning, they must understand how they would measure it. What gets measured gets done. This is not to say a learning target would not have words that need further definition, exploration, and redefinition over time. What, for example, does *understand* entail? It's easier to say *I can define* or *explain* or *identify*. But it is important to consider what metric or manner would help students make meaning of their ability along the way. If *understand* is the verb, how will students know it when they experience it?

Extendable

If teachers present a new target each day, learners will become overwhelmed by the sheer number, and they will quickly see the futility of investing in their learning if they have no built-in opportunities to improve on each target after it's introduced. Nicole Dimich (2015) recommends listing the multitude of learning targets that emerge from the standards and placing them in a ladder-like structure, with the easiest targets at the bottom and the hardest at the top. Then circle the few (teachers decide what number is manageable) at the top to translate into student-friendly language and share with students. Generally, the easiest targets at the bottom are subcomponents of the more challenging targets at the top, so the top targets assume the lesser ones. For example, a kindergarten learning target might be, "I am learning letter sounds and blends so that I can read words." The learning objective for a single lesson might include learning the *bl* blend. While that smaller target is important for students to see during a discrete lesson, it serves as a subpart of the larger, more focused target to learn letters, sounds, and blends. Otherwise, learning something like the alphabet could end up generating an overwhelming number of learning targets (lowercase, uppercase, multiple sounds, and blends for each letter) to make visible. Students discover early that one-and-done learning targets are hard to invest in.

Questions to ensure learning targets are measurable and extendable include the following:

- Are the targets measurable?
- Have we agreed on what proficiency will look like (naming quality criteria), and do we have ways of making those expectations clear to the learners as we engage them in the work of mastering the learning targets over the course of study?
- Are the targets able to be monitored over time, allowing students the ability to self-assess, set goals, and track their progress in meaningful and productive ways? Will the data they gather about their progress support their ability to make strong instructional decisions so they can be successful? (Erkens, 2015b)

In the end, learning targets work for both teachers and students. They must help teachers accomplish two things: (1) make learning visible and accessible to the learners, and (2) support teachers in spiraling the learning to build a rich depth of knowledge. "When teachers take great care to incorporate the criteria for quality learning targets in their development phase, they create a visible pathway to success for everyone on the learning journey" (Erkens, 2015b).

Learning Criteria

Learning intentions must include the quality criteria for success; otherwise, students know only *what* they need to learn. In the absence of *how well*, the picture of what they are striving to accomplish remains murky. *Learning criteria* are the list of aspects or standards used to judge or critique something. They are derived from the standards as well as from the field of expertise—for example, what do exemplary writers deem makes proficient writing? Or, what do expert musicians use to identify quality music?

Criteria help clarify "what constitutes quality in mastering the learning target" (Chappuis, 2015, p. 51). Quality criteria also help students answer the question, Where am I going? Chappuis (2015) states, "It makes sense that if students are to be able to self-assess, they must first understand the concepts that define quality" (p. 51). When developing quality criteria, it's best to keep the number of criteria to a manageable few. Too many criteria cause confusion and can quickly overwhelm learners.

During the learning phases, teachers have a better chance of inspiring student investment if they invite their learners into the identification and creation process. So, while teachers should already know the quality criteria for the tasks at hand, using examples shared during the formative phases (from earlier in the school year or from previous years) helps teachers elicit what quality looks like from the students. These examples would strategically reveal the range of performances along the novice-to-sophisticated continuum. Imagine, for example, that a teacher showed a two-minute video of students engaged in an academic conversation and then asked the students to notice the parts of the conversation that were exemplary and the parts that were not. Once students named the parts, the teacher could tease out the criteria involved. If the class noticed that in a quality academic conversation, the videoed participants were referencing specific text passages with quotes or paraphrases, then the teacher might ask, "How would we qualify and categorize that?" The criteria that might emerge are reliable evidence- or text-based responses.

Once the criteria are identified, the teacher can flesh out the specific proficiency levels by continually using work samples to explore characteristics and levels of quality.

Chappuis (2015) notes the strategy of letting students practice with strong and weak work examples refines "students' evaluative thinking by letting them practice making judgments about accuracy or level of quality with carefully chosen assessment items and examples" (p. 71). Chappuis (2015) adds, "The goal is to help students come to hold an understanding about accuracy and quality similar to yours before they engage in extended practice with the target" (p. 71).

The goal would be to generate a like-minded image of quality among the teacher and all students in the classroom. That can happen only if the teacher places the criteria into rubrics and constantly revisits the rubrics for the purpose of calibrating scoring with examples of strong and weak work.

At the highest level of student investment, teachers activate learners as resources to themselves and to each other (Wiliam, 2018a). For this to occur, students must have an image of the learning intentions that matches the teacher's. Anything the teacher can do to involve students in creating, refining, and evaluating learning targets and quality criteria will help create the sense of safety necessary for students to begin engaging in intellectual risk taking.

Part 4: A Learning Continuum for Implementation

Assessment purpose centers how learners use their assessment information to deeply understand how they learn, what they are learning, where they are in their learning, and how they can move forward. This idea of moving learning forward is all about using assessment information to help students see themselves as clearly as possible. When they feel that learning is possible and doable, students have a much higher likelihood of investing and engaging in that step. This type of engagement is not about compliance (although it is always nice when students do as teachers ask); it is about noticing how students learn, detecting where they are at in using their assessment information, and guiding them to notice their learning on their own.

The journey will often begin with a teacher-directed practice and move to teacher-centered actions (see figure 2.2, page 52). As teachers develop a clear vision of student investment, practices move to more learner-centered approaches and then learner-directed ones while students unlearn relying on the teacher for understanding their learning. Each step on the continuum provides teacher actions that signify where one is on the journey. It is important to note that while this figure is offered as a continuum leading to student investment (learner-directed action), there will be times when teachers and students move back and forth on this continuum as they notice the impact a given move or practice has on student achievement and confidence.

	Teacher Directed	Teacher Centered	Learner Centered	Learner Directed
Our school, team, or classroom employs assessment practices for specific purposes that ensure forethought and planning, clear targets and criteria, and metacognition.	**Forethought and Planning** • Teachers plan all assignments and assessments, directing each step along the way. **Clear Targets and Criteria** • Teachers share standards and learning goals with students. **Metacognition** • Teachers share with students their overall strengths and areas of improvement based on assessment results. Students are invited to reflect on their learning; teachers invite students to reflect on their assessment information.	**Forethought and Planning** • Teachers plan most assignments and assessments, directing students' planning along the way. **Clear Targets and Criteria** • Teachers share standards and learning goals with students. Teachers engage students in dialogue about the targets and criteria. **Metacognition** • Teachers share with students their overall strengths and areas of improvement based on assessment results. Teachers design	**Forethought and Planning** • Students and teachers work together to define learning and determine the assessment evidence that will show relevant mastery of the intended learning. Students reflect on the instructional methods that will best support their learning. **Clear Targets and Criteria** • Students co-construct criteria and qualities of learning with teachers. Students can apply these qualities to their own self-reflection and can track their progress over time.	**Forethought and Planning** • Students and teachers work together to define learning and reflect on strengths and next steps in learning. Students make choices about what kind of practice they need and how they will show mastery. **Clear Targets and Criteria** • Students co-construct criteria and qualities of learning with teachers. Students develop clear language and can articulate what quality looks like. Students can apply these qualities to their own self-reflection and

instruction and assessment based on these observations. Teachers ask students to reflect on their own work. Students are invited to reflect on their learning; teachers invite students to reflect on their assessment information.	Metacognition • Students receive prompts to reflect on their learning and what helps them the most. Teachers and students reflect on the results of their individual and collective assessment information. Students articulate (with teacher prompting) what next steps will help them grow. • Students can confidently explain how they learn, what they are learning, and where they are in their learning.	can track their progress over time. Metacognition • Students reflect before learning occurs to consider the best way to learn more; reflection happens during learning to make adjustments based on how the learning is going; and reflection happens after learning to understand what worked and what could change in the future. Students track their learning over the course of a unit and across multiple units.

Figure 2.2: Continuum for nurturing student investment through assessment purpose.

Part 5: Tips for Moving Forward

Many teachers wishing to be data driven are simultaneously struggling with data themselves, especially when the results come from assessments they do not design or when there is confusion about the design and use of the balanced formative–summative assessment system they do control. It's so important to begin the work of generating student investment by first mastering the science of effectively designing high-quality assessments that produce reliable results, and then mastering the art of effectively employing those results in ways that motivate the students. Because teachers are naturally assessing every day, there are some manageable quick starts that teachers can use to create and employ better classroom assessment systems.

- **Start small:** Mr. Stroelle was right to start with just his biology class. For him, feeling overwhelmed meant beginning with only one of his classes. For other teachers, it may mean something different. The point is that teachers give themselves permission to start where they are already doing things, where they are most comfortable beginning the change of practice, or where they can most easily envision potential changes in the immediate future. Using assessment results formatively is a new habit for some teachers, let alone the learners, so slowly building new habits is the fastest way to ensure their permanent place in a culture of learning.

- **Think of assessment as more verb than noun:** Labeling an assessment *formative* does not make it so; it's only formative when it is *used* formatively. Creating the opportunities (making space) to build student investment is different from increasing the number of events that feel more summative. While Mr. Stroelle's students did a lot of tracking, they did little to respond to the results in a way that focused on *what's next*. This is where assessment purpose is connected to architecture; if teachers know the purpose is formative, then they should design assessments to elicit evidence that learners can use to identify their own next steps.

- **Know your standards:** Teachers need to intimately understand the cognitive complexity of curricular standards to bring students inside the formative and summative purposes. Clarifying the learning goals (and the targets that underpin those goals) makes it clearer to learners how assessment results are to be prioritized. When learners are clear that the priorities are practice and next steps, they will come to know that the focus is on a descriptive, not judgmental, response.

Help learners understand how sophisticated their demonstrations should be and how the demonstrations either connect to the big picture (formative) or are the big picture in themselves (summative). A balanced assessment system makes purpose the primary driver; *why* is the information that results from the assessment necessary, and how will it be utilized? When teachers know their standards, learners will too. When learners know, they are better positioned to understand how daily activities and goals act as scaffolds toward proficiency.

- **Employ strategic tracking:** There is a significant difference (or at least there can be) between that which is tracked and that which contributes to a learner's report card grade or level. While teachers prioritize *using* the results in the formative purpose, learners still can track their results—numerically or anecdotally—to have a running record of their growth toward proficiency. The balance comes in the middle. At the most granular or basic level (namely, in simple recall questions), tracking may have little benefit if the standard is much more sophisticated (such as if the standard relates to strategic thinking). The granular demonstration, while important, may bear little resemblance to the standard itself. However, along the growth trajectory, tracking may play a more impactful role, as learners, as well as parents, will be able to monitor the students' levels of readiness for reaching the standards. The closer the formative demonstrations are to the standards, the more beneficial they might be to track. And while the orthodoxy of assessment research might suggest *formative score* is an oxymoron, learners will be able to use the results to assess their own readiness. Even if tracking occurs in the form of a journal that emphasizes description instead of levels, the longitudinal tracking of successes, challenges, and growth will create opportunities for investment.

- **Prioritize useful feedback:** Grades, scores, and levels identify *what was*, but for the purpose of learning, emphasize *what's next*. While strategic tracking can be useful for learners, it is imperative that learners think descriptively about how they can respond to assessment results—especially when the purpose is formative. Again, assessment purpose reveals the intended *use* of the results, so the subsequent action should mirror that. Even when the purpose is summative, *what's next* feedback or direction can still be prioritized in the process.

Part 6: Questions to Guide Your Conversations With Students

Traditionally, assessment was often something done *to* students rather than *with* students. Good questions can generate conversations with students, and the resulting answers can provide invaluable feedback to the teacher, the team, and the school regarding how individual students and groups of students may invest in their learning in deeper ways. When assessment is done with students, they come to understand why they are being assessed, what the purpose is, and how the elicited evidence is intended to be used. Simply asking for feedback has powerful implications for the culture of a classroom, but being specific about assessment's purpose goes a long way toward securing a collective student mindset that assessment is about not just evaluating but also advancing learning. Being transparent about which feedback informs classroom policies and practices can have further powerful effects on the trust that teachers build with students. This trust leads to a culture of learning where students feel they can engage and learn at high levels. Use the following questions to engage in and facilitate dialogue among students and teachers. Use them to prompt writing and more deeply understand how to involve students in developing student investment in learning and school. (Visit **go.SolutionTree.com/assessment** for reproducible versions of these questions.)

Questions to elicit conversation on purpose include the following.

- What is the purpose of assessment?
- When is assessment helpful and engaging? When is assessment frustrating and challenging?

Questions to elicit conversation on growth include the following.

- How do you use practice work to improve?
- How do you transfer your knowledge and skills across units of study?
- What kind of instruction helps you learn the most?
- How can assessment help you and your teachers understand strengths and next steps in achieving learning?
- What kind of learning and support do you think teachers need in order to help you invest in your learning?
- How could tracking your progress be engaging and motivating? How could you track your learning progress?

Questions to elicit conversation on reflection include the following.

- What kind of reflection is most helpful? What kind of reflection is frustrating or challenging?

- To what extent can you articulate what you are learning? How do you know what learning looks like?

- How do your teachers and your school currently get your input on how school is going for you?

Part 7: Dangerous Detours and Seductive Shortcuts

Although many educators can quickly define formative and summative assessment with ready terms and metaphors that make sense, the truth is the work of engaging in a truly balanced assessment system is nuanced. As noted, there are times when formative becomes summative and summative becomes formative. It's important to always attend to the purpose of the moment and then elicit the desired evidence that will support that exact purpose. The evidence should support the purpose in a manner that leverages the instructional decision making that *both* teachers and students need to engage in. To dig deep, educators must avoid the detours and shortcuts that so often trap their decisions in traditional paradigms.

- **Focusing on labels:** Labeling an assessment doesn't make it so. Be cautious not to think that simply calling an assessment *formative* means the students have done formative assessment. The subsequent actions—not the labels—are what make the distinction.

- **Focusing on the size and scope:** Take caution not to think that an assessment is inherently formative or summative by the nature of its size and scope. The subsequent action is what matters, not how large or small the assessment is; every assessment can be used formatively or summatively—and even those purposes can morph over time as new evidence is gathered.

- **Defaulting to methods:** The method of assessment is irrelevant to the purpose, so don't believe that by utilizing a variety of assessment methods, learners engage in both formative and summative assessment. Methods are more or less appropriate given the intended learning and its cognitive complexity. Learners benefit from having the opportunity to show what they know in various formats, but that has nothing to do with how the learners use the resulting information.

CHAPTER 3
ASSESSMENT ARCHITECTURE

Learn stuff that matters. If I can look it up, I probably don't need to memorize it.

—Ninth-grade student

Assessment architecture—the plan or blueprint teachers develop to map out the assessment evidence they will use to monitor learning and determine proficiency throughout a unit of study—is the more clinical side of assessment design. While assessment architecture tends to be more technical in nature and perhaps, at first glance, paradoxical to emotional investment, teachers need it to purposefully and predictably create opportunities for students to fully invest in their learning. Purpose and predictability occur when assessment evidence is intentionally planned in advance and is clearly focused on measuring the intended learning. Assessment design is too often positioned as a technical action and focused on a singular, limiting type of method, such as a test. Shifting assessment from completion of work to meaningful evidence of learning creates an intentional focus on designing assessment evidence, or the assessment architecture, that communicates learning.

This shift allows students to identify their strengths and specific areas of growth. Focusing on strengths and using assessment evidence to understand learning leads to increased student confidence and emotional investment as students begin to believe they can learn. James McMillan (2020) notes the important connection between student emotions and assessment evidence: "Assessment information is only fully understood by consideration of social interaction and emotions" (p. 81). When assessment architecture is intentionally planned and communicated in terms of learning to students, investment takes hold (Brookhart, 2013a, 2020; Willis & Adie, 2016).

Part 1: Case Study

Mr. Sprig was a beloved middle school history teacher, recognized for his soft heart and his willingness to give his students second chances. He was known for his humor, his captivating storytelling, and his ability to keep even the most bored students' attention for an extended period as they learned about tedious historical details. Many details Mr. Sprig loved to share weren't even in the history books, or the standards for that matter. But he weaved interesting stories around those details, and Mr. Sprig knew middle schoolers love to feel like their teacher is providing more than they are supposed to get from the dull curriculum. Plus, their rapt attention indicated they loved to hear those stories.

While his entertaining, direct instruction had consistently been one of the strongest features of his teaching, Mr. Sprig wanted to make his assessment options equally engaging. He worked overtime to provide his students with interesting choices for demonstrating their learning. He always valued performance assessments—and he knew from experience that his students loved doing activities—but he found them a little challenging to design and use in history courses. He decided to challenge himself to increase his performance-based opportunities in a unit he knew needed to be more fascinating: the rise and fall of ancient civilizations.

Mr. Sprig first made sure he was looking at his state standard: explore the development of ancient civilizations (for example, Mesopotamia, ancient Egypt, the Roman Empire, ancient Greece, and the Xia dynasty) and the factors that led to their collapse (Louisiana Department of Education, 2019). He thought it important that each of his assessment options include things his students would enjoy. Then, using his curriculum and past assessments as a guide, Mr. Sprig created a tic-tac-toe approach to his assessment system (see figure 3.1).

Mr. Sprig gave students the tic-tac-toe options and asked that they select three options from within a single row, column, or diagonal (for example, A/D/G or D/E/F or A/E/I). Students also received three separate dates for submissions, so each project would have at least five days for development. That way, Mr. Sprig reasoned, he would not get three projects per student on the last day of the unit.

Though each project would be very different, Mr. Sprig wanted consistent parameters for quality on all projects, so he created a checklist outlining his expectations.

A: Develop a rap song highlighting the details of one or more political figures of that culture.	B: Build a diorama of the ancient civilization.	C: Create a mask or other piece of artwork that would have come from that civilization.
D: Write five blogs (that span a period of time) from the perspective of a citizen trapped in one of the famous skirmishes involving that culture.	E: Deliver a possible speech the leaders of that civilization might have given to try to prevent the end of their civilization.	F: Design the Facebook page for one of the key leaders of that civilization, and add dialogue exchanges between several key leaders on that page.
G: Create an animated story or video outlining the daily life of a religious citizen in that culture.	H: Create a topographical map highlighting the import and export options available to that civilization.	I: Develop a pictorial timeline depicting the civilization's rise to dominance and its ultimate decline.

Figure 3.1: Tic-tac-toe approach to assessment example.

- All provided historical details are accurate.
- One or more of the following systems is thoroughly addressed: social, economic, political, or religious.
- The project is creative. Ingenuity is involved in some way.

Each attribute on the checklist would be worth ten points. To increase the likelihood that he would not face a grading nightmare at the end of the unit, Mr. Sprig promised that if all students turned in each of their three projects by the deadline, the class could host a Death of a Civilization party on the unit's last day. Students could bring fun foods from home, dress in period costumes from that civilization, listen to music (loosely linked to the culture of study), and play some games. To make it even more exciting, Mr. Sprig would award one pass from a class period (to go to the library or student lounge for the hour or to skip the homework assigned that day) to the student who wore the most convincing costume.

It did not come as a surprise to Mr. Sprig that the students loved his ancient civilizations unit. He used the Roman Empire for their unit of study, and students seemed enthralled. The party was a blast, complete with decorations some of his students had made. And the unit projects did show some ingenuity. The wide array of projects helped students see the big picture of the Roman Empire. However, at the conclusion of the unit, the students did not do well on his final test about the social, political, religious, and economic features of that empire. Worse, they seemed unable to transfer what they had learned about the rise and fall of the Roman Empire to the later explorations of Mesopotamia, ancient Egypt, ancient Greece, and the Xia dynasty. Had all the time he'd put into preparing and scoring those activities been worth it? Maybe, he concluded, performance assessment didn't belong in the social studies curriculum.

Reflection

Like Mr. Stroelle from chapter 2 (page 38), Mr. Sprig recognized the importance of designing backward. He understood he must consider his assessment architecture during his preplanning phases, since "assessment is most effective when it is planned, purposeful, and intentionally sequenced in advance of instruction by all of those responsible for delivery" (Erkens et al., 2017, p. 5).

Efforts at assessment architecture are especially significant if teachers are going to differentiate assessment options with any degree of accuracy in measuring standards. Even though Mr. Sprig thought he did the right technical work, and even though his lessons and party activities captivated students, his best efforts did not generate his desired results for increasing achievement *through* engagement. It seemed to him as if he had increased engagement *at the expense of* achievement. Why? What went wrong?

Part 2: Celebrations and Considerations

While Mr. Sprig's attempts to fully engage his students included much to celebrate, there were some aspects of his plan that predictably contributed to his underwhelming results. Mr. Sprig had the right idea: student investment increases when learners are having fun, when they are interested, and when they are empowered through choice so students care about the content.

Mr. Sprig's attention to captivating student interest was laudable. For students to fully engage, all parts of the teaching and learning process—standards, assessments, curriculum, and instruction—must be tailored to nurture investment opportunities. Mr. Sprig used appropriate strategies for increasing interest and empowerment during both instruction and assessment activities: choice, relevance, and multiple engagement opportunities.

His instructional strategy of storytelling offered a fantastic mechanism to captivate learners. Storytelling, like in this historical context, can bring key ideas to life, adding emotion, visualization, and connections to make the learning memorable.

The challenge in telling an instructional story is to ensure the learning intentions—the clear learning targets or learning outcomes for the story—are front and center throughout the entire story and to then find multiple points and various ways within the story to make connections to the learning expectations for the listeners. Stories can be captivating in the moment, but if they don't lead the learner to understand the learning expectations, they miss the mark. When teachers employ storytelling, they must always ensure that the intended learning is transparent and understood by engaging students in dialogue or reflection on the key takeaways. Without both transparency and reflection, storytelling is at best a memorable experience, and at worst an entertaining pacifier.

Fortunately, Mr. Sprig's instructional efforts to increase student investment served as a conduit to his assessment design efforts. So, in addition to ensuring his assessment system would enable his students to navigate the learning in manageable and meaningful ways, Mr. Sprig designed more relevant performance assessments and gave his students choices in a popular tic-tac-toe format for differentiating products. What he discovered, though, is that *hands-on* doesn't always equate to *minds-on* in important learning activities. Just like storytelling, performance assessments must be designed to reveal the learning expectations in transparent and metacognitive ways so student thinking emerges.

Assessment architecture includes designing or choosing varied, engaging, meaningful, and relevant assessment evidence. Ensuring that students are experiencing a variety of assessment methods that clearly demonstrate the intended learning creates a pathway to student investment. Assessment methods such as creating a video or playing or designing a game can be fun. There is, of course, nothing wrong with having fun while learning; the important thing is that the fun leads to critical learning outcomes all students need in order to succeed. Meaningful and relevant assessment methods can include having students produce something for an audience outside the classroom; for example, students could create potential ways for a city government to ensure families can access fresh fruits and vegetables when they do not have a car or other transportation. These solutions could appear in the form of a letter, a proposal, a video, or a presentation slideshow for the city government's consideration. The learning could include researching, reading, and formulating an argument with credible evidence. Assessment architecture focuses on intentional planning so the learning being measured is clear and the evidence generated is meaningful and relevant. Clarity, variety, meaning, and relevance in assessment design lead to deep student investment.

It's true that performance assessments can increase engagement. But, as education professor Suzanne Lane (2013) affirms, "It is also important to clearly delineate the content and cognitive processes that need to be assessed" (p. 314). As intricate as his assessment system might seem, Mr. Sprig's challenges began and ended with gaps in his assessment architecture—specifically, the integration of his standards, the missing formative pathway he should have utilized to ensure readiness, the inaccuracy and inequity of his final summative choices, and the lack of clarity on how he would determine proficiency.

To begin, Mr. Sprig had a complex standard—to explore the development of ancient civilizations and the factors that led to their collapse—but he limited his interpretation of the standard to be about defining the civilizations' cultural features. He was seeking recalled information about the important features of any working society. In this case, students were simply listening, reading, or viewing to capture and retain important snapshots of information to reproduce later. Even in the case of only seeking recalled details, Mr. Sprig's content expectation was too broad. Was the economic system of more or equal importance compared to the political, religious, and social systems? Were students meant to drill down into the art and music of a civilization? If so, how far? Without more clarity for the students, they wandered aimlessly through Mr. Sprig's captivating instruction, gathering only the points that resonated with them the most.

More importantly, however, Mr. Sprig did not capitalize on the opportunities to integrate meaningful content and skills into his unit or his performance assessment design. His selected standard highlights two significant skills that he could easily have embedded in his unit of study in the form of learning targets: (1) inquiry and exploration and (2) justification and argumentation regarding the factors that led to societal collapse. Imagine the benefits if Mr. Sprig had created clear learning targets for his content as well as the inquiry and justification skills for his ancient civilizations unit. He could have done the following.

- Used the content and skills to engage student thinking
- Clarified the purposes behind each assessment and even each assessment item
- Targeted specific thinking skills in various assessment choices so his choice board had a more balanced set of opportunities
- Created a formative pathway in which he used small formative tasks to ensure students got the feedback they needed for achieving the standards and to monitor student growth or gaps prior to the summative assessment

The beauty of performance assessments is they allow for the integration of skills and content that can reveal degrees of student understanding in the final products. In such a scenario, students would not just be gathering information about all things Mesopotamia; rather, they'd be exploring and gathering key information to justify which of the many underpinning systems of Mesopotamia may have led to its ultimate demise. These systems could include the exclusive language of the Sumerians who lived there, the nomadic tribes that wandered the expansive desert spaces between the rivers, or any other of Mesopotamia's hallmarks. With those realities in place, learners would shift to using the same exploration skills to study their own culture. Then, they would build their arguments on which modern systems in their current reality could most likely threaten *this* civilization and what plan they would implement to protect it.

With more robust options for summative assessments, Mr. Sprig could have established a formative pathway where he used smaller tasks to check for students' grasp of cultural features, students' skills with exploring and gathering information, and students' ability to argue and support claims. This would have given him better opportunities to check results along the way and prevent surprises—by students and himself—at the conclusion of his unit.

Attending to assessment architecture could have allowed Mr. Sprig to ensure his tic-tac-toe choice board design was robust and equitable. As they stood, the choices did not ensure that the three options one student selected would be of equal value to any three options other students selected. If, for example, a student picked the first row, then all the evidence the student generated would have remained at a low cognitive level wherein the primary purpose was to share specific details in creative avenues. On the other hand, a student who selected the second row's options would have engaged in more robust cognitive activities where inferencing, justifying, and arguing were required. However, if Mr. Sprig had incorporated thinking skills and planned his assessment pathway in advance, he could more strategically have set up a choice board that graduated in complexity. He could have ensured that each line of three options included multiple content features he wanted to ensure students understood, a task that involved an inquiry feature, and a task that involved an argumentation feature that tackled the preservation of cultures.

Equally problematic, Mr. Sprig's project expectations did not lend clarity regarding his learning criteria for the work's quality, and they did not illuminate the proficiency levels students should have tried to reach. Instead, his expectations offered a checklist of details that left many questions in students' minds and prohibited students' ability to drive their own learning. Figure 3.2 (page 66) outlines the questions students likely had about the detail-oriented checklist.

Mr. Sprig would have been more likely to generate student investment and monitor growth over time if he had developed a rubric that he could use over time on all his standards that addressed inquiry or argumentation. In that way, students would have understood his expectations more clearly and could have remained focused on making improvements over the course of multiple assessments. An inquiry rubric, for example, would likely have included criteria such as questioning, planning, executing, analyzing, evaluating, and communicating. An argumentation rubric might

Mr. Sprig's Checklist of Expectations	Unanswered Questions for Students
All provided historical details are accurate.	Which historical details? Is there a degree of sufficiency for the historical details? How deep of a dive is needed in each detail?
One or more of the following systems is thoroughly addressed: social, economic, political, or religious.	Is *or more* required for an A, or can one system addressed thoroughly qualify for an A? Does the level of proficiency increase with each additional cultural system? Is one system more important than another?
The project is creative. Ingenuity is involved in some way.	What does *creativity* look like or mean? Is creativity found in the product that is produced or in the way the content is interpreted? What happens to a grade if a student is not deemed creative?

Figure 3.2: *Clarifying questions when quality criteria are not present.*

have included criteria such as quality claim, accuracy and sufficiency of evidence, reasoning, and presentation. In a rubric, each criterion is more fully described, outlining the various levels of proficiency. Though clarity around the criteria is never instantaneous, teachers can achieve it through activities that repeatedly use such tools and allow students to frequently revisit the ideas, explore the criteria in examples of strong and weak work, and provide both self- and peer feedback with the criteria.

Such work requires much forethought and planning. Measuring the demands of learning cannot be left to chance. In the absence of a tight, preplanned assessment blueprint, both teachers and students can wander aimlessly through content and *hope* they hit the mark by the end of the unit of study.

Part 3: Action to Take

Assessment architecture is the intentional planning teachers and teams do to clearly sketch out what students will be learning, the assessment evidence teachers will use formatively to provide feedback so students grow, and the evidence teachers will use summatively to determine students' level of mastery of the standards. Designing assessments to generate the desired evidence before beginning to engage students in the learning leads both the teacher and students to clarity as to what mastery of the intended learning looks like throughout the instructional unit. The clearer teachers are in sharing what is to be learned and providing a relevant and meaningful purpose for the targeted learning, the more students invest (Andrade, 2013; Briggs & Furtak, 2020; Brookhart, 2020; Willis & Adie, 2016).

Clarity begins with laying out the pathway to achieve the intended learning. Here, professors Derek C. Briggs and Erin Marie Furtak (2020) note the significance of teachers using learning progressions to develop clarity around their own learning theory, which in turn helps them generate meaningful questions and activities on the progression pathway that will define how students come to the intended learning:

> Research on learning progressions represents one tangible response to a key recommendation from *Knowing What Students Know*, namely that all assessment activities should be motivated by, or at least motivate reflection about, theories for how students learn in a given subject domain. The presence of a learning theory is important because once established, it is more general and comprehensive than any single assessment event. A good theory helps teachers to pose the questions best suited to their students, so ideally it is learning theory that eventually drives student assessment, and not the other way around (Shepard, Penuel, & Pellegrino, 2018). Moreover, theories about how students learn can help teachers discern instructionally relevant insights from the answers that students give on assessment items. Because learning progressions are premised on testable hypotheses, the learning theories that they embody can and should be modified and refined over time. (pp. 146–147)

Teachers work together to create and refine learning progressions that they share with students. They co-create the meaning of these learning progressions with students through assessment that is embedded within a unit of study. Assessment architecture is the plan that grounds teachers' instruction and assessment. This grounding increases teachers' ability to communicate with students so students gain clarity about the qualities of learning.

This clarity leads to the conditions that cultivate student agency, which is an integral aspect of student investment. During the co-construction process, teachers intentionally build student agency when they seek feedback from students to deeply understand students' interests, lived experiences, and worldviews. Student agency is about creating relevant and meaningful opportunities with students so they can make informed decisions about what they learn, how they learn, and how they show evidence of their growth and mastery of intended learning. Integral to student agency is the teacher's ability to gain understanding of all that students bring to the classroom. With a strong assessment architecture in place, teachers foster classroom and school practices where students have agency and develop investment in their learning as they see their work and what they are learning as integral to their current and future success. Learning progressions and student agency practices have specific nuances that lead to student investment through assessment architecture.

Learning Progressions

Learning progressions provide a blueprint for instruction and assessment that makes clear to teachers what and when to assess (Andrade, 2013). Learning progressions are made up of the learning targets crafted from standards or competencies and laid out from simple to complex in cognitive demand as a pathway to achieving the learning intentions. They are a very important assessment design idea (Shepard, Daro, & Stancavage, 2013) since they highlight the intimate relationship between classroom instruction and assessment—something often missing when it comes to large-scale standardized testing. For students, learning progressions make the sequence of instruction more obvious and transparent; students can invest in learning they can see.

There are certainly a wide range of working definitions of *learning progressions*, but according to formative assessment expert Margaret Heritage (2013), they all coalesce around (1) laying out the successive, increasingly more sophisticated steps in learning and (2) describing development over an extended time. In the past, teachers have often hidden, been opaque about, or haphazardly shared what students are to learn. This learning, defined in the assessment architecture, is now seen as a critical part of how students learn and how teachers can purposefully sequence instruction and assessment for a more efficient and effective learning experience. D. Royce Sadler's (1989) conceptualization of formative assessment posits that students must be clear on what they are supposed to be learning, and they must have the capacity to monitor and adjust their own work. Sadler's three formative assessment conditions—(1) students understanding their performance goals; (2) students having an opportunity to compare the performance goals against their actual performance; and (3) students having an opportunity to close the gap revealed between their desired performance and their actual performance—lend themselves to three questions: (1) Where am I going? (2) Where am I now? and (3) How do I close the gap? These questions serve as the model framework for subsequent models of formative assessment from Black and Wiliam (1998), John Hattie and Helen Timperley (2007), Jan Chappuis (2015), and others (Brookhart, 2020). According to Andrade (2013), theories of formative assessment argue that the agency for learning resides with the students, which makes it even more critical for teachers to give students opportunities to learn how they can manage their own learning.

Terminology matters when it comes to learning progressions. While many terms are used interchangeably (for example, *learning progressions* and *progress maps*), it is important to make clear the distinction between a vertical learning progression through multiple grade levels and the more finite progression from simple to sophisticated within a sequence of lessons or a unit of study. For the purposes of this book, the term *learning progression* refers to the latter while the term *vertical alignment* refers to the former; students' investment through assessment architecture is much more associated with the simple-to-sophisticated structure of a lesson sequence or unit.

Understanding the Value of Learning Progressions to Student Investment

Learning progressions have value related to student investment in their use as purposeful sequences of instructional goals verified by formative assessment information that guides learning. For students, this sequencing can be pivotal in their ability to self-regulate their learning. Barry J. Zimmerman (2011) highlights the importance of having students engage in a continual cycle of setting goals and plans, self-observing, and self-reflecting if they are to be more self-regulatory; the learning progression makes it possible for students to have the clarity they need along the instructional sequence to fully engage in their actions.

Being able to fully carry out cognitive, affective, and behavioral practices and procedures is vital (Zimmerman & Schunk, 2011). If students are to be the agents for learning, then they can no longer remain passive recipients simply along for the ride. Teachers must purposefully create meaningful opportunities to neutralize this default disposition. Student investment begins with awareness of the learning goals and the necessary steps to get there. Once that level of transparency is achieved, the opportunities for students to invest through assessment architecture become that much more obvious.

Developing Learning Progressions

Prior to developing the learning progression, educators unpack standards to determine learning targets or learning intentions. Unpacking a standard is where educators interrogate the standard and analyze all the learning students need to do in order to achieve the standard. The resulting discrete learning expectations are often described as *learning targets* or *learning intentions*. Teachers develop learning progressions from the learning targets and learning intentions they tease out while unpacking the standard. Once educators have unpacked the standards into enabling targets, they need to purposefully arrange the standards to properly scaffold the learning to the appropriate cognitive complexity. Anyone who has taught a child how to swim or to ride a bicycle understands the need for a progression of learning. There is an intentional, step-by-step process one engages in to learn to swim or ride a bike. In fact, most teachers instinctively plan and teach with a progression in mind; it's just that they often inadvertently hide the progression from students or do not explicitly share it. If students are not clear about the learning progression, it can prevent them from seeing the bigger picture or ultimate learning goal.

Tom Corcoran, Frederic A. Mosher, and Aaron Rogat (2009) of the Consortium for Policy Research in Education identify five essential components of a learning progression. Table 3.1 outlines those five components in the left-hand column, with the addition of specific implications for student investment (not present in Corcoran and colleagues' [2009] text) in the right column.

Table 3.1: *Essential Components of Learning Progressions for Student Investment*

Essential Component	Implications for Student Investment
1. Learning targets or clear end points that are defined by societal aspirations and analysis of the central concepts and themes in a discipline	1. Clear learning targets make the learning goals transparent, which allows students to set goals, examine self-efficacy, and formulate plans moving ahead.
2. Progress variables that identify the critical dimensions of understanding and skill that are being developed over time	2. Identifying the *critical dimensions* of understanding and skill development gives specificity to what the end points look like; here, students can see the potential iterations of proficiency.
3. Levels of achievement or stages of progress that define significant intermediate steps in conceptual and skill development that most children might be expected to pass through on the path to attaining the desired proficiency	3. The stages of progress define the intermediate steps to illustrate to students the milestones necessary to reach proficiency. The milestones allow students more frequent successes (akin to learning to hold one's breath underwater when learning to swim), which can positively impact hope and confidence that success is within reach.
4. Learning performances, which are the operational definitions of what children's understanding and skills would look like at each of these stages of progress, and which provide the specifications for the development of assessments and activities that would locate where students are in their progress	4. Learning goals need success criteria: how students will show they know, understand, or can do. This *vision* of what understanding looks like allows students the opportunity to self- or peer-assess not only at the end point but also at all points along the progression.
5. Assessments that measure student understanding of the key concepts or practices and can track their developmental progress over time	5. Students can—where standards are negotiable—be allowed inside the assessment process to co-create assessments, codefine success, and track their own progress over time.

Source: Adapted from Corcoran et al., 2009.

Some learning standards and targets are clear enough to both students and teachers to post as is; however, others may be clear to teachers but not so clear to students. In the latter case, it may be wise to translate the learning targets into student-friendly language (Chappuis, 2015). Teachers can make learning targets student friendly in one of two ways. First, teachers can define what key terminology means. For example, a teacher could take the concept of developing a hypothesis and write, "I can develop a hypothesis. This means I can argue a logical proposal that can be tested to establish whether it is true." In this case, the integrity of the terminology is maintained. Second, teachers can rephrase the target itself; for example, they could redefine "compare and contrast" as "find what is similar and different." The point is not to compromise the acquisition of key vocabulary but to make the learning accessible. That can be accomplished by teaching up to key terminology or by redefining relatively complex concepts; the teachers must decide what matters most for their students.

Student Agency Through Assessments

A second route educators can take to improve assessment architecture in ways that ensure student investment is to promote student agency. *Student agency* means students have meaningful, relevant, and authentic opportunities to drive their learning through their own interests; it means giving them a voice and a choice in what their assessment experience is going to look like. With assessment, something often done *to* students, teachers can create opportunities for students to fully invest in the assessment process by ensuring students have agency. Teachers can ensure this by engaging students in relevant assessment tasks and by offering choices in how students show their learning. This is not a zero-sum game; teachers remain fully and actively involved in the assessment process *while* students enter the design process.

Agency Before the Assessment

Agency does not mean students are set free to do whatever they want; teachers and students still have to work within the mandated curricular standards. That said, most standards have some level of negotiability in assessment when only the learning process or the content is prescribed. Though standards may prescribe the outcome, *how* the students demonstrate that outcome could be up to them (or jointly negotiated). Most standards and learning outcomes do not dictate the assessment method. So while it is still important to match the right method to the learning target or standard since assessment methods are not interchangeable (Chappuis & Stiggins, 2020), students can have some voice and choice in showing their teacher what they know, understand, or can do.

In *Personalized Learning in a PLC at Work: Student Agency Through the Four Critical Questions*, Timothy S. Stuart, Sascha Heckmann, Mike Mattos, and Austin Buffum (2018) cleverly turn the four guiding questions of a PLC at Work (usually targeted to the adults) into questions that guide student agency:

1. What do *I* want to know, understand, and be able to do?
2. How will *I* demonstrate that I have learned it?
3. What will *I* do when I am not learning?
4. What will *I* do when I have already learned it? (pp. 16–17)

The first two questions are integral to the assessment design phase; moreover, the answers to those questions can be co-constructed with students, making the learning expectations transparent and serving as a springboard into student agency. While some people might argue that true agency is not possible within the sphere of mandated standards since students are not allowed to select their own outcomes (Richardson, 2019), the first two questions do allow for a good amount of student voice and choice even with prescribed standards. The foundation for inquiry-based learning is tapping into student curiosity—posing the focus of a unit of study in terms of questions and wonderings about the topic or process. Problem-based learning (also known as *project-based learning*) engages students in solving real-world problems or complex problems. Good problem solvers need to be good *problem finders* (Tishman & Clapp, 2017), so it is incumbent on teachers to create opportunities where students find problems, even within the mandated state standards or provincial curriculum. For example, with a prescribed standard such as, "Design, build, and refine a device that works within given constraints to convert one form of energy into another form of energy" (HS-PS3-3; NGSS Lead States, 2013), students could choose to explore alternative fuel sources. Or they could choose to explore ways in which atypical energy sources could be used in everyday products; a mandated standard does not mean voice and choice are not possible.

On the one hand, inquiry-based learning clearly is a way to foster student investment since, at its core, it means tapping into students' curiosity and intrinsic interests. On the other hand, inquiry-based learning receives somewhat mixed reviews in academic literature. While some studies show a significant increase in student achievement (Pandey, Nanda, & Ranjan, 2011), others (Hattie, 2012) reveal only a moderate effect size. Researchers find thorough research challenging because of the wide variety of what is called *inquiry based* (Friesen & Scott, 2013). Given all of that, teachers would be wise to focus on the *timing* and the *quality* of the experiences they afford their students.

Since the goal of inquiry-based learning is to foster an experience where students identify an area of curiosity to explore, the timing is important. Fostering this experience before students have foundational knowledge from which to explore their own curiosity about a topic would obviously be premature. Likewise, using inquiry to explore fundamental knowledge would seem an inefficient use of instructional minutes.

Teachers would also be wise to ensure the experience is high quality—that the experience challenges students to explore deeper, more sophisticated aspects of the subject discipline. Ensuring students are analyzing, critiquing, or creating will fulfill the promise of going deeper and having students fully invest in their self-identified area of inquiry.

The concept of student agency often creates a false dichotomy in the minds of educators, which they have been wrestling with for years. Educational reformer John Dewey believed that thinking of the student and the curriculum as separate creates this dualism between the agent (student) and the structure (curriculum; as cited in Nikolaidis, 2018). Pediatrician A. C. Nikolaidis (2018) asserts that the solution to this dichotomy lies in the collapse of this progressive-versus-traditional view. Educators don't have to choose the one they value more and go all in. Again, agency is not a zero-sum game where an increase in student investment leads to a decrease in teacher involvement; both can and should exist simultaneously.

Agency Through Relevance

Assessment and evaluation expert Ralph W. Tyler (1950) professes that "no single source of information is adequate to provide a basis for wise and comprehensive decisions about the objectives of the school" (p. 5). He suggests that a study of the learners themselves would be a valid source to identify the objectives of education. Tyler (1950) adds:

> It is essential to see that education provides opportunities for the student to enter actively into, and to deal wholeheartedly with, the things which interest [them], and in which [they are] deeply involved, and to learn particularly how to carry on such activities effectively. (p. 11)

Perpetuating the either-or dichotomy is not helpful here, as Tyler (1950) also suggests that contemporary life and subject specialists (among several sources) be used to determine outcomes. His point is that students can be a source for determining objectives, and while Tyler may not have had models of student-sourced interest in mind, the point still holds.

Zimmerman (2011) conceptualizes the self-regulation of learning as having three phases: (1) forethought, (2) performance, and (3) reflection. During the forethought phase, learners need opportunities to determine their self-motivation beliefs and interests (among other things) in order for them to invest in the learning that is about to unfold. Relevance offers the *why* of learning, which can be expeditiously identified if sourced from the learners themselves. Rather than trying to retrofit relevance, teachers who offer interest and curiosity as starting points allow agency to emerge more authentically and give learners the chance to drive their experiences, even within the expectations of a mandated curriculum.

Relevance in design lets learners decide how they demonstrate that they have reached their goals. In consultation with their teacher or autonomously, learners can shape their demonstrations to include their talents, passions, and interests. Most curricular standards do not dictate the assessment format, so while teachers will need to enhance their ability to infer quality via atypical demonstrations of learning (movies, projects, games, music, and so on), the opportunity for students to show what they know in various, more personalized formats exists nonetheless.

Relevance in the reflection phase occurs when students discover more about themselves (interests or noninterests, skills and challenges, effective or ineffective strategies for addressing the challenges, and so on) based on their experiences and results. In this way, assessment is both a window and a mirror—it helps the teacher see in to how the student is understanding or advancing their learning while also helping the student explore the self from an internal vantage point and a natural curiosity.

Agency Through Inclusivity

To promote student agency through assessment architecture, teachers must create the most inclusive learning environments possible. Inclusivity does not just narrowly center on those who qualify for special education. In fact, the qualification for special education is irrelevant to a student's need for support (Jung, 2017). While students who qualify for special education are certainly part of an inclusivity effort, a broader view of inclusivity that includes culture, language, race, and sensitivity to harmful gender norms is more desirable. Inclusiveness scholar William Ayers (2001) articulates key phases to understanding who students are and connecting their experiences with student agency:

> A first step is becoming the student to your students, uncovering the fellow creatures who must be partners to the enterprise. Another is creating an environment for learning, a nurturing and challenging space in which to travel. And finally, the teacher must begin work on the intricate, many-tiered bridges that will fill up the space, connecting all the dreams, hopes, skills, experiences, and knowledge students bring to class with deeper and wider ways of knowing. (p. 122)

In response to these key steps, leading scholar in the area of culturally responsive teaching Geneva Gay (2018) articulates the need for a broad definition of inclusiveness and concludes that "teaching is most effective when ecological factors, such as prior experiences, community settings, cultural backgrounds, and ethnic identities of teachers and students, are included in its implementation" (p. 28).

Another critical aspect of inclusivity is teachers having what Yvette Jackson (2011), in her book *The Pedagogy of Confidence*, calls a "fearless expectation and support for all students to demonstrate high intellectual performance" (p. 13). If teachers believe that high levels of performance are possible for all learners, then they will relentlessly pursue strategies to meet students' diverse experiences and needs. In addition, educators will seek constant feedback from their students to inform the actions and strategies so they create the classroom environment where all learn at high levels. Teachers expect and attain this high achievement by deeply seeking information about how students learn and what connections will lead to developing confidence, understanding, and investment.

Many educators have turned to Universal Design for Learning (UDL) as an organizing framework for inclusivity and equity. UDL is about eliminating barriers so every student can succeed (Novak, 2016). Briefly, the UDL framework guides the design of learning environments that are both accessible and challenging for all. The fundamental idea is to create multiple means of engagement for purposeful, motivated learners; representation for resourceful, knowledgeable learners; and action and expression for strategic, goal-oriented learners (Meyer, Rose, & Gordon, 2014). Student agency through assessment architecture converges particularly through optimizing relevance, value, and authenticity as well as minimizing threats and distractions. It could be argued that there is no greater threat to students than being excluded, minoritized, or *otherized* through the assessment process. Teaching for inclusivity at its most effective will have teachers "create a learning climate in the classroom and devise activities that allow all children to feel safe, respected, and valued for what they have to contribute" (Katz, 2012, p. 3).

The Mr. Sprig vignette (page 60) has much to capitalize on for meaningful inclusivity. For example, storytelling is a prominent oral tradition within Indigenous cultures, so Mr. Sprig's attempt to create student investment through storytelling, while poorly executed, was aimed in a favorable direction. Teachers can collapse the dominant Eurocentric view of what a successful learning demonstration looks like if they create culturally relevant opportunities where individuals can demonstrate their learning or where students come to know the validity of oral traditions as part of an authentic classwide expression. As well, these opportunities encourage all learners to appreciate and deeply accept that, even within the parameters of a prescribed curriculum, they can define and source success; all they need is the chance.

Part 4: A Learning Continuum for Implementation

Assessment architecture forms the foundation of rooting student investment in learning and not simply in the completion of work. More often than not, teachers and teams engage in the work of identifying what students will learn, how they will learn it, and how they will measure levels of proficiency or mastery. This backward-design process (see also chapter 2, Part 2: Celebrations and Considerations, page 39) has been well explored and implemented in educational settings for a long time and has had varying levels of success in clarifying for students what they are learning, why they are learning, and how assessment connects to their learning (versus just a grade or score). When assessment architecture begins to attend to student investment, the process of assessment architecture intimately engages students in defining learning, choosing evidence, and guiding their learning as teachers notice and observe what is working for students and what is a struggle. Teachers, in observing, make moves to ensure students learn how to progress in their learning and how to reflect on the strategies and things that help them take the next step and stay deeply engaged or re-engage.

The journey often begins with a teacher-directed practice and moves to teacher-centered actions (see figure 3.3, page 78). As teachers develop a clear vision of student investment, practices move to more learner-centered approaches and then learner-directed ones while students unlearn relying on the teacher for understanding their learning. Each step on the continuum provides teacher actions that signify where one is on the journey. It is important to note that while this figure is offered as a continuum leading to student investment (learner-directed action), there will be times when teachers and students move back and forth on this continuum as they notice the impact a given move or practice has on student achievement and confidence.

Students' unique needs, strengths, and experiences play an essential part in students' and teachers' working together to design and execute the assessment architecture and to ensure an inclusive and rich environment for all students.

Part 5: Tips for Moving Forward

Designing an assessment architecture can feel overwhelming, especially if educators feel they never received instruction on how to design quality assessments, never received feedback on their existing designs, never realized how challenging such work could be, or simply never experienced or needed to engage in the work because of existing curriculum-based assessments. But the truth is teachers are assessing all day, every day—even in the day-to-day, moment-to-moment instructional questions they choose to employ. Being purposeful and strategic about the design can lead to a more informed and intentional response that better ensures the desired outcomes are accomplished. Teachers can take the following small, deliberate steps to advance their assessment architecture efforts in service of generating better learner investment.

- **Create learning progressions of increasing complexity:**
  A learning progression is much more than a sequencing of topics; it is a purposeful progression from simple to sophisticated based on the increasing cognitive complexity of the learning targets and standards. Learning progressions are often the answer to the "Why do we have to learn this?" question that arises when students do not see how the current learning targets, or intentions, connect to the

bigger picture. Investment through architecture begins with clarity on how sophisticated the learning targets, or intentions, are and the purposeful pathway to reach them.

- **Ensure learning progressions are transparent and accessible:** Learning progressions need to be accessible to all learners; at no point should students wonder where learning is going. Most teachers have a progression in mind as they are teaching; however, ensuring the students have clarity about the progression can sometimes be a different story. Part of transparency is accessibility, which means teachers can use student-friendly language to describe the progression so they avoid any extra hurdles in understanding. That said, if terminology is essential to the learning, then *teaching up* to the vocabulary is more desirable than simplifying it.

- **Plan assessment within the progression:** Assessment architecture is most effective when it is planned and purposefully sequenced in advance of instruction (Erkens et al., 2017). Planning for where both formal and informal formative assessment strategies will be employed allows teachers more purpose and more flexibility. The most crucial aspect of this planning is to ensure students are ready for the increase in complexity. Rather than creating an epic assessment at the end that assesses all levels of complexity, consider assessing readiness at the most relevant times throughout the cycle or unit (often checks for understanding). Proactive planning prevents the last-minute surprise that students have not yet secured the foundational skills, and it ensures that the assessment used to indicate a level of mastery is at grade level and not below (or too focused on the prerequisite skills).

- **Make interest an instructional routine:** Although the existence of curricular standards does create some structure and definitiveness to learning, there is often much flexibility within those parameters. Tapping into student curiosity and interest can accelerate student investment through relevance. Teachers could, in advance of any unit of study, take inventory of what previous knowledge students are bringing to the learning and what they are particularly interested in learning about. Educators can also gauge interest at any moment by using cues, questions, or prompts to draw out of students what they find most intriguing about a topic or issue. Through prompts such as, "What have you always wondered about how the United States emerged as a superpower in the 20th century?" or "What do you find most fascinating about electricity?" teachers can foster student interest as a source throughout the instructional progression.

	Teacher Directed	Teacher Centered	Learner Centered	Learner Directed
Teachers and teams intentionally develop their assessment architecture by crafting learning progressions and cultivating student agency.	**Learning Progressions** • Teachers and teacher teams design learning progressions from competencies or standards. • Teachers share learning progressions with students. • Teachers design instruction and assessments that mostly align with the learning progressions. **Student Agency** • Students engage in instruction and assessment guided by the teacher. Regular prompts by the teacher ask students to reflect on their learning, how their	**Learning Progressions** • Teachers, along with their teams, develop learning progressions and accompanying assessment evidence and instructional practices to ensure students are intentionally learning to achieve the essential standards. Learning progressions guide the choices in assessment design and instruction. **Student Agency** • Students provide feedback and ideas after teachers have designed the progressions and assessments.	**Learning Progressions and Student Agency** • Teachers gather feedback and input from students on their interests and perceptions of how they learn. Teachers use this feedback to design assessment and instruction that clearly center the learning progression versus simply completion of work. • Students reflect on their assessment evidence, guided by the teacher. Students are able to articulate their strengths and next steps according to the learning progression.	**Learning Progressions and Student Agency** • Teachers design learning progressions collaboratively with students. Students consistently and regularly use the learning progressions to understand where they are and where they need to go. The learning progressions guide goal setting and are an integral part of students' conversations about their learning and progress. • Students are integrally involved in determining the evidence that will show their learning

learning is going, and how it is meaningful. • Students may ask, "Why do we need to learn this?" and the response is mostly driven by the teacher or reasoning that insinuates this is the way it has always been done. There is a test. • Students may have some opportunities to learn in different ways, and there is some connection to different interests or experiences students bring to the classroom. Instruction, assessment, and learning are mostly the same for all students.	• Students reflect on their assessment evidence, guided by the teacher. Students are able to articulate their strengths and next steps according to the learning progression. • Teachers provide choices for students in helping them take their next step toward mastery. This involves analyzing errors and working on misconceptions or incomplete understanding. These choices provide some opportunities to learn in different ways.	• Students reflect on the ways they learn best and make plans to take the next steps in their learning. • Students, with teacher guidance, uncover their strengths and next steps. • Students and teachers create learning choices based on what the students and teachers notice works and what gets in the way of the learning process for individual students and groups of students.	across the learning progression. This happens prior to the beginning of a unit. • Students set goals and make action plans within the unit that clearly align with the learning progression. • Students articulate and demonstrate their growth through the assessment evidence they produce and collect. • Teachers work with students who are not showing progress and collaborate with them to take a different approach.

Figure 3.3: Continuum for nurturing student investment through assessment architecture.

- **Be thoughtful about the timing of student-driven processes:**
  While curiosity and interest can always be natural parts of instructional routines, engaging learners in student-driven experiences (that is, inquiry- or problem-based learning) is advantageous when they have a foundation of knowledge. Knowing *something* about a topic enhances their curiosity. So while priming the pump of interest is good at all times, revisiting students' interest and curiosity at a time when they have a foundational understanding will likely result in a more authentic identification of what could be the source of an investigatory learning experience.

- **Be thoughtful about the quality of student-driven processes:**
  Similar to the timing of student-driven processes, the quality of student-driven processes is essential to meet the promise of *relevance* and *depth*. Developing the assessment architecture prior to beginning a unit aids teachers in planning how to put students in the driver's seat. Teachers might consider beginning with a particular aspect of the curriculum for which they have more intimate knowledge or at least the aspect of the curriculum for which it is easiest to envision engineering authentic and rich student-driven opportunities. Part of the challenge at the beginning of learning is to also teach the process of inquiry. For example, it is important to get off to a strong start and not let inexperience with the process be compounded by a limited vision of what the process could look like. Teachers are experts in their content areas or grade levels, but that expertise often comes via a teacher-centric lens; the student-driven process takes time to build as the new norm. Quality over quantity is always a favorable way to begin something new.

- **Build inclusivity from the inside out:** Begin by taking advantage of the diversity that exists in the classroom. Language diversity, cultural diversity, racial diversity, learning diversity, and gender diversity exist in the majority of classrooms. A possible starting point could be the learning traditions that currently exist in students' personal communities or homes. Clearly, teachers need to handle these conversations with care, but building relevance and inclusion from the inside out creates a foundation on which to build. Relevant sources of diversity within the larger community (not in the school or classroom) can also provide opportunities for inclusivity that are transferable beyond just learning. Here, teachers might consider the cliché, "Think big, but start small," as they should always consider social norms and sensitivities when creating these essential opportunities.

Part 6: Questions to Guide Your Conversations With Students

At the core of student investment is intentionally bringing students in as partners in designing their school experience. This includes bringing learners in as part of the architecture of their learning. Some students have the knowledge and skills to take part in this without much guidance while others need modeling, instruction, encouragement, multiple opportunities, and feedback. When students are invested in their learning, they, along with their teachers, have ongoing conversations about what they are learning, how they are learning it, and how they will show their learning. The following prompts are designed to facilitate conversations and actions teachers and students can take to create the conditions for student investment when designing assessment architecture.(Visit **go.SolutionTree.com/assessment** for reproducible versions of these questions.)

Questions to elicit conversation on learning progressions include the following.

- How do you know what you are learning?

- To what extent is it clear that the assessments and instruction you are doing relate to what you are learning?

- "I know what I am learning." To what extent do you agree with this statement—strongly, mostly, somewhat, or not at all?

- How have your teachers shared what you are learning with you?

- Have there been times when you decided what you wanted to learn? What did this look like?

Questions to elicit conversation on student agency before the assessment include the following.

- How often do you learn something about yourself through classroom assessments?

- Do you ever feel over-tested? When has this happened?

- Do you feel like there is too much assessment? Why do you think that is?

- What kind of practice do you get before you feel like you have to know something?

- What kind of practice or feedback helps you learn the most?

Questions to elicit conversation on student agency through relevance include the following.

- What kind of relevant work are you doing? What has been most meaningful?

- Is it clear that the work you are doing is meaningful and will help you learn things essential for future success?

- To what extent are you learning things that are interesting and current—all the time, sometimes, rarely, or not at all?

Questions to elicit conversation on student agency through inclusivity include the following.

- Do you feel there are lots of different ways to learn in school that really attend to what your strengths are or how you learn?

- Can you articulate the ways you learn best and the ways that don't help you learn? If so, why? If not, why not?

- Do you get to show your learning or what you have learned in lots of different ways? Do you get to do lots of different types of assessments (tests, projects, recordings, and so on)?

- How do your teachers learn about the ways you learn best, your interests, or the kinds of topics that interest you?

Part 7: Dangerous Detours and Seductive Shortcuts

The path to quality assessment architecture is fraught with many opportunities for various types of errors along the way. Given such challenges, it would be easy to look for shortcuts and simple tricks. However, the process of designing accurate assessments, employing them thoughtfully, and then responding to the results in highly effective ways is most certainly *not* the venue in which to cut corners. Instead, teachers must strive to get students to accept and interact with their own results in meaningful ways. The following common errors—albeit well intended in application—can actually distract teachers and students from the right work.

- **Having a singular focus:** The idea that a teacher *only* does inquiry or *only* does problem-based learning is unnecessarily and artificially limiting. Likewise, fostering inclusivity only along cultural lines while ignoring (or giving only lip service to) language or gender diversity is equally unhelpful. While it is important that teachers start slowly to ensure quality experiences, remaining stuck limits student investment through assessment architecture.

- **Increasing testing:** Having an effective assessment plan does not mean increasing the frequency with which teachers test or quiz their students. There is certainly a place for those assessment types; however, an effective assessment plan uses assessment formatively, where feedback, readiness, and subsequent action are prioritized. Teachers plan these formative assessment strategies for both singular lessons and moments where the cognitive complexity of learning toward meeting the standard is at hand.

- **Being *too* interest driven:** Interest-centered learning does not mean learning is a free-for-all. Nurturing interest and curiosity is important, but it is also important to ensure that certain learning outcomes and standards are being met; interest-centered learning is not an either-or proposition. It is not about being reactive to students' whimsical musings day to day; it's about allowing interest and agency within the high expectations of rigorous learning experiences.

- **Defaulting to methods:** The method of assessment does not guarantee rigor or higher-level thinking. Selected-response or constructed-response items and even some performance assessments can be quite routine; a paragraph prompt could ask students to simply recall—in long form—what the teacher covered in class. The chosen method must be designed to elicit evidence at the appropriate cognitive complexity, but it's the sophistication of the tasks themselves that will determine how deep and rigorous the assessment is.

CHAPTER 4
INTERPRETATION OF RESULTS

We're told that the grade you get on a test doesn't define who you are—but how, when those who succeed are honored and those who fail are shamed?

—Twelfth-grade student

Assessment evidence, both formal and informal, contributes to students' making inferences about their potential to learn and their being motivated to persist in learning more (McMillan, 2020). Interpretations and inferences are critical aspects of how teachers analyze assessment evidence in the moment and, more intentionally, how that analysis leads to action that prompts students to learn more. Students need guidance in how to interpret assessment evidence so they can tease out their strengths and understand their next steps; that way, they can see possibility in those steps' leading to more success.

Student investment occurs when students' interpretation of assessment evidence leads to a sense of possibility and progress toward a goal. This progress, when made explicit to students, prompts momentum and fosters a belief that progress is not just possible but likely. This momentum fuels students' investment because they have clarity in where they are going, where they are, and how they can close the gap (Gay, 2018; McMillan, 2020; Sadler, 1989). Interpretations that are inaccurate, deficit focused, or too general or overwhelming for students lead them to experience apathy, boredom, and anger, and even to give up. Teachers can enhance student investment by implementing processes that assist students with interpretation of their assessment results.

Part 1: Case Study

The staff at Cargas Elementary School wanted students to invest in their learning with more consistency and accuracy for the upcoming school year. During a spring workshop, staff read some research on the power of self-regulation and loved the idea of using data notebooks to help students monitor their own progress. At a follow-up staff meeting, they decided to implement student data notebooks across the entire building. It was an exciting time! First, the sheer notion that students might finally be able to drive their own learning was exhilarating; and second, for the first time in a long time, all staff members were on board with a new initiative.

To make the initiative feasible, the principal used the parent-teacher organization's leftover funds from last year's book and cookie sales to purchase a four-inch three-ring binder for every K–6 student in the school. To make it manageable, teachers added subject dividers and made schoolwide agreements to color-code the various sections of the notebooks (for example, all mathematics pages would be green, all English language arts pages would be blue, and all science pages would be yellow). They also made agreements on the frequency and types of data that the notebooks would need to include. Those data included the following.

- The schoolwide positive behavior agreements and individual classroom rules, if needed

- Classroom grading policies

- Monthly reports from the school's computer adaptive testing system in both mathematics and language arts

- Quarterly reports from the district's benchmark assessments

- Biannual reports from the state testing system (a formative one and a summative one)

- Data from classroom tests, assessments (like running records), or projects

- Worksheets and artifacts or projects from weekly efforts (at least one contribution per week)

- Notebooks from class note taking (the four-inch three-ring binder could accommodate several notebooks if they were also three-hole punched)

- Student SMART goal sheets—one per subject

- DynoWards (certificates earned for good behavior or high achievement scores that could be turned into currency to purchase small items at the school store)
- Any other certificates or honors earned (for example, student of the month, sports achievements, and so on) that could show students in their best light

All computer-generated reports would be three-hole punched so students could place them behind the appropriate tab as directed.

Students in the intermediate grades (grades 3–5) would engage in peer-assessing the binders so teachers could be certain those students were including all the appropriate materials. Intermediate students who demonstrated a strong command of their own data notebooks or personal achievement gains could earn DynoWards by visiting the primary classrooms (preK to grade 2) and reviewing and approving the primary students' data notebooks or flagging those that were missing or misplacing important data. In this way, teachers could feel more certain that data notebooks were comprehensive and accurate when parent-teacher conferences took place.

To make data notebooks fun and personal, students could use special bright-colored markers to write their names on the binders. Each teacher would ask students to decorate their notebook covers with markers or stickers in a manner that would help their teacher best understand their individual strengths as learners. The data notebook should serve as a celebration of learning.

The shiny new notebooks and bright-colored markers were distributed, and students and teachers alike launched the new year with great enthusiasm and a deep commitment to learning. Because of the agreements to add classroom policies and procedures, pages were added early in the year so students could immediately experience filling the notebooks.

But by the end of the first week, problems began emerging. First, the binders were too fat to fit within desks, so they always had to remain on top of each student's desk, and they took up a lot of space. With the binders consuming valuable desktop real estate, students could not put up their chairs at the end of the day for easy cleaning. Plus, the big binders were too heavy and large for the primary students' little backpacks, so it was impossible to take the binders home for parents to sign off on key data sheets.

By the end of the first semester, everyone—teachers and students alike—was tired of filling the notebooks. Worse, teachers did not notice an increase in student motivation *or* achievement. It seemed the only students benefiting from the entire experience were those who didn't need to increase motivation or achievement in the first place. The learners who liked learning appreciated the opportunity to document their success while the learners who typically struggled seemed to loathe documenting their results.

Reflection

When working to generate student investment, it's important to understand that "the interpretation of assessment results must be accurate, accessible, and reliable" (Erkens et al., 2017, p. 5). The Cargas Elementary School staff aspired to make the students' results transparent, trackable, and applicable for future learning. Isn't that the same thing? They applied well-intended, detailed, and diligent efforts to involve students in comprehensive ways. What went wrong?

- Why were students only marginally invested, to almost the same degree as they were before the data notebook launch?

- Were the research articles the staff read wrong? Should the school have given up the data notebooks altogether?

- Were the researchers right but the process just didn't work with the Cargas Elementary student population?

- Were the researchers right but the school's system was missing something? Should the school have kept data notebooks but tweaked efforts so students would eventually invest?

In the end, the Cargas staff felt as unsuccessful and unempowered as they feared their students did.

Part 2: Celebrations and Considerations

The Cargas faculty took a unified and proactive stance to address a common concern: students did not seem as invested in their own learning as teachers would prefer them to be. To their credit, the faculty had engaged in examining the research so they could identify best practices before they launched, and they worked to build consistency in their chosen approach across the entire campus. Moreover, they shared agreements on the frequency and types of data to gather while still attempting to personalize the data from grade level to grade level and student to student. They readily agreed that students at all grade levels could monitor their own growth, and they adopted the popular educational trend of using data notebooks to do so. Each of their decisions seemed to align with best practices, so their frustration is understandable.

The Cargas staff tried to be proactive. They anticipated that some students would not be inclined to track personal data of their own volition, so they generated positive DynoWards to encourage the issue. Extrinsic rewards are still immensely popular in schools despite a consistent body of evidence indicating their adverse effects on learning and motivation (Chappuis, 2015; Pink, 2009; Ryan & Deci, 2000a, 2000b). The research is not new. In their 1999 meta-analytic review of extrinsic rewards' effects on intrinsic motivation, Edward L. Deci, Richard Koestner, and Richard M. Ryan note that providing extrinsic rewards only serves to "undermine" people taking responsibility "for motivating or regulating themselves" (p. 659). In fact, studies reveal that extrinsic rewards can have an even greater negative impact on any task of cognitive significance such as learning (Hattie, 2012; Pink, 2009).

This is not to suggest that all reward systems are instantly flawed or detrimental to learning. Extrinsic rewards, however, are beneficial *only* to the degree that they direct students' attention to the learning and facilitate a burgeoning awareness of where to remain focused throughout the remainder of the learning without additional rewards being necessary (Hattie, 2009; McMillan, 2020; Pink, 2009; Reeve, 2018). In general, extrinsic rewards like the DynoWards contain no helpful feedback that can lead to new learning and no supportive task information that can lead to consistent repeat performances.

When students see and feel success, they are more likely to invest in their learning and persist (Brookhart, 2020). Assessment evidence, at its best, is interpreted to inspire hope and possibility and lead to action that increases learning and success. Michael T. Kane and Saskia Wools (2020) articulate interpretation's central role in making high-quality decisions about what instruction students need and guiding students to understand their strengths and next steps in a way that generates a productive response—one that increases achievement and confidence:

> The bottom line in validating classroom assessments (as in all assessments) is to identify the qualities that the assessment results need to have, given their particular interpretations and uses in the context at hand, and then to examine whether the assessment results meet these requirements. (p. 12)

Accurate interpretation involves all types of assessment evidence and the process of teachers and students noticing, observing, interpreting meaning (asking, for example, "What does this evidence say about students' understanding, misconceptions, errors, and next steps?"), and then communicating and taking action. To increase the accuracy of these interpretations, teachers must work with students to create a clear learning progression and then engage in defining the success criteria so students can deeply understand their progress and self-assess using their assessment evidence. Success criteria are the qualities that need to be present to show mastery of the learning. The success criteria help guide students' progress while they come to engage in the process of learning.

As students work with teachers to determine the learning that is most essential for them to achieve, goal setting becomes an important part of setting expectations and a clear outcome. Students work with teachers to set goals around essential learning intentions. Learning targets along the learning progression help students monitor progress through reflecting on their assessment evidence along the way, or throughout the unit of study. This reflection centers on students interpreting their assessment evidence to uncover their learning strengths and their next steps in growing toward achieving the intended learning. The goal orients both teacher and student to what the end learning looks like so the teacher can be instructionally responsive to the evidence gathered and help the student reflect and interpret the assessment evidence.

Surprisingly, the data notebooks themselves—if used to develop a student's personal strengths, talents, or interests—can become the necessary motivator without the addition of external rewards. Jackson (2011) states, "Developing an individual's strengths (or talent) provides the individual with a sense of self that is likely to motivate the individual to exhibit those strengths more frequently, leading to a reinforcing, generalizable cycle of success" (p. 91). Success truly does breed success (Jackson, 2011; Kanter, 2004; McMillan, 2020). Had the Cargas team found ways to highlight and leverage successes within a few key focused goal areas for students, the intrinsic reward system could have easily eliminated the need for DynoWards.

Research in the field of classroom assessment indicates that learners of all ages can and will likely invest in their own learning (Brookhart, 2013a, 2017; White, 2022; Wiliam, 2018a; Wiliam & Thompson, 2008), but certain conditions must be in place to enhance students' ability and willingness to invest. A key prerequisite is that students understand and own their results. As McMillan (2020) states, "The degree to which classroom assessment information is useful for learning depends in turn on how each student perceives, prepares for, and reacts to assessment, and how assessment affects each student's learning and motivation" (p. 85). Facilitating guiding conversations and reflections on students' motivations and what helped them learn or shut them down can help students uncover their perceptions of and reactions to assessment evidence. Exposing students to their personal data can make their results accessible, and asking students to reflect on their results can facilitate a shared interpretation of the data between student and teacher. Unfortunately, the efforts are certainly insufficient when it comes to ensuring the results are accurate or reliable. In truth, *visible* is not synonymous with *accessible*, so it's even debatable that *showing* students their results or having students self-manage the documentation of their results will suffice to make the data understandable or influential—key features of accessibility for students. It is through explicitly understanding students' thoughts and perceptions and then helping students make sense of those thoughts for their own learning that teachers can best influence productive responses from students. Productive responses are the bedrock of student investment.

The Cargas staff asked students to track way too many data. As if the sheer magnitude of trackable data was not challenging enough for teachers to track, the additional challenge of asking students to track a plethora of data that they did not understand, find personally relevant, or immediately pertinent doomed the effort. When students do not understand what the data mean, they cannot activate themselves as resources to address the chasm between where they currently are and where they need to be.

To activate themselves or each other as resources in moving their own learning forward, students must first be able to identify targeted areas for improvement, isolate the specific types of errors to address within those areas, and select clear and actionable strategies to *learn forward*. Of course, embedded in this requirement is the prerequisite understanding that (1) the learning expectations will be revisited in the context of the error so the student *can* improve, and (2) the new evidence will replace the old evidence so early mistakes never compromise the resulting level of proficiency during the summative phase.

Moreover, if the data to be tracked appear as marks, grades, or scores without the benefit of detailed feedback or the clear understanding of where and how to make the recommended improvements on future assessments, then students will be unable to *use* the data in meaningful ways (Andrade, 2013; Black, Harrison, Lee, Marshall, & Wiliam, 2004; Brown & Harris, 2013). Data notebooks are so often about numerical data and visible tools for tracking learning trajectories; as a result, specific feedback— the qualitative data regarding how best to improve—is left out. If students are to invest fully, they require more diagnostic and detailed information that empowers them "to move forward, to plot, plan, adjust, rethink, and thus exercise self-regulation in realistic and balanced ways" (Hattie & Yates, 2014, p. 66).

Part 3: Action to Take

Any educator who intends to create opportunities for students to gather, monitor, and celebrate learning is on point with the work of classroom assessment. Interpreting assessment evidence is rooted in noticing and intentionally reviewing what students say, do, and produce. Gathering these observations and artifacts to understand where students are in achieving the intended learning is important to shifting to a culture of learning. In order to foster student investment through interpretations, educators create pathways for students to see their growth, monitor their progress, and celebrate their learning. The Cargas staff had the right idea to gather and monitor evidence of learning through data notebooks, but in implementation, the staff lost sight of the process and purpose of collecting this evidence. Data notebooks might have *data* in *notebooks*, but they don't always lead to a student's ability to accurately document the data, carefully monitor and interpret the data, and successfully celebrate the learning (and not simply increase the quantity or number). In fact, the contents can become more of a collection of artifacts or large-scale assessment results that are not conducive to student investment or learning. The existence of data notebooks is a good start, but their utility for learning and investment matters more. Teachers can use data notebooks to prompt deep reflection on assessment evidence in relationship to success criteria along a learning progression toward achieving the standard.

Educators interpret many different types of assessment evidence at all levels of the school system. They can interpret these different assessment methods in ways that empower the system (district leadership teams and staff, school leadership teams and staff, teacher teams, teachers, and students) to make effective practice and policy decisions that increase student investment, including student achievement and confidence. Assessment evidence is the center of interpretation that leads to practices that guide students to collect, interpret, and invest in their learning. Interpretations inform the action educators take to foster student investment. Success criteria guide students and teachers to create a common understanding of what quality looks like when students have achieved the essential learning. Finally, goal setting is positioned to help students identify their targeted learning. Students use assessment evidence and the accompanying success criteria to monitor progress and determine when they have met this goal.

Explicitly teaching students how to self-reflect and self-assess is critical, as it develops students' ability to learn how to learn. This ability to self-assess accurately and reflectively leads to more targeted and effective goal setting, monitoring, and growth documentation (McMillan, 2020). According to McMillan (2020):

> Self-assessment is a student-centered activity in which the student evaluates his or her performance. Wylie and Lyon (2020) describe three steps in self-assessment: understanding the desired performance, monitoring progress, and taking action to improve their proficiency. As such, it is clearly related to self-regulation: evaluating and setting goals, being aware of learning, and comparing performance to intended learning (Brown & Harris, 2013). (p. 86)

Implementing data notebooks is a practical strategy of this process of interpretation. Critical to the effective and impactful implementation of data notebooks is a student's ability to define success criteria, self-assess, and set goals. Large-scale assessment is best used to assess system and school effectiveness over time; it does not provide the best data for individual students to monitor their ongoing progress toward achieving standards or learning intentions. Classroom assessment evidence is best used for monitoring progress and determining expectations; it is noted here to help educators move away from large-scale assessment data, which are frequently misused or overused in day-to-day classroom investment. Large-scale assessment data are important for the system, district, and school leadership teams to monitor, including interpreting results to understand the impact of practices and curriculum approaches being implemented. Large-scale assessment data can help the teams determine which groups of students they are serving well and which students they are not, meaning educators need to do something different. These data do *not* lead to student investment when used as the end goal. Achievement of the essential standards or learning is the end goal.

Large-Scale Assessments

Large-scale assessments are best used to understand system effectiveness. Inferences and interpretations made from large-scale assessments are most reliable when analyzed over the course of years and across a large body of students specific to an identified territory, so as to identify trends and anomalies within the larger data set. Relying on large-scale assessments to inform student learning day to day or unit to unit is often misleading. Data notebooks are intended to be used for reflection and progress to help students make connections to what they are learning, their actions, and their growth. A data notebook's contents need to align with the initial goal. If students are going to use the contents of their data notebooks to achieve the goal of self-regulating and investing in their learning, for example, then those contents need to represent a more frequent cycle of data analysis. Including data that are available only once or a few times per year, such as large-scale assessment data, is not useful when day-to-day student investment is the goal.

There is a place for large-scale assessments (state or provincial annual assessments or benchmark assessments), provided they are used at the appropriate and applicable level; every level (classroom, school, district, or state or province) of assessment can be valid, but every level needs to stay in its place. The value (or lack thereof) of large-scale assessments comes in the use (or misuse) of the results. This is neither an advocacy for nor a statement against large-scale assessment. Rather, the point is to keep each level of assessment at its most valuable level. *If* large-scale assessments are a reality, then educators must diligently work to ensure their classroom designs will align with the specifications of the large-scale assessment (areas of focus, standards, levels of rigor, expected proficiency), but the instrument itself will not unduly influence their targeted instruction. This means that large-scale assessment data are not useful to track or reflect on for a classroom assessment tool, such as a data notebook.

Large-scale assessments should influence large-scale decision making. For example, it's fair for states and provinces to ask whether the educational programming is effective for most if not all learners. Medium-scale assessments (such as districtwide interval benchmarks) are appropriate for medium-scale decision making—for example, asking, "Is our school's approach to literacy producing the desired results?" That leaves classroom assessments for more granular decision making. In the case of data notebooks, where the goal is to have students invest in their own learning on a day-to-day basis, the majority of the contents should reflect that and be grounded in the learning progressions.

Success Criteria

Success criteria are the qualities that lead educators and students to understand how they are progressing toward achievement of the intended learning. Learning progressions provide a road map toward achievement of the standard, competencies, or intended learning. Success criteria help guide self-assessment and teacher interpretation of where students are and where they need to go next.

Teachers can make success criteria transparent by purposefully having students co-construct the success criteria. Thinking about what quality looks like increases the effectiveness of self-assessment (Andrade, 2013; Ross & Starling, 2008). Goal setting and criteria co-construction need to be inextricably linked; goals set to established and co-created criteria lead to more seamlessness in learning. Co-constructing criteria serves as the backdrop for more effective goal setting; if the criteria are *learning focused*, then the goals are likely to be as well.

The process for co-constructing criteria is actually quite simple; the complexity comes in consistently utilizing the process, ensuring the criteria are learning focused, and predictably using the criteria to advance proficiency. In *Instructional Agility*, Erkens, Schimmer, and Dimich (2018) describe co-construction as follows:

> When students have a clear understanding of both learning intentions and success criteria, it is more possible for them to mobilize on behalf of themselves. Students can hit any target they can see (Stiggins, 2008). They make decisions at every point along their learning continuums; however, not every decision they make is necessarily on point or feeds their advancement to proficiency, especially when they base their decisions on an incomplete or faulty understanding of the learning outcomes.
>
> Once teachers clarify the intended learning outcome, they can deepen students' understanding of what successfully achieving that outcome looks like by involving them in constructing the success criteria. As Anne Davies (2007) writes, "When we involve learners in co-constructing criteria, they grasp important ideas more readily because they are translating expectations into language that they understand" (p. 39).
>
> Most students have some idea of what quality work looks like, even if their views are incomplete or faulty in some areas. Involving learners in co-constructing criteria has nothing to do with teachers relinquishing any control or influence; teachers must still be the final arbiters of the criteria. However, by co-constructing criteria, teachers put students in a position where they must consider the end result and the possible iterations of what success looks like. Co-constructing criteria can also serve as a formative assessment strategy since through that process, the teacher learns

what the students know and don't know about the task, skill, or process at hand. (p. 113)

In their book *Setting and Using Criteria*, Kathleen Gregory, Caren Cameron, and Anne Davies (1997, as cited in Erkens et al., 2018) outline a simple four-step process teachers can use to co-construct criteria with their learners.

1. **Brainstorm.** Brainstorm a list of ideas of what quality work looks like. Teachers often use a question or prompt to elicit ideas from the students. A few possibilities include the following: *What does quality writing look like, sound like, and feel like? What are the important aspects of a quality science lab report? What does a great speech sound like?* The point is to prompt students to put into their own words what it will be like to succeed; the teacher ensures that, in most cases, they describe quality in generic terms, which allows the criteria to apply across multiple demonstrations.

2. **Sort, group, and label.** Students then sort and group the ideas into logical clusters. They label these clusters with generic headings that organize the criteria. For example, they may organize all the ideas for *what makes a great speech* into categories such as *explanation of ideas, organization, supporting materials, integration of technology, nonverbal actions,* and *voice.*

3. **Make a T-chart.** The learning demonstration's cognitive complexity dictates how detailed the criteria are, but in any event, students should organize groupings into a chart that clearly articulates what success looks like. The left side of the chart lists the cluster labels, while the right side lists students' brainstormed ideas.

4. **Use the criteria to guide the work.** Ideally, the teacher posts the T-chart or otherwise makes it accessible to students so they can, while producing their work, consistently refer back to the chart to check where they are against where they need to be. (p. 113–114)

Erkens et al. (2018) go on to say:

While there are few steps, it is important that teachers not rush the process to provide ample time for students to reflect on what proficiency looks like. As well, teachers may develop a rubric with greater specificity from the established criteria. Sharing that with students would eventually be beneficial, but in the early stages it may be advantageous to keep the explanation of the criteria as simple as possible by simply articulating *here's what success looks like* without clouding the process with levels of success. (p. 114)

Once teachers and students have established criteria, examining exemplars can deepen students' ability to recognize quality in their own work and self-assess to further develop. Most often, through the collaborative examination of high-quality exemplars, teachers can engineer opportunities where learners hypothesize and brainstorm what aspects of quality are consistent among the exemplars. Teachers lead students in discussions about the qualities present in various exemplars. This discussion leads to deeper understanding of the success criteria. Once the class has exhausted the possible aspects of high quality, teachers and students engage in discussion to cluster the aspects into logical groupings they agree belong on the rubric. When they reach consensus on the groupings, the final step is to describe a natural progression of quality along however many levels have been identified; the levels usually connect to the larger scale agreed on at the school or district level for both formative and summative purposes.

When the primary purpose is formative and the advancement of learning is the priority, most teachers will organize the criteria into either an analytic rubric or a single-point rubric. For most, the term *rubric* conjures visions of an analytic rubric, which identifies the aspects of quality down the left side, the levels of quality across the top, and individual descriptions in all boxes where aspects and levels of quality intersect. Figure 4.1 depicts an analytic rubric on critical thinking (Erkens et al., 2019).

The advantage of these multipoint tools is all levels of quality have an individual description, making it easier for learners to pinpoint where they are along their own learning trajectory; the downside is they can be labor-intensive to create and verbose for novice learners to use effectively.

However, the other effective format is the single-point rubric, which identifies only the highest level of quality and articulates it down the center of the tool. In this rubric, space on one side is reserved for specific feedback on aspects of strength while the other side is reserved for specific feedback on aspects in need of strengthening. Figure 4.2 (page 98) exemplifies the structure of the single-point rubric. The advantages of single-point rubrics are that they do not reveal criteria for any level less than the exemplary level of performance, they allow for individualized feedback, and they are much easier to create. The potential downside is that they lack any specificity for those not performing at the highest level and may leave novice learners wondering what advice to give to themselves or their peers.

Students won't fill in every box; rather, the spaces are available to articulate details of what is particularly strong and what needs strengthening. There is no perfect rubric; teachers and students need to utilize the format that makes the most sense given the learning at hand.

Aspect of Quality	Initiating	Developing	Achieving	Advancing
Explanation of the issue	Minimally states and describes the issue with little specificity; significant gaps in information exist	Ambiguously states and describes the issue; some gaps in information evident	Adequately states and describes the issue; articulates most of the necessary information	Clearly states and thoroughly describes the issue; articulates all necessary information
Gathering and analysis of evidence	Minimally gathers the evidence and information and presents a limited view of the issue; superficially analyzes the quality of the available evidence for credibility and authenticity	Limitedly gathers the information and presents a narrow synthesis of the issue; minimally analyzes quality of the available evidence for credibility and authenticity	Sufficiently gathers the evidence and information and presents a complete synthesis of the issue; analyzes the quality of the available evidence for credibility and authenticity	Thoroughly gathers and presents evidence with an insightful synthesis of the issue; thoroughly analyzes the quality of the available evidence for credibility and authenticity
Personal hypothesis or position	Presents a singular, limited (simplistic or unclear) view of the hypothesis or position	Presents a limited view of the hypothesis or position; addresses some alternate points of view, but needs to address some gaps in logic	Presents a diverse view of the hypothesis or position; clearly and logically addresses several alternate points of view	Presents a diverse and thorough view of the hypothesis or position; clearly and logically addresses a comprehensive wide range of alternate points of view
Justification and assessment of resolution and its implications	Offers limited justification and minimally examines the potential implications of the resolution	Supports justification and inconsistently examines the potential implications of the resolution	Supports justification and completely examines the potential implications of the resolution	Thoroughly supports justification and comprehensively examines the potential implications of the resolution

Source: Erkens et al., 2019, pp. 33–34.

Figure 4.1: *Analytic critical-thinking rubric.*

Aspects to Strengthen	Exemplary Aspects	Aspects of Strength
	Aspect of quality	
	Aspect of quality	
	Aspect of quality	
	Aspect of quality	

Figure 4.2: *Single-point rubric structure.*

Goal Setting

Student investment through the interpretation of assessment results begins with students and teachers being clear on success criteria. This leads to goal setting, which, when students see and feel progress on targeted learning, becomes an integral part of motivation and learning (McMillan, 2020; Schunk, 2003). During the learning, students need to be able to judge not only their performance toward the standard at hand but also their progress toward what often amounts to an interval goal along the learning progression. Without the goal itself, that interval comparison would not be possible. For example, the chart in figure 4.3 indicates the goal and the success criteria and provides a document to track progress across three texts on any given scientific concept.

The existence of goals does not automatically enhance motivation and learning. Dale H. Schunk (2003), renowned expert in the self-regulation of learning, argues that certain properties—specificity, proximity, and difficulty—ensure goal setting has its desired effect. Rather than a generic goal of *do your best*, Schunk (2003) argues that specific goals are more likely to enhance and reinitiate learning. As well, he asserts that short-term goals (those closer in proximity) result in increased motivation and efficacy because students achieve them more quickly. Finally, Schunk (2003) insists that moderately difficult goals are ideal. Too easy, and learners tend to exert less effort; too difficult, and learners believe the goal is impossible to achieve. Finding that balance is essential so students perceive the goal itself as plausible and feel encouraged to exert effort toward the goal. In this way, teachers can raise motivation and self-efficacy—students' belief that their effort will result in growth. This sense of belief in their own ability to grow leads to a sense of hope. When hope is present, motivation follows.

Another mitigating factor could be the focus of the goals themselves. If self-assessment results in students giving themselves feedback to advance their own learning, then teachers would be wise to consider the importance of distinguishing between task-based feedback and learning-based feedback. Dylan Wiliam (2018b) asserts that "the purpose of the feedback is to improve the learner, and not the work" (p. 17). The

Goal: By the end of unit 3, I will apply scientific information to pose solutions to complex scientific problems.

Learning Progression	Success Criteria	Text 1	Text 2	Text 3
Apply information to solve complex problems (my goal). Make connections independently to other material with similar or different central concepts. Ask and answer evaluation and analysis questions about details in the text.	Students clearly describe scientific concepts using specific examples. Students clearly explain connections among scientific concepts. Students use information to clearly pose a solution to the problem. Questions are evaluative and analytic. Questions lead to solutions.			
Ask and answer questions about key details in a text. Retell information including key details, and demonstrate understanding of the central concept or lesson. Apply information to solve problems.	Questions and answers provide evidence that the text is understood. Details support the general meaning of the text. Explanations use the information accurately to pose basic solutions to set problems.			
Identify details in a text. Apply information to routine problem-solving situations.	Students describe general details. Explanations supply solutions to problems described previously.			
Students receive guidance or prompting from the teacher in order to complete assessment.	Teachers guide students to generate explanations.			

Figure 4.3: Sample progress-tracking document.

distinction between the work and the learner is critical since focusing on the *task* can improve performance on the task but have no impact (or even have a negative impact) on long-term learning. For example, a statement like "I will identify an accurate theme for *The Grapes of Wrath*" focuses on the task, whereas "I will grow in my ability to explain how the evidence in the examples supports the theme in a given text" focuses on the qualities of the learning. Setting goals to improve the task keeps the goals limited to the task and does not lead to transferable skills. For example, "I will learn how to put the data from my fingerprint lab into a line graph" focuses only on the task, whereas "I will learn how to collect data and represent them in multiple and meaningful ways" focuses on skills the student will use in other circumstances. For teachers, the ramifications for goal setting are quite clear: goal setting should focus on the *learning* the task is meant to reveal and not on the task itself.

Self-Assessment

The pivot point of student investment arises when students judge the quality of their own learning to determine what's next and to keep learning on track. The act of self-assessment draws on what Zimmerman (2002) calls *metacognitive competencies*, which can improve students' self-regulatory skills. The self-assessment process makes students the definitive source of formative assessment information (Andrade, 2013) and reinforces the centrality of learners in their own learning.

Research studies tend to group self-assessment methods into three major types: (1) self-rating, (2) self-estimation, and (3) criterion-based assessment (Brown & Harris, 2013). A *self-rating* is where students judge quality along a predetermined scale or rating system; these systems could feature levels of satisfaction (that is, the degrees to which students are pleased with the results) or levels of learning (that is, levels like exemplary, proficient, developing, and novice, accompanied by brief explanations). A *self-estimate* is where students literally estimate the degree to which they reached the learning goals before they know the results; this could be as simple as articulating how well they did on a test or as complex as providing specific details as to why they made the estimates they did. Finally, a *criterion-based assessment* (rubric), arguably the most common form of self-assessment, is where students use the established (co-constructed) criteria to judge the specific aspects of quality; the rubrics themselves will always be presented as incremental progressions of quality regardless of whether scores are attached to each level.

Another consideration with self-assessment is accuracy. Accuracy cannot be assumed, which reemphasizes the importance of setting goals and co-constructing criteria. This is not an advocacy against self-assessment but merely an important aspect to be aware of. In their book *Using Self-Assessment to Improve Learning*, Gavin T. L. Brown and Lois R. Harris (2013) wisely remind educators, "Consistent with reliability theory, . . . we consider that all self-assessments, no matter how privileged the self is in terms of knowing what the self has done, are imperfect indicators of competence" (p. 370). This suggests that teachers prioritize a formative focus on the self-assessment process and that they diligently ensure learners have a view of quality that aligns with the collectively agreed-on, co-constructed criteria.

Data Notebooks

Data notebooks (folders or portfolios) give learners an effective way to gather (on a large or small scale) authentic evidence of learning and any supporting documentation. Cargas Elementary was right to pursue data notebooks, but the targeted content completely missed the mark. Self-assessment on singular demonstrations of learning is essential, but data notebooks with multiple, random demonstrations of learning can generate a sense of *everything* being equivalent in value, which will distort a student's capacity to focus on what matters most. Whether they use a notebook, a folder, or a portfolio (tangible or electronic), students should receive a purposeful opportunity to invest in the big picture.

Professor of education Susan F. Belgrad (2013) defines *portfolios* as "authentic collections of student work that represent who students are as learners" (p. 332), which means the terms *data notebook* and *portfolio* are essentially interchangeable. She further adds the research is clear that being definitive about their purpose is key to using portfolios successfully. Belgrad (2013) has synthesized the four main purposes of portfolios as follows.

1. **Learning portfolio:** "Captures evidence of knowledge and skills to provide a holistic picture of learning and achievement over time" (p. 332).

2. **Developmental portfolio:** "Demonstrates the continuing growth and development as readers, writers, thinkers, etc." (p. 332).

3. **Assessment portfolio:** "Captures evidence of the achievement of benchmarks or standards, how criteria are met, and plans for improvement" (p. 332).

4. **Showcase portfolio:** "Invites students to focus on, communicate, and celebrate individual achievements or talents" (p. 333).

All four purposes are valid; the point is that a data notebook or portfolio cannot be everything simultaneously. Even more critical is that teachers, by way of assertion and execution, ensure data notebooks or portfolios fulfill the purpose. This is especially important when using e-portfolios—or an electronic collection of assessment and reflection on learning—where efficiency can easily surpass effectiveness. For example, school staff could easily claim that an assessment e-portfolio is going to replace the antiquated report card system to create a system that captures evidence of the achievement of standards, how criteria are met, and plans for improvement. However, in execution, the e-portfolio is nothing more than a showcase since what it is sharing has no substantive support. If students and parents are unclear about the purpose, the portfolio could be counterproductive. Again, there is nothing wrong with making *showcase* the purpose as long as that was the intended purpose in the first place. No purpose is inferior to the others; any mismatch between purpose and execution is what needs attention.

For student investment in learning, only the showcase purpose falls flat. Cargas Elementary could have chosen any of the other three purposes and then tailored the contents accordingly. Data notebooks can't be everything to everyone, so identifying the specific purpose leads to the specific contents that allow students to authentically track their growth, measure their achievement, or reflect on what is next along their learning trajectory.

Part 4: A Learning Continuum for Implementation

Interpretation of results is all about *noticing*. Teachers and teams of teachers notice and make inferences about students' strengths, misconceptions, misunderstandings, and errors. Those inferences lead to decisions that teachers and their students make about a student's next steps, the kind of instruction needed, and the probability of learning more.

The journey often begins with a teacher-directed practice and moves to teacher-centered actions (see figure 4.4, page 104). As teachers develop a clear vision of student investment, practices move to more learner-centered approaches and then learner-directed ones while students unlearn relying on the teacher for understanding their learning. Each step on the continuum provides teacher actions that signify where one is on the journey. It is important to note that while this figure is offered as a continuum leading to student investment (learner-directed action), there will be times when teachers and students move back and forth on this continuum as they notice the impact a given move or practice has on student achievement and confidence.

Part 5: Tips for Moving Forward

Educators often exclaim in frustration over the sheer number of assessments they are expected to give and the scores they are required to post on a weekly basis in the virtual gradebook. The volume alone can be overwhelming. The shortest and fastest route would simply be to score, record, and advance in an ongoing iterative cycle. However, this rinse-and-repeat cycle is especially dangerous when it comes to helping students generate a valid, reliable, and accessible interpretation of their own results. Helping students do this will take time—most likely more time than teachers generally feel they have the luxury of providing—but such time and effort is paramount to the teachers' success in generating the necessary understanding and buy-in on their students' behalf.

Teachers can use the following strategies to help students achieve a more accurate and accessible understanding of their results.

- **Front-load:** Student investment through the interpretation of assessment results depends on the setup. Providing the time and space for setting goals and co-constructing criteria pays dividends on the back end. These processes are essential to ensuring the interpretation of results holds its place between the *before* and *after* of learning.

- **Set goals with guidance:** As discussed, goals need to be specific, proximal, and at the appropriate level of difficulty; students won't set such goals automatically. Effective goal setting comes from teachers guiding their learners to dig deeper into those three elements to ensure that goals are not simply impossible-to-miss platitudes. *Doing one's best* can vary from day to day and is useless to advancing learning. Again, the up-front time investment is worth it.

- **Keep learning at the center:** Sometimes, the distinction between learning and performance can feel like one of semantics; however, it is critical to keep learning at the center of the self-assessment exercise. Learners' *performance* on a task is meant to reveal how much they have learned and what comes next. Yes, the line between learning and performance can sometimes be blurry, but remember that any task is just a means to an end—and the end is learning.

- **Co-construct . . . up to a point:** Co-constructing criteria is unquestionably a worthwhile endeavor, but teacher expertise matters also. As students brainstorm, cluster, and shape ideas about what high-quality learning looks like, teachers need to stay actively involved in the process to ensure that learning criteria do not omit critical aspects of quality. With finesse, teachers can insert ideas of quality in the form of cues or questions that elicit the aspects of quality from the learners. The co-constructing process is undermined if, in the end, the teachers just tell the students the criteria.

- **Emphasize quality over quantity:** Throughout all aspects of student investment, the quality of the experience makes the biggest difference. Rather than trying to race through the processes described in the Action to Take section (page 91) to cover as much as possible, teachers would be wise to slow down, especially

	Teacher Directed	Teacher Centered	Learner Centered	Learner Directed
Teachers and teams engage students in interpreting their assessment results and use that insight to foster success and confidence.	Large-Scale Assessments • Teachers may frame something as important to learn because it may appear on a large-scale assessment. Criteria • Teachers share the learning goals and criteria with students. Some learning targets are posted and on assessments. Self-Assessment • Teachers guide students in reflecting in general on their strengths and areas of growth. Responses to areas of growth are generally developed for all students. Goal Setting • Students set goals in a general way, and	Large-Scale Assessments • Teachers frame large-scale assessments as information for the system and adults to understand the effectiveness of the program overall and its effectiveness for groups of students. These assessments are not used for any individual student goal setting or as a single measure for any major decisions about what to take and what not to take. Co-Constructed Criteria • Teachers share learning goals and engage students in conversation about criteria and elements of quality (perhaps through looking at examples of strong and weak work, and revising and sharing	Large-Scale Assessments • Leadership teams use large-scale assessments as one component of understanding the effectiveness of programs and practices. They are positioned for families as system evidence and not individual student achievement indicators. Co-Constructed Criteria • Students and teachers share and reflect on learning goals and the learning progressions. Together, from examples of student work and other artifacts, they develop criteria to further understand what proficiency looks like. Students, in collaboration, examine samples of work,	Large-Scale Assessments • Leadership teams use large-scale assessments as one component of understanding the effectiveness of programs and practices. They are positioned for families as system evidence and not individual student achievement indicators. Systems incorporate other authentic assessment information to substantiate understanding of the effectiveness of critical learning and school experiences. Co-Constructed Criteria, Self-Assessment, and Goal Setting • Students execute and teachers facilitate the use of criteria, self-assessment, and goal setting in an ongoing

	teachers set generic strategies for all students. The emphasis remains on achieving points versus quality of learning.	models of how to move from where a student currently is to the next level of quality). Self-Assessment and Goal Setting • Teachers guide students to set goals and develop strategies for achieving those goals. Goals are related to the criteria. • Students collect evidence of learning related to the criteria, their self-assessment, and goals. This evidence is collected and tracked through portfolios, data notebooks, or the equivalent.	compare them to their own work, and revise their work from this co-constructed set of criteria. Self-Assessment and Goal Setting • Students set goals on essential standards or competencies and use their assessment information to self-assess and criteria to measure progress and set new goals. Self-assessment is part of each assessment experience to ensure students see assessment as related to their learning.	manner. Students reflect on learning progressions and develop criteria from samples of student work and other artifacts. Students use this ongoing understanding of criteria to self-assess and set goals. Self-assessment is part of each assessment event or experience, and goals are set based on the criteria and self-assessments. • Students receive guidance from teachers to notice and interpret what their assessment information means for their learning. This assessment information may come from quizzes, tests, discussions, activities, presentations, or other processes and products that students engage in.

Figure 4.4:* *Continuum for nurturing student investment through interpretation of results.

when initially making student investment a purposeful part of classroom routines. This way, they can guarantee that each aspect is meaningfully fulfilled and that students deeply learn and experience the practices. The impact, not the existence, of the practices is what will positively affect student learning.

- **Audit self-assessments:** Inaccurate student self-assessment is counterproductive. Educators cannot assume accuracy; they still need to verify that student self-assessment is accurate so subsequent responses align with improved learning. This is especially true for novice learners, who can suffer from a sort of double whammy: they both don't know and don't know what they don't know.

- **Keep the purpose and execution of data notebooks aligned:** Every purpose of data notebooks or portfolios is valid, but each purpose is pointless if, in execution, the contents and actions are a mismatch. Resist the temptation to make the data notebook the catchall. This relates to the notion of quality over quantity. If quantity is the focus, students may feel overwhelmed by the sheer volume of content they are asked to gather.

Part 6: Questions to Guide Your Conversations With Students

Assessment information is personal. How students interpret the results can involve a combination of how the results are communicated and what the expectations of the results are; both are influential in determining what a student might believe is possible in the future. It is imperative to consider how students perceive assessment information and to find ways to help and guide students in positioning assessment as information about one's progress and not an evaluation of one's worth. The following prompts are designed to facilitate conversations and actions teachers and students can take to create the conditions for student investment when interpreting assessment results.

Questions to elicit conversation on shared understandings include the following.

- What helps you understand the expectations for your learning?

- When you get assessments back, what do you look at? How do you use the information you get?

- What kind of feedback do you get on your assessments?

- How do you currently set goals? What is the purpose of goal setting? When are goals successful? When are they unsuccessful?

- What do you need to set quality goals? What do you need to help achieve your goals?

- How do you track your learning progress? What assessments indicate you are making progress? What gets in the way of your progress?

- Do you ever feel overassessed? Talk about why or why not.

- Does all your work—assignments, assessments—align with the learning goals and criteria that are the focus of your course or grade? If so, how do you know? If not, where do you see misalignment?

Questions to elicit conversation on large-scale assessments include the following.

- What is the purpose of large-scale assessments? What is the best use of large-scale assessments?

- What do large-scale assessments tell you? What don't they tell you?

- In your opinion, what does it take to do well on a large-scale assessment?

- What is the best information to use when accurately showing what you know and can do?

Part 7: Dangerous Detours and Seductive Shortcuts

The validity of teachers' scoring and grading practices has long been called into question (Brookhart, 2013b). Are teachers sharing accurate, consistent, and reliable interpretations of their results? It can even be a challenge to know that teachers have equitably and consistently applied a single rubric across a range of student work within a single assignment. Watch for the following common errors during student interpretation of results.

- **Rushing:** Teachers often feel pressure to cover massive amounts of curriculum, so they always have the temptation to rush through it; however, that never works. It's ironic that student investment work has a significant impact on learning, yet many claim to not have the time for it. Make the time; less is more. Let each step along the student investment continuum breathe and have a chance to produce the desired outcomes.

- **Cutting corners:** Likewise, skipping or omitting important processes predictably leaves students and teachers disappointed. The interpretation of assessment results takes time; students will be challenged at first to efficiently identify aspects of quality when co-constructing criteria and to accurately infer quality once they have demonstrated their learning. Anything longer in the setup feels daunting, as time is of the essence. Trust the effectiveness of the process, and allow efficiency to emerge with time.

- **Setting immeasurable goals:** Related to rushing and cutting corners is allowing the quality of student goals to be immeasurable. Teachers can be tempted to applaud the existence of goals rather than their quality, but judging quality requires specificity. Audit the goals and push the students to be specific so they will better understand how much they've grown and how well they've achieved when the self-assessment process unfolds.

- **Using task-based criteria:** Too often, school is about completing tasks and gathering points. Of course, doing well on any given assignment is important for learners, but the assignment's connection to the intended learning matters most. Criteria that heavily focus on the task may produce some short-term wins; students will perform better on that particular task. However, the students may not realize how *doing better* actually translates into *learning more*. Don't leave the connection to long-term learning to chance; make sure the criteria are learning focused.

- **Packing the portfolio:** While overflowing data notebooks or portfolios may initially look impressive, it's the utility of the content that will have the desired impact on student investment. Remember, the portfolio can't be everything to everyone, so continue to align the stated purpose with the execution. If data notebooks are packed with data and other supporting materials, the students may not even be able to make sense of their own progress. Remember—less is more.

CHAPTER 5
COMMUNICATION

When there's so many comments, I ignore it. I usually read one and that's all.

—Third-grade student

From a very young age, learners make decisions about what they will or will not accept from the feedback they receive. For teacher communications about student results to work, they must generate a productive response from all learners (Erkens et al., 2017). Though it may be glaringly obvious, the *how, what, when,* and *why* of learning a teacher communicates have a direct link to whether students invest in the expected learning. Teachers use in-the-moment communication as the primary intervention strategy, so it's important that the feedback succeeds; yet well-intentioned teachers struggle with the best ways to generate high levels of student engagement through their communications.

Part 1: Case Study

Ms. Mending was a high school English teacher who prided herself on providing her learners with copious feedback, especially when it came to their writing. She knew from her own experience as a writer that feedback was a very powerful tool to improve her students' understanding and individual skill levels. Coupled with purposeful, direct instruction, she reasoned, feedback was individualized, targeted, and timely. To that end, Ms. Mending created a comprehensive and multilayered feedback system, and she committed to spending hours of her evenings and weekends writing all the feedback.

Ms. Mending took great care to design assessment tools in advance of her instruction. She wanted to make sure that her assessments aligned with her standards and that her students would have the opportunity to be successful because they knew her criteria beforehand. Because each type of writing was so different, each assignment had its own rubric, and each rubric was accompanied by a form that students could use to document her feedback, peer feedback, and even their own feedback throughout the writing process. She even added a color-coding system so that students could easily distinguish feedback they received for the initial draft from the feedback given during each of the editing rounds.

When Ms. Mending handed the students their rubrics and their accompanying feedback forms for the upcoming writing assignment, she also gave them an exemplar that showed the students what a quality piece of writing would look like for that specific rubric. Each time she distributed those materials, she tried to use different activities that made it so the students would need to read and discuss the rubric. For example, for the argumentation paper, Ms. Mending asked the teams of students to argue, using evidence from the exemplar, as to why the work scored high. On the narrative paper, she asked the teams of students to describe the characteristics of an unexemplary paper for that rubric. She made sure the groupings of students varied from one paper to the next so that students were always hearing multiple perspectives.

Each year, it continued to amaze her that even after she took time to share the rubric with students, most of them still didn't seem to understand it, and few could use it accurately when giving peer feedback. As a result, she found herself allowing for fewer and fewer opportunities to employ peer feedback, which meant she had to either increase her own feedback or give fewer rounds of feedback for improvement. As much as she might have wanted to, she couldn't stay focused on one or two papers for an entire year.

During the writing phases, Ms. Mending was careful to give the students feedback on everything, making sure they didn't miss big concepts or little details in their writing. And she made sure her feedback was directive, telling the students exactly what they needed to do to get a better grade on that paper. She was trying to make it as easy as possible for them to improve. To her surprise and dismay, she noticed that only some of her students cared about improving the quality of their writing, while the majority opted to accept the early grade and ignore her feedback altogether.

Though it felt like she was doing the right work, Ms. Mending grew increasingly tired (and a little exasperated, if she were being honest) as the year progressed. Small tweaks to her system over time always seemed to generate similar results; namely, she was still working harder than her students. She'd moved over to a digital system for writing and tracking feedback a few years prior, and that helped her alleviate the stress on her hand from writing, maintain a better-documented improvement trajectory, and increase the quantity of feedback she could provide, but the payout seemed minimal. She was too tired to keep doing this with so little return on her investment. She felt like she barely had a personal life anymore. Next year, she was going to try to incorporate more student conferencing regarding the given feedback, but if that didn't work, she'd have to either forgo giving all that feedback while teaching English or consider a career change that wouldn't require her to work so hard for so little return.

Reflection

A fundamental factor for increasing student investment requires that "the communication of assessment results must generate productive responses from learners and all stakeholders" (Erkens et al., 2017, p. 5). Committed to excellence, Ms. Mending understood this, so she took great care to give extensive specific feedback. Why wasn't it working? Why weren't her students using the feedback and choosing to improve their grades? What should she have done differently?

Part 2: Celebrations and Considerations

Ms. Mending was accurate in her perception that feedback is a powerful instructional strategy to reduce discrepancies between where a student is and where a student needs to be (Erkens et al., 2017; Marzano, 2019; Marzano, Pickering, & Pollock, 2001; Wiliam, 2013, 2018a). But the fact that her students were not buying into her feedback clearly indicated she wouldn't see the desired achievement gains, even after all her hard work. She understood that if her communication of their results did not produce productive responses on behalf of the individual students, then her feedback was not serving its primary purpose. While her efforts were working for *some* students, that seemed insufficient. She was putting so much in for such little return that it felt as if her efforts were an exercise in futility.

Still, there is so much about Ms. Mending's feedback system that's worth celebrating. Using feedback as an instructional intervention—its core purpose—she embedded feedback as a steady construct that she consistently leaned on. Her efforts aligned with best practices in that she employed feedback as her primary, customizable instructional intervention to reduce discrepancies in *each* of her students' learning. Moreover, her allowance for student revisions provided a bridge that both permitted and encouraged students to continue their learning and improve their grades.

She was careful and methodical. Her preplanning strategy of designing assessment and feedback tools in advance enabled her to anticipate needs and next steps because of the types of feedback she was likely to provide. Her strategy allowed her to forecast student needs, employ prior assessment results to improve future instruction, and monitor individual students' growth over time. She used feedback as an intervention, and she attempted to activate the self-regulation skills of persistence through revision. Committed to helping students improve by giving targeted, meaningful feedback, she strived to engage her students by helping them understand the rubrics through activities and exemplars so that she could incorporate a steady dose of self- and peer feedback.

It seems as if she had all the right stuff, so what was wrong? Why weren't her students improving when she had taken great care to give copious and detailed feedback? To begin, Ms. Mending was *over-feedbacking* when she offered too many comments on each paper. Teachers need not indicate everything that needs improvement at one time. Too much feedback can overwhelm students to the extent that they shut down completely. Worse, in such a situation, when a student sees more that is wrong than right, the opportunities to increase hope and build efficacy are eradicated instantly. Also, when there is so much feedback, the likelihood that the feedback is directive regarding specific changes increases—meaning that Ms. Mending ended up doing all the thinking for the learners. In such a situation, the revision becomes compliance oriented; in other words, students don't need to do their own original thinking to solve the problems at hand. In an ideal world, feedback does not do the thinking for the learner but rather sets the learner on a deeper investigatory path (Chappuis, 2015).

In addition, Ms. Mending's use of so many different rubrics required her to teach each rubric separately. The first problem with such an approach is that learners do not have enough time and experience with each rubric to develop inter-rater reliability. The second problem with such an approach is that learners cannot make improvements between assessments when the rubric keeps changing.

Whenever teachers gather to calibrate scoring on student work, they must spend a considerable amount of time revisiting, redefining, and clarifying their original intentions behind the criteria they've already developed. Consistent scoring with common tools does not happen overnight, even with well-informed educators who likely co-constructed the tools in the first place. Imagine being a student who's seeing the tool for the first time, or even the second time. Just like teachers, students might co-construct the criteria but still require collaborative conversation, routine practice, and ongoing analysis to deeply understand what was meant by the criteria and proficiency levels on the rubric. So, it stands to reason that if the rubric changes frequently, students can't generate inter-rater reliability with the teacher, much less their peers.

If Ms. Mending's students were to have repeatedly used a task-neutral rubric—a tool with generalizable criteria that is usable across multiple tasks and multiple standards—they would have had a better chance at consistently understanding and applying the criteria to their own and each other's work. Task-neutral rubrics focus on the critical skills and competencies that learners would have employed in all writing in Ms. Mending's classroom. For example, if she had focused on the six traits of writing—(1) ideas and content, (2) organization, (3) voice, (4) word choice, (5) sentence fluency, and (6) conventions (Education Northwest, 2021)—she could have provided consistent feedback across the various genres of writing that she was expected to teach (narrative, informative, and argumentative). While each genre has some unique features, the core processes remain the same. Ms. Mending could have affixed a few additional criteria at the bottom of each consistent rubric that teased out a specific genre's features. Figure 5.1 (page 114) illustrates how task-neutral rubrics might look for three genres of writing.

While the few criteria to highlight in genre-specific writing might require students to revise that specific paper for genre expectations, the core criteria for quality writing should remain consistent from paper to paper. In this way, students can invest in improving the quality of their writing skills over time and setting goals, revising, and monitoring improvement over the course of multiple assessments.

Imagine, for example, that a student of Ms. Mending's learned she needed to improve her word choice and sentence fluency after writing her narrative paper. She knew she must incorporate that feedback to be a better writer and to earn the top marks in her English language arts course. She knew that the protocol required her to (1) set a goal in those areas; (2) solicit peer feedback in her drafting phase regarding those two areas; (3) write the exact feedback, the exact personal goal, or both regarding those two areas at the top of her next paper—the information paper; and (4) use a yellow highlighter to highlight her areas of improvement with word choice and a pink highlighter to highlight her areas of improvement with sentence fluency within the paper before she submitted it to Ms. Mending. In this way, both student and teacher could immediately track the student's efforts to make achievement gains *between* assessments, and both could keep a laser-like eye on the individual's application of past feedback.

Also, in this way, the feedback Ms. Mending so painstakingly offered could generate a more productive and focused response on her own behalf. Both she *and* her students would gain traction in their follow-up instructional decisions to ensure the learning continued.

Part 3: Action to Take

Researchers of classroom-based assessment always highlight feedback as the area that needs more study—likely because the impact of feedback is contextual and nuanced. Erkens, Schimmer, and Dimich (2017) note, "The communication of assessment results must generate productive responses from learners and all stakeholders" (p. 5). Teachers can apply the commonly understood criteria for quality feedback—it must be timely, specific, and constructive—in a manner that still creates a sense of hopefulness

Narration Rubric
Writing a story that may be factual or fictional

	1	2	3	4
Purpose and organization				
Elaboration of ideas				
Conventions				
Narration				
Story elements				
Dialogue				

Information Rubric
Writing a nonfiction text with the intent to inform

	1	2	3	4
Purpose and organization				
Elaboration of ideas				
Conventions				
Information				
Research and citations				
Fact and opinion				

Argumentation Rubric
Writing a nonfiction text with the purpose of arguing, defending, or countering a position

	1	2	3	4
Purpose and organization				
Elaboration of ideas				
Conventions				
Argumentation				
Evidence				
Reasoning				

Figure 5.1: Task-neutral writing rubric for three genres.

on behalf of the student. Feedback is the instructional pathway that students use to eliminate the gap that exists between where they currently stand and where they need to be with the learning intentions. It is the tool students leverage to activate themselves as primary instructional decision makers. Students *will* employ that pathway. But if the feedback doesn't set them on the right path with a bright future, students are likely to make the wrong instructional choice, opting for no response or even the unhealthiest option: to refuse participation in future learning opportunities altogether (Kluger & DeNisi, 1996; Wiliam, 2013).

As an instructional intervention, quality feedback should not lead to compliance-based editing. Instead, it must ensure students still learn during a singular experience—in the case of the previous example, a writing experience—and across multiple other opportunities. In figure 5.2, the acronym of *LEARNS* (modified from Erkens, 2019) incorporates the best practice research on quality feedback (see Brookhart, 2017;

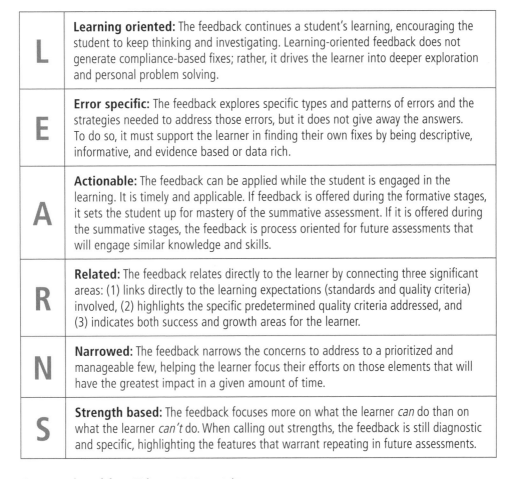

L	**Learning oriented:** The feedback continues a student's learning, encouraging the student to keep thinking and investigating. Learning-oriented feedback does not generate compliance-based fixes; rather, it drives the learner into deeper exploration and personal problem solving.
E	**Error specific:** The feedback explores specific types and patterns of errors and the strategies needed to address those errors, but it does not give away the answers. To do so, it must support the learner in finding their own fixes by being descriptive, informative, and evidence based or data rich.
A	**Actionable:** The feedback can be applied while the student is engaged in the learning. It is timely and applicable. If feedback is offered during the formative stages, it sets the student up for mastery of the summative assessment. If it is offered during the summative stages, the feedback is process oriented for future assessments that will engage similar knowledge and skills.
R	**Related:** The feedback relates directly to the learner by connecting three significant areas: (1) links directly to the learning expectations (standards and quality criteria) involved, (2) highlights the specific predetermined quality criteria addressed, and (3) indicates both success and growth areas for the learner.
N	**Narrowed:** The feedback narrows the concerns to address to a prioritized and manageable few, helping the learner focus their efforts on those elements that will have the greatest impact in a given amount of time.
S	**Strength based:** The feedback focuses more on what the learner *can* do than on what the learner *can't* do. When calling out strengths, the feedback is still diagnostic and specific, highlighting the features that warrant repeating in future assessments.

Source: Adapted from Erkens, 2019, p. 147.

***Figure 5.2:** LEARNS acronym for quality feedback.*

*Visit **go.SolutionTree.com/assessment** for a free reproducible version of this figure.*

Chappuis, 2012, 2015; Chappuis & Stiggins, 2020; Dweck, 2013; Hattie & Timperley, 2007; Kluger & DeNisi, 1996; Pink, 2009; Ruiz-Primo & Li, 2013; Ryan & Deci, 2000a; Wiliam, 2013).

Feedback is an instructional intervention that teachers use to ensure every student learns. Often, teachers spend countless hours writing comments on students' work, and "research has made clear that students hardly read teachers' written feedback or know how to interpret it" (Cowie, 2005a, 2005b, as cited in Ruiz-Primo & Li, 2013, p. 225). That's unfortunate because teachers can empower learners to drive their own instructional decision making through the intervention tool of feedback. More importantly, teachers can build hope and efficacy for their learners through feedback.

It's easy to become overwhelmed when considering all the components of quality feedback. Clearly, a rubber stamp of generic feedback—albeit easiest or most convenient for the teacher—often falls short of inspiring learners to continue or deepen their learning. But students deserve quality feedback. The good news is there are efficient strategies that can help teachers create a laser-like focus in their feedback. Figure 5.3 outlines several options.

Feedback happens at all points in the learning process. To maximize the potential of feedback, educators must consider the following.

- The LEARNS qualities of feedback
- Student involvement in feedback
- Grading

Educators can use each of the qualities of feedback to increase student involvement and improve scoring and grading conversations.

The LEARNS Qualities of Feedback

To most effectively elicit student investment in learning, high-quality feedback should follow the LEARNS acronym and be:

- Learning oriented
- Error specific
- Actionable
- Related
- Narrowed
- Strength based

Highlighting	Use highlighting to quickly draw attention to key areas.
	Highlight areas of concern. Return work to students, ask them to identify the types of errors behind the highlights, and instruct them to fix the work for resubmission.
	Ask students to submit their work, highlighting their own areas of concern within the submission. If students highlight in yellow, for example, then teachers can highlight in another color, like blue, to confirm a mistake exists in that location. Where yellow and blue overlap, the highlight turns green. If a highlight remains yellow, the teacher does not deem it a mistake, and if there are blue highlights, the teacher found mistakes the student did not.
	Have students highlight on a rubric where they think they are with given criteria and then highlight in the submission where the evidence matches the score they self-assigned.
Goal Focusing	Have students write their goal (based on previous teacher feedback) at the top (or in front) of a new submission. Then have them highlight any evidence within the submission of places they believe they have improved relative to that goal; for example, a student who is focused on improving arguing from evidence will highlight key sentences or words that provide the evidence directly linked to the claim.
Group Feedback: My Favorite No **See video called "My Favorite No" on YouTube (Alcala, 2015)**	Have students complete a single task on a three- by five-inch card. Collect the cards and quickly sort them into piles (right or wrong or levels of proficiency like 1, 2, 3, and 4) in front of the students but without revealing any student's identity.
	If right and wrong piles were created, use one favorite wrong answer. Rewrite it in teacher handwriting and engage the class in diagnosing all that was right about the work before analyzing where the mistake happened in the work.
	If levels of proficiency are present, select *one* card and type it or rewrite it in teacher handwriting for all to see. Engage teams of students in determining what level of proficiency they think the teacher would assign. Have them argue from evidence and try to convince their peers they have accurately determined the score the teacher would assign.
	In either case, be sure to end with group-wide clarity on what types of mistakes occurred with that particular type of task.
Peer Feedback	After students have developed inter-rater reliability with teacher scoring through constant practice, engage them in peer feedback, but make sure the author of the work is the one writing out the peer's spoken feedback. This leads to more questioning and probing, and deeper understanding of the feedback being offered.

Figure 5.3: Fast feedback strategies.

continued ➔

Compact Conference	Use a three- or four-minute compact conference protocol. This protocol can be used when students are setting goals, seeking feedback, formalizing revisions, or reflecting on the final product. Each minute of the conference has a designated purpose, and the student maintains ownership of the process and the follow-up documentation. With this form, a student can choose to invite feedback and support from peers or other adults in addition to the teacher. Once an assignment is complete and students have filled in a form regarding their own strengths and opportunities for growth, they solicit and document feedback from others. A timer is set at the start of the conference.
One-Minute Checkpoints	Randomly approach students, require them to quickly point to evidence that supports their ability to accomplish the learning task at hand, and have them share why they think that is a good example of their skill level, what they are working to improve, or both. Or hand students a fast single-item task to complete, and then circle back to check in on where students think they are strong or limited in that task.
Sampling	After students have completed a task, ask them to select from among their work the best part, the most challenging part, or both (for example, their fourth paragraph) for teacher attention. Have them provide a written rationale as to why they want to focus on that area.
Selection of Appropriate Feedback	Write feedback on separate sheets of paper without student names attached (but code it in some way so as to remember which feedback goes with which student submission). Put students in teams, return to each student their initial submission with no feedback on it, and give the students the corresponding strips of feedback for all submissions within that team of students. Ask students to decide which strip of feedback goes with which student project and why.
Dotting	*Option 1:* Place dots at the ends of lines of text that contain errors (one dot per error), and ask students to find, name, and fix the errors. *Option 2:* Walk around the room, place three dots on each student's practice work next to items that may be right or wrong, and have students redo the work to ensure it is right, explaining their thinking as they do so.
Snip, Drag, and Drop	Snip images of the rubric language, and drag (copy and paste) it directly into the student work where it best applies. Put a plus sign (+) next to the image where the work strongly exemplifies the rubric criteria and a caret (^) next to the image where the student should check for improvements.

Learning Oriented

Feedback is any description, observation, or question that guides students to reflect on their learning and gain new understanding and increase the quality of their work, leading them to take their next steps to achieving the standard, competency, or intended learning. This feedback can come in the form of verbal or written observations that emerge from an instructional activity, from the work students produce on a test, in a draft of an essay, or in any other product. Feedback requires educators to make observations about what students are doing, saying, and producing and then communicate to them their strengths and next steps. For feedback to increase confidence and learning, it must cause the student to think and act. It must help the student recognize where they are and where they need to go next. In the *SAGE Handbook of Research on Classroom Assessment*, Maria Araceli Ruiz-Primo and Min Li (2013) assert:

> Students are essential players in the feedback process. In addition to being recipients of feedback, the students have a role as partners in each of the formative feedback activities . . . and as feedback providers and developers of actions to be followed. (p. 221)

When feedback is communicated to students and it leads to improved learning—that is, when students see and feel they have learned in a manner that positively impacts their results—investment begins to take root and grow (Brookhart, 2017; Chappuis, 2015; Dweck, 2013; Pink, 2009; Wiliam, 2013, 2018a).

Students are more likely to invest when the feedback continues their learning within the context of opportunities to improve their marks, grades, or scores and ultimately encourages them to continue their thinking and sustain investigation. Learning-oriented feedback avoids compliance-based fixes that do not lead to improved understanding.

Error Specific

Descriptive feedback explores specific types and patterns of errors and the strategies needed to address those errors, but it does not give away the answers. Rather, it supports learners in finding their own fixes by being descriptive, informative, and evidence based or data rich (Chappuis, 2015; Erkens, 2019). *Descriptive in nature* means students receive written or verbal feedback that describes the quality of the work instead of simply pointing out what is wrong (Chappuis, 2015; Erkens, 2019). The descriptions relate to the learning targets and the success criteria and may be in the form of comments or questions that drive the learner back into a discovery mode. These comments illuminate for the student what the teacher noticed about their work in terms of the desired qualities.

This does not mean that feedback should only be related to errors; rather, it highlights the need for clarity around what needs improvement. In fact, if students are to have hope and efficacy, then they should know *more* about their strengths than they do about their weaknesses following a given set of feedback. Error-specific feedback isolates specific gaps in knowledge or skill, but it does not tell students what to do. For examples, see figure 5.4.

Instead of Saying _____ (Traditional Feedback)	Try Saying _____ (Error-Specific Feedback)
"You have seven out of ten correct."	"In the three errors you made, you had an insufficient sample of evidence before you drew your conclusion. Work to gather more evidence first so you have a full picture of the details before drawing your conclusion."
"Put the proper mathematical operation symbol here and here and here." (Circled marks show where operation signs should be placed.)	"There are three times on page 2 of the test where you forgot to indicate which operation you were using in your math. See if you can find the errors and make the necessary changes."

Figure 5.4: *Examples of error-specific feedback.*

Actionable

Feedback should cause action and not just invite it or suggest it. When students do not understand how to act on the feedback, teachers will see inaction, confusion, frustration, or even indifference. However, when students act, it indicates the feedback was successful and impactful (Brookhart, 2017; Chappuis, 2015; Erkens et al., 2017; Wiliam, 2013). When there is inaction, teachers must examine the strategy or method of feedback to determine how they can adjust the feedback to ensure it causes thinking and then learning.

Students should be able to apply actionable feedback while engaged in the learning (Chappuis, 2015; Dimich et al., 2017; Hattie & Timperley, 2007; Wiliam, 2013, 2018a). Actionable feedback should be timely, applicable, and forward facing. If a teacher offers feedback during the formative stages, it should set the student up for mastery of the summative assessment. If the teacher offers it during the summative stages, the feedback should be process oriented so the student will succeed on similar future assessments that will access the same kinds of concepts and skills. For examples, see figure 5.5.

Instead of Saying _____ (Traditional Feedback)	Try Saying _____ (Actionable Feedback)
"More information needed."	"Before submitting your science report, recheck your charts and graphs to ensure *all* the relevant information is included. It will help if you look back at the sample we constructed as a class to compare the kinds of information included there to what you have provided here."
"You have a 2 on the argumentative rubric."	"In this argument essay, you forgot to include the counter-perspective so you could discredit it. You will want to incorporate this feature in the upcoming debate unit because it will strengthen your argument."

Figure 5.5: Examples of actionable feedback.

Related

Feedback that is related strives to connect three things to one another: (1) the learning expectations, (2) the quality criteria, and (3) the learner's needs (Erkens, 2019).

First, feedback should always link directly to the learning expectations (learning targets or academic standards; Chappuis, 2015; Chappuis & Stiggins, 2020; Hattie, 2009; Wiliam, 2013). In fact, teachers should strive for feedback to incorporate the specific language involved in those expectations. If, for example, teachers give an assessment to ensure learners understand how to evaluate the quality of evidence provided in an argument, then feedback should specifically reference each student's ability to evaluate the quality of the evidence and should not get lost in tangential details, such as a resulting paragraph being unorganized. When feedback wanders into territories that do not address the specific targets of the assessment, learners quickly become confused and teachers miss the opportunity to further the instruction on the standards at hand.

The learning targets outline *what* is being assessed, while the quality criteria indicate *how well* the targets must be met. Both features, targets and criteria, are necessary to help students develop a mirror image of the teacher's expectations. Teacher-directed feedback that reaches outside students' understanding of the learning criteria can cause frustration, as students often do not know how to interpret such feedback or do not know what *quality* looks like. If teachers give teacher-directed feedback, they may spend hours commenting on students' work yet subsequently see little evidence of growth. Students may not know what to do to make their work increase in quality even if they have seen exemplars.

Students need explicit instruction to understand the criteria as well as exemplars so they can see the criteria in action. Co-creating criteria and developing rubrics with students gives the teacher's expectations a clear focus. (See also "Learning Criteria," page 50, for more information.) Feedback, then, should remain on point and help the learners examine their work in lieu of that exact focus.

Rubrics clarify gradations of quality. Learners need to see the specific features both in the rubric and in the teacher feedback using the rubric so they can perceive how to move from one level to the next. To this end, modeling how to move from one level of quality to the next can help students see and feel the work needed to move, including the struggle and the thought process.

In the research on the effectiveness of quality feedback, Hattie (2012) finds a 74 percent gain in student achievement. Feedback, an instructional intervention that teachers use to reduce discrepancies between where learners are and where they need to be, is a powerful first line of intervention (Erkens, 2019; Marzano, 2019; Wiliam, 2018a). Hattie's bodies of research (2009, 2012; Hattie & Timperley, 2007) have consistently highlighted the substantial potential that feedback has to improve student achievement. The trick is to generate feedback that consistently produces productive responses on behalf of every learner (Erkens et al., 2017). Hattie, Fisher, and Frey (2016) sum it up best when they state, "Unfortunately, although getting teachers to provide feedback is relatively easy, getting students to receive that feedback is complicated."

The very reason that providing quality feedback to students can be so challenging is the recipient must be amenable to receiving the information. Learners are all unique— not only in what they need to address in the work to master the learning expectations but also in their levels of readiness or personal preferences for how to receive the information. Some students prefer that teachers quickly get to the heart of the matter without worries about being gentle in their feedback, while others prefer a softer, possibly less critical approach. Some students are comfortable with a group discussion about opportunities to grow, while others prefer a private one-on-one conversation. Some prefer to talk, while others just want written notes. The best way to accomplish customizing feedback so the recipients can receive it is to develop strong relationships with students and thereby gain clarity on the individual students' needs and preferences.

In sum, related feedback should directly connect the learning expectations and the quality criteria to the student in a manner that the student can best receive the feedback. Feedback must be nuanced and intentional if it is to deeply take root and initiate focused improvement. For examples, see figure 5.6.

Narrowed

Too often, students get so much feedback they don't know where to start. It can be hard, as a teacher, to resist commenting (verbally or in writing) on everything a

Strategies to Personalize	Strategies to Focus on the Learning
Ask students their preferences for receiving feedback either in a survey or on a "learner profile" index card where students share important things about themselves that they want teachers to know. • Do you prefer your feedback in oral form or in written form? • Do you prefer feedback that is gentle or feedback that is direct? • Do you prefer feedback that is kept secret or feedback that can be explored in protected conversations with peers (for example, there are guidelines for confidentiality)?	Avoid language that directs the students' attention to what the teacher likes or loves. Instead of saying, "I like how you . . ." or "I love that you . . . ," try keeping the focus on expertise. For example, say, "Master mathematicians always check their work for accuracy by using the opposite operations when possible. Try using opposite operations to ensure you get the same answer more than once."
Give students the option to select the piece of feedback that they believe will be most helpful to advancing their work.	Incorporate the language of the standards directly into the scoring tools.
Allow students to self-assign feedback first and then respond to their insights about what's working and what needs improvement.	Cut and paste exact sections of the rubric directly into the student work where they are relevant.

Figure 5.6: *Examples of related feedback.*

student must change or revise, but as stated previously, the quantity of comments can have diminishing effects. When students receive too much feedback, they feel overwhelmed by the amount of feedback or confused about what to prioritize (Hattie, 2012; Hattie & Timperley, 2007). So, focus feedback on a few qualities that have been identified in the assessment architecture or unit plan as essential. Quality feedback narrows the concerns a student must address to a prioritized and manageable few, helping the learner focus their efforts on those elements that will have the greatest impact in a given amount of time.

Showcasing how much a student is missing merely stifles student investment. It's far more appropriate to select one or two of the most significant components in need of fixing and provide the feedback that will empower the learner to make incremental improvements. Sometimes, the larger changes a student makes will automatically fix the little details.

Examples of narrowed feedback include the following.

■ "You have one piece of growth feedback in the lower-left corner and one piece of success feedback in the upper-right corner. Use your growth feedback to pair up with one or more classmates for whom that area was a success. Work together to find ways to improve your growth areas. Be sure to share your success with others as well!" (White, 2022).

- "Transfer the most important piece of growth feedback from the bottom of your current assessment to the top of the blank page for the next assessment. Complete that assessment with an eye to making the improvements from that feedback. When you are done, use a yellow highlighter to highlight all the places in your work where you think you've shown improvement based on that same piece of feedback."

Strength Based

Strength-based feedback focuses more on what the learner *can* do than on what the learner *can't* do. When calling out strengths, the feedback is still diagnostic and specific, highlighting the features that warrant repeating in future assessments. When learners are struggling with confidence and morale, use strength-based feedback to build a foundation and get students back in a mindset of possibility. When learners are doing well, use strength-based feedback to help guide their thinking about the quality of their work versus only the grade. Lead learners to recognize what is high quality about their work and shift from answering, "Is this right?" to answering, "What do you think and see in your work?"

Examples of strength-based feedback include the following.

- "You retold the story, including all the important details, in the right order. You even added some of your own inferences in the retelling so that the story included your insights along the way."

- "You have elicited concise information from the text to interpret the most significant concepts. In your interpretation, you make solid, defensible judgments about the reasoning of the author and the quality of the evidence that was provided."

- "Just like a scientist, you constructed a model using all the essential components from familiar contexts, and then connected those components to a less familiar context to examine a new idea. As a result, you have the beginnings of a new investigation."

Student Involvement in Feedback

Feedback is successful only to the degree that it activates learners to be a resource to themselves and to peers (Wiliam, 2018a). So, ideally, feedback supports self-regulation by enabling learners to make independent, healthy instructional choices while inspiring them to continue doing so. Once feedback launches the self-regulation process, it must feed the learning forward.

Teachers take notice if the feedback is causing students to learn more, but it's equally important to note if students are better able to self-assess accurately. Feedback should lead to students understanding how to recognize quality and next steps in their own work (Brookhart, 2017; Chappuis, 2015). Any feedback move by teachers should cause recognizable increases in learning and confidence.

At the conclusion of all feedback, learners should experience an increase in achievement as well as new personal insights due to reflection caused by the feedback experiences along the way (Brookhart, 2017; Chappuis, 2015; Wiliam, 2013). Powerful feedback moments shed light for learners (and teachers) on what helps them learn and what does not. Reflection for students involves deepening their learning while simultaneously exploring insights into how they prefer to learn. Reflection for educators is key, as it helps guide the practices that impact learning while also developing confidence and commitment to which practices work (and which don't) for each individual learner and for groups of students. Ultimately, feedback creates the tone that fosters hope and efficacy for the learner.

Students' understanding of the learning is magnified when they engage in developing inter-rater reliability with teachers. In this way, learners can activate each other as resources (Wiliam, 2018a) and build both intellectual and social capital (Hargreaves & Fullan, 2012). Such scoring conversations help learners develop a shared understanding, and scoring rehearsals with examples of strong and weak work will then lead to improved accuracy and a clearer vision of what the standards look like when achieved. Students, in collaboration with their peers, review multiple samples of student work at each level of quality so they can accurately score the work as the teacher would. In this way, learners build consensus around the plethora of samples, which ultimately leads to a clearer understanding of quality. When that happens, students become informed and empowered to offer quality feedback to themselves and their peers. They can then get in the driver's seat to improve their own demonstrations of learning.

When teachers notice students can articulate the expected qualities of feedback as well as isolate specific strengths and outline next steps, teachers can consider it time to move these conversations to peer-to-peer feedback. Quality feedback should lead to improved, more accurate, and more meaningful conversations for students and their peers about their learning (Brookhart, 2017; Chappuis, 2015; Dimich et al., 2017). When students work in a group, in collaboration, or get peer feedback, do they learn more? Does the quality of their work improve? If teachers notice and students comment on a lack of accuracy and productivity in peer-to-peer feedback conversations, they may need to take a step back to further develop students' understanding of quality.

Feedback and practice in reviewing work, noticing what is strong about work and what needs to change, and seeing models of how to change the work can also lead to and set the stage for high-quality self-assessment. Feedback, at its best, should provide students with understanding of quality so they can notice quality in their own work. Andrade (2013) notes:

> In general, the research on feedback shows that it tends to be associated with learning and achievement but that not all kinds of feedback are equally effective. Feedback is most effective when it is the right kind (e.g., detailed and narrative, not graded), delivered in the right way (supportive), at the right time (sooner for low-level knowledge but not so soon that it prevents metacognitive processing and later for complex tasks), and to the right person (who is in a receptive mood and has reasonably high self-efficacy). (p. 25)

Learners' ability to notice what's working and what's not, as well as their ability to accept teacher feedback and apply it to their work, leads students to invest in their next steps and have the confidence to take those next steps. Providing students with feedback is serious business.

Grading

Grading is an evaluative form of feedback. As such, grading has the power to stop learners from investing altogether. But it doesn't need to be that way. As Schimmer (2016) states, "Anchoring grading practices with a focus on accuracy and confidence leads to grading decisions that are on point and aligned with what we know to be in the best interest of student success" (p. 23). Helping students increase their accuracy with scoring and facilitating processes that enable learners to improve their grades over time will increase the students' confidence. When this is done well, students and their families can articulate what grades mean as a measure of learning rather than as a tally of points earned from the completion of expected work.

Grades become a distraction when they are weaponized as carrots or sticks to inspire motivation or force accountability. Student investment is not about getting students to be compliant. Investment is rooted in learning and knowing that when students learn more and they know it, they will gain confidence (Brookhart, 2013a, 2017; Dweck, 2006, 2013). When students are more confident, they start to believe learning is possible. This sense of possibility leads to persistence. In the absence of grades meaning something in terms of learning, the emphasis remains on accumulating points. Unfortunately, this mindset that grades motivate students continues to plague systems and can often weigh heavily on both teachers' and students' minds. This heaviness leads to the focus on accumulating points. In fact, David T. Conley (2018), in his book *The Promise and Practice of Next Generation Assessment*, describes additional issues that emerge with grades:

Many high school students conflate a grade with their perception of what the teacher thinks of them. Others garner decent grades without mastering content by being savvy about how the system works, possessing good test-taking skills, being able to charm teachers, or having aggressive parents. Even students who work diligently and learn the material well and get good grades don't necessarily receive explicit feedback or guidance on what they did well or how to improve their learning skills. The result is that many students across the full range of high school grade point averages, from high to low, enter college without much awareness of what it takes to be successful learners. In fact many have to unlearn behaviors that were effective in high school but don't work as well in most college courses, such as relying on copious amounts of extra credit to make it over the bar. (pp. 41–42)

Conley (2018) articulates the myriad reasons traditional grading systems do not serve students well. So many grading practices run counter to a culture where students even have an opportunity to invest in their learning, as the practices lead to a focus on compliance and accumulation of points. In addition, the grading practices often do not clearly communicate or describe a student's learning, way of learning, and future possibilities.

It takes a fierce commitment to grading for learning to reverse this trend. First, teachers must adopt a grade-for-learning mindset: "Grades must be a reflection of student proficiency, not a reward for compliance" (Schimmer, 2016, p. 23). Second, teachers must intentionally infuse their grading system with attention to accuracy and a commitment to increasing student confidence. Both features are key to student investment. Finally, teachers will likely have to find temporary work-arounds in a digital gradebook that they do not control.

Though it takes time and intentionality to shift grading from documenting compliance and tallying completion to creating grading practices that inspire deeper learning and generate student confidence, the work is possible and necessary if teachers expect students to invest in personal improvement efforts. Table 5.1 (page 128) describes the shifts in assumptions and practices that educators must constantly pursue to make this fierce commitment and create the conditions for student investment. This commitment and these conditions will result in high achievement and deep investment from and with students.

These important maneuvers capture the most important aspect of grading for communication that is clear and not muddy. As with any complex and comprehensive change, it is incredibly important to notice the impact *each* practice is having on student confidence and grading. A teacher's ability to notice, reflect, and adjust is what will lead to grading and feedback that clearly empower students to invest—thereby

Table 5.1: *Shifting Assumptions for Student Investment*

When Educators Focus on Compliance, Coverage, and Points	When Educators Focus on Qualities and Learning
Assumptions: Assessments and assignments with evaluative scores (grades or percentages) communicate clearly to students. Points will get students to complete work, and if they complete work, they will learn. Penalizing students by reducing points will change academic behaviors. Grades motivate all students to do work. If students do work, they will learn.	**Assumptions:** Assessments and assignments are evidence of learning and need qualities to clearly communicate student learning using symbols. Evidence of learning is more important than completion of work. Completion of work doesn't necessarily equal learning or proof of responsibility. Learning takes time. Getting it faster doesn't mean you get it better. Feedback, when based on strengths, focused on next steps, and requiring action, creates the conditions for deep learning, motivation, and engagement. Strength-based feedback builds student confidence, which creates trust and a sense of openness to persisting.
Practices: Assignments and assessments have a grade or percentage assigned. Communication to students is largely focused on getting things completed and turned in. Zeros are used to indicate missing work (making the grade rise and fall with small and big assignments and assessments).	**Practices:** Assessments and assignments are evidence of learning and need qualities to clearly communicate student learning using symbols. Grades and percentages are explained by learning goals, standards, and criteria on every assignment and assessment. Work collected serves as evidence of learning instead of just completion of work. Feedback and revision are about increasing learning, so students experience multiple opportunities and get full credit for those opportunities. Feedback is strength based, focuses on next steps, and requires action. Learning is situated in what is most essential and relevant.

achieving high levels of learning and developing confidence on the journey. The following sections examine four such practices: (1) recording evidence; (2) giving fewer grades, more feedback; (3) focusing on evidence of learning; and (4) communicating transparently.

Record Evidence

A concrete move teachers can make is to record evidence of learning by standard or learning target instead of by assignment. Figure 5.7 (page 130) outlines a workable framework designed to indicate a student's level of proficiency by each individual learning expectation, whether it is a standard, a target, or a characteristic of quality. In the sample provided, each learning target offers multiple spaces to record the results from the multiple points of evidence a student produced for that target. (Please note: figure 5.7 is an example only, illustrating how to score. In practice, multiple evidences can be used, not just the three shown in the figure.)

In a structure such as this, teachers can (1) allow for mistake making, (2) monitor for improvement over time, and (3) generate a true reflection of where the learner ended up in the learning by grading based on the most recent or most frequent median score. They can use all categories to determine a final grade. In this model, it is very clear where students are strong and where they need work. Three pieces of evidence are indicated as an example, but the general idea is that teachers would need ample evidence to ensure the score is consistent and as accurate as possible when reporting. Figure 5.7 (page 130) is simply an example. Teachers have many options for helping students focus on the learning expectations (standards, targets, criteria, or common skills like the mathematical or science and engineering practices) so as to concentrate on the areas of growth most needed to improve (see Reibel & Twadell, 2019; Schimmer, 2016; Schimmer, Hillman, & Stalets, 2018; Townsley & Wear, 2020). When combined with opportunities to improve, a laser-like focus on targets for improvement can increase student investment. More accurate and targeted information gives students power and focus to take specific actions in their growth.

Give Fewer Grades, More Feedback

Any sort of evaluative mark or grade tends to distract students from continuing to learn the assessed concepts (Schimmer, 2016; Schimmer et al., 2018; Townsley & Wear, 2020). If a grade indicates something is completed, it's challenging to get students to continually reinvest. Reducing the amount of grading makes room for more feedback. When there are fewer assignments and assessments, students focus on completing meaningful work and using feedback to improve the quality of their work. Once the work has reached a minimum level of proficiency, a grade is appropriate. This reduction in assignments and grades dramatically reduces the work teachers do when they are recording, leaving more space for interactions with students to support continued learning.

Two issues regularly arise with the *less grading, more feedback* concept. The first is a policy issue. Often, grading policies require teachers to record a certain number of grades each week so stakeholders have an ongoing way to monitor achievement over

	I can explain my reasoning with a viable argument.			I can create a model to represent my solution.			I can use primary sources to analyze and explain geographic and population phenomena.			Academic behaviors and work habits			Overall Most recent or most frequent median from each category
	Evidence 1	Evidence 2	Evidence 3	Evidence 1	Evidence 2	Evidence 3	Evidence 1	Evidence 2	Evidence 3	Evidence 1	Evidence 2	Evidence 3	
Student 1													
Student 2													
Student 3													

Figure 5.7: Template for grading based on learning targets.

time. While it is vital that all stakeholders have such information in a timely and ongoing manner (DuFour et al., 2016), this practice leads to a culture of completion instead of quality. This problem can be solved without sacrificing one option for the other because it's not an either-or proposition. Educators have many electronic options for keeping communication channels about progress open, and there are many things to share that do communicate a student's progress (teacher feedback, student goals, student tracking forms, and so on).

The second concern in a system of less grading, more feedback involves the algorithms used to determine the final grade (Schimmer, 2016; Schimmer et al., 2018; Townsley & Wear, 2020). A tallying of point accumulation is misleading, especially when points are based on assessments that might not provide clear and concrete evidence of mastery of the concepts. Assessment evidence should be grounded in what students are learning. Ample evidence is important so that the teacher is confident a grade reflects where a student is, but it is not so important if it is more of a reflection of perseverance and quantity of work completed. No algorithm, no matter how sophisticated, can properly compensate for the accuracy of professional judgment based on a body of evidence. *Professional judgment* means agreed-on standards of excellence have been applied to a significant body of evidence that accurately reflects the depth of understanding or skill a student demonstrates (Cooper, 2022; Hargreaves & Fullan, 2012).

So, an approach centered on less grading, more feedback leads to a culture of investment because of the focus on meaningful work related to learning needs. Such a system allows for flexibility, as it's no longer about filling in blank boxes in the gradebook; rather, it is about seeking evidence of understanding and skill based on individual student needs and then making an informed judgment about that learner's abilities based on the preponderance of evidence. Exploring these practices on a unit or two can help teachers, teams, and schools consider the kinds of practices that increase grading accuracy and develop more confidence in students' ability to reflect and focus on learning.

Focus on Evidence of Learning

When educators focus on evidence of learning instead of completion of assignments, they have much less work to do. Instead of trying to get students to complete assignments that they may or may not find helpful or relevant to them, teachers center their work on collecting evidence of understanding (Schimmer, 2016). For learning goals and standards, teachers should articulate the related assignments and assessments. When there is evidence that students have mastered the concepts or skills, teachers can then let go of assignments that involve the same learning, as relying on those assessments will only lead students to focus on getting work done instead of help them learn more. If students didn't do the homework but showed mastery on the assessment, it most likely means the homework was not essential to their learning. This also gives students an incredible opportunity to make choices about the assessments and assignments they feel will help show their mastery. This type of decision making (along with teachers' guidance of student reflection) develops a deep sense of ownership and relevance within the learners.

Communicate Transparently

It's important to communicate results transparently and frequently to all stakeholders. Students need to see feedback and grading as part of a system of communication. The grade is only one part of the system of communication (Erkens et al., 2017). Each week, students should be getting feedback that informs their work, their next steps, and any focused revisions. The grade rarely helps students who don't know how to fix their work learn more. It most often shuts down their learning and motivation. Communication involves helping students and families understand the meaning of grades, how they are determined, how feedback is given and used, and what assessments mean in terms of learning (Schimmer, 2016; Schimmer et al., 2018; Townsley & Wear, 2020). This broader understanding of how grades and feedback work together to clearly communicate must be an ongoing conversation among educators, students, and families. A teacher's written communication in syllabi and on websites needs to articulate the school's commitments to the preferred communication protocol and what various forms of communication will entail to best help students know where they are going, where they are currently, and what to do next.

Part 4: A Learning Continuum for Implementation

Communicating student learning is an overall process that includes many components. A teacher should design their communication strategy to address the overall goal of having students and families clearly understand student strengths and areas of growth. Grades signal levels of proficiency in moments in time, while feedback along the way is geared toward providing insight into students' strengths and the next steps in their learning. Both, along with all the varied strategies that encompass formative feedback and grading, are designed to communicate to students and families. That communication needs to be accurate. Students need to know what they are strong in and what they must work on.

As teachers develop a clear vision of student investment, practices move to more learner-centered approaches and then learner-directed ones while students unlearn relying on the teacher for understanding their learning (see figure 5.8). Each step on the continuum provides teacher actions that signify where one is on the journey. It is important to note that while this figure is offered as a continuum leading to student

	Teacher Directed	Teacher Centered	Learner Centered	Learner Directed
Our school, teams, and teachers create a clear and powerful system of communication through implementing feedback and grading practices that allow students to invest.	• Teachers provide students with feedback around learning criteria and invite students to act on it. • Teachers base grading on the accumulation of points with some emphasis on learning.	• Teachers provide students with feedback and lessons in how to act on the feedback. • Most students act on feedback and improve their learning. • Students self-reflect on their learning based on assessments and feedback as prompted by the teacher. • Teachers report grades by learning goal, and there is still much emphasis on completing work or getting work turned in versus an emphasis on quality of work and ample evidence.	• Students use feedback to improve their work. Teachers guide students in interpreting the feedback and ensure that feedback is moving students forward in their learning. • Feedback leads to self-reflection and more independence for students. • Grades mostly reflect learning and separate work habits from achievement indicators. • Teachers clearly articulate communication methods to students and families in multiple ways.	• Students consistently use feedback to improve their work and articulate how it influences their learning. Teachers work alongside students to help them interpret and act on feedback. Teachers facilitate conversations to ensure that feedback leads students to reflect on their own learning and gain confidence in describing where they are going, where they are in their learning, and where they will go next. • Teachers give grades only when students have reached a level of proficiency. • Teachers' mindsets consider assessments and assignments evidence of learning. Thus, all assessments and instruction focus on what is to be learned. Investment centers on teachers prompting students for evidence of learning and *not* completion of work. • Teachers clearly articulate communication methods to students and families in multiple ways and in all communication.

Figure 5.8: Continuum for nurturing student investment through communication.

investment (learner-directed action), there will be times when teachers and students move back and forth on this continuum as they notice the impact a given move or practice has on student achievement and confidence.

Part 5: Tips for Moving Forward

The idea of changing or improving the way a teacher is already giving feedback can seem overwhelming and certainly time consuming. The goal is to create a feedback system that is productive for *both* the teacher and the student. Fortunately, teachers have some manageable ways they can begin the process so neither they nor students are overwhelmed while engaged in the feedback loop.

- **Start with strengths:** Feedback doesn't always have to be about critique; begin by reaffirming that which is strong so learners feel like their decisions through the learning are validated. As students invest in self-assessment, create routines that typically have them identify strengths first. It is always more *efficient* to just focus on what's next, but it may not necessarily be as *effective* since hearing about only what's wrong can take its toll.

- **Have smaller, more frequent cycles:** Teachers and students can tend to think that each moment of feedback has to be epic. All learners, but especially novice learners, can easily feel overwhelmed by the sheer volume of feedback they receive. The goal of feedback is to initiate more learning, which need not happen all at once. While an overwhelming number of aspects may need improvement, teachers are wise to focus feedback on what is most immediate; through more frequent cycles, learners can address the same number of deficiencies but in a more palatable way. With self-assessment, the same principles apply. Frequent reflection and a mindset of constant improvement are the ultimate goals.

- **Target the learning:** Teachers and learners alike find it challenging when the criteria keep changing; this happens when the criteria focus on the *task* instead of the learning. In Ms. Mending's class, each assignment had its own rubric. Rubrics (criteria) need to be taught, so each time a rubric changes, it could lead to inefficient use of the available instructional minutes. Feedback is most effective when it addresses the *learning* the task is meant to reveal; the task is a means to an end in most cases. Learning-focused criteria can transfer to several tasks when the same learning goals are at hand, and they increase the likelihood that feedback will have a positive impact. Divert learners' attention away from doing better on the task, and have them more deeply reflect on what's next for them to keep learning.

- **Make learners think:** Again, when teachers focus on initiating more learning, their feedback repertoire opens up. Utilizing feedback in the form of questions, cues, prompts, or highlighters directs learners' attention to what is strong and what needs strengthening without necessarily giving away the *what's next* answer. This feedback can be effective in peer-assessment situations as well, provided learners have enough proficiency to prompt, cue, or question; novice learners might still need more teacher involvement.

- **Teach learners *how*:** Feedback, whether sourced from the teacher or from the self, is most effective when it's acted on; however, not all learners know how to strategically act on the feedback they receive or identify. At first, be purposeful about embedding subsequent actions within classroom routines. While this may be redundant for some students, most will benefit from some direction or advice on how to approach improvement. Leave nothing to chance.

- **Grade only when necessary:** Grades aren't necessary for learning. In fact, sometimes grades can be counterproductive to initiating more learning. Using assessment results for the summative purpose is valid, but grading is not a strategy or an intervention, which makes drawing a line between *how you grade* and *how you improve learning* erroneous. Grades are not instructive, as no symbol, score, or level identifies what the learner should do next. Verifying the degree to which learners have learned and reporting that to others in a synthesized manner is a non-negotiable part of a balanced assessment system, but initiating (or reinitiating) learning and verifying it are two different purposes that are best kept apart, especially if learners settle for scores, grades, or levels that they find satisfactory but that are far from exemplary.

- **Be mindful of emotions:** No matter how focused feedback is on the quality of learning itself, there is always a chance that learners will take it personally; it is their work, and the feedback reflects what the teacher thinks of its quality. Directly, pay close attention to how learners might interpret routines, phrasings, and semantics. Indirectly, pay close attention to students' nonverbal cues (that is, body language, facial expressions, and so on) once they receive the feedback. Verbal cues can help, but the majority of what teachers communicate comes from nonverbal cues. The emotional side of assessment, including the communication of assessment results, is an influential force on learners.

Part 6: Questions to Guide Your Conversations With Students

Feedback and grading are essential components of a comprehensive communication approach for ensuring high-quality assessment practices and policies. The following prompts are designed to facilitate conversations and actions teachers and students can take to create the conditions for student investment when considering communication. (Visit **go.SolutionTree.com/assessment** for reproducible versions of these questions.)

Questions to elicit conversation on feedback include the following.

- What kind of feedback helps you learn the most?
- When do you tend to act on feedback?
- When does feedback shut you down?
- How can feedback help you self-assess?
- When you offer feedback to peers, how confident are you that your feedback is accurate?
- When you get feedback from peers, how does it help you?
- Does feedback help you learn more? In what ways?

Questions to elicit conversation on grades include the following.

- What do grades mean?
- What does it take to get "good grades"?
- When are grades most accurate?
- When do grades build your confidence?
- If you work hard and turn everything in, do you get a better grade?
- When are grades most useful?
- What should a grade mean?
- Do grades help you learn more?
- What kinds of grading practices or policies would be important to make sure grades are meaningful and helpful?
- What are the best ways to communicate to you and others progress on learning and academic behaviors?

Part 7: Dangerous Detours and Seductive Shortcuts

It's fairly common in the field of education to provide students with feedback that addresses the three most popular criteria for feedback: (1) timely, (2) specific, and (3) constructive. Unfortunately, those three criteria do not inherently increase productive responses from students. In fact, sometimes timely, specific, and constructive feedback can eradicate hope and efficacy in a heartbeat. When that happens, students make unproductive decisions to walk away from learning, eliminating the possibility of increasing student achievement altogether. Providing quality feedback that produces productive responses isn't always easy, and educators have some dangerous detours and seductive shortcuts to avoid along the path to improving the quality of feedback.

- **Turning feedback into an epic event:** For all the right reasons, teachers are often guilty of giving too much feedback; this turns feedback into an epic event. Epic events are exhausting and give teachers a false impression of the amount of energy it takes to provide feedback. The consequent exhaustion could lead to long stretches in between feedback moments since teachers need time to catch their breath. Quantity may have external, superficial appeal; a high quantity of feedback will let other people (including parents) know that teachers have thoroughly examined the students' demonstrations of learning, but it may be counterproductive to actually improving learning.

- **Giving feedback that is too sophisticated:** Having cognitively complex learning goals and sophisticated criteria does not necessarily mean all feedback should reference those things in the moment; feedback needs to be within reach. For many novice learners, feedback that references the exemplary level of understanding may be too sophisticated for where they are now. Feedback that is slightly above the learners' current status is more likely to cause a reinvestment in their learning, as learners will see that what is being suggested is plausible.

- **Relying on grades:** Technically, grades are a form of feedback, but in terms of advancing learning, grades miss the mark. Grading is not a strategy or an intervention (which are what improve learning), so expecting grades to improve learning is erroneous. Increasing the frequency with which one grades is not akin to increasing the use of effective feedback. There is a place for grading, as using assessment for the summative purpose is valid; grading is just not the same as providing guidance on what's next in the learning.

- **Giving feedback that is too prescriptive:** Following explicit directions does not always require thinking. Teachers, especially teachers of elementary learners, may be guilty of being too prescriptive with their feedback, thereby removing any need for students to invest in their learning, as teachers have done all the investment ahead of time. Leave the heavy lifting to the students, and facilitate feedback through the use of cues, questions, or prompts.

- **Expecting automaticity:** The existence of feedback does not cause an increase in learning, so remind yourself that although providing feedback is important, it is incomplete without any subsequent action. As they develop feedback routines, teachers should also consider the protocols students will follow to independently (or with guidance) use the feedback to further advance their learning.

CHAPTER 6
INSTRUCTIONAL AGILITY

When [my teacher] responded to my need for help with
frustration, I learned that it's wrong to ask questions. I
stopped asking questions because I was afraid of feeling
dumb and slow in front of a whole class of people.

—High school student

It's completely natural for a learner to have questions during instruction, and it's therefore predictable that a classroom full of learners may have a wide array of questions to support their understanding. Instructional agility occurs in the classroom when teachers respond to the emerging evidence with both precision and flexibility in their maneuvers. To make this happen, teachers must intentionally solicit the evidence to which they can respond. In other words, they must assess as they teach. "In a classroom where assessment is used with the primary function of supporting learning, the divide between instruction and assessment becomes blurred" (Thompson & Wiliam, 2008, p. 5). Quality instruction *is* formative assessment in action.

Part 1: Case Study

Mr. Stifton was a hardworking third-grade teacher, striving to increase his students' achievement on the annual state test. His students usually performed average when compared to the state median on those exams. However, last year was rough, and his students scored well below average. It would have been easy for him to blame last year's students (they were a pretty tough group) or even the test itself (it did seem to change often, and no one ever provided clarity on what was changing or why it was changing). But he knew *he* needed to do something different this year to be more responsive to his students' needs and to truly get the students ready for the test. He did not want a repeat of last year's scores, no matter the cause.

To make this work manageable, Mr. Stifton decided to fully integrate the online adaptive testing system StaxUp (a fictitious entity) into his curriculum planning and instructional activities. The state recommended StaxUp, the system that his campus was already employing for test preparation, as a local option to monitor student readiness in mathematics and reading. Mr. Stifton created his own classroom rotation for activating and interacting with the StaxUp program. In the first and third weeks of the month, students took the reading test on Mondays. In the second and fourth weeks of the month, students took the mathematics test on Wednesdays. The testing system generated an immediate, individualized student report and a resulting proficiency level for each student while specifically highlighting the strands in which the student needed support. Mr. Stifton planned to use the proficiency data to create appropriate student groupings and intervention center activities.

To pace the work to make it more manageable, he'd limit the intervention stations to three groups (one low, one middle, and one high) for both mathematics and reading. And he'd put the mathematics interventions in the reading testing weeks and the reading interventions in the mathematics testing weeks. That way, he reasoned, an entire week would have a focus on both mathematics and reading, and he'd have time after the testing to review the data and create the groupings for the week following a test.

In his esteem, the new system seemed responsive, but there were some significant challenges that he would have to overcome. For example, he realized he was grouping students by scores and not by the specific learning strands they had missed on the StaxUp assessment. He did his best to give each group learning activities and tasks that might hit most of the group members' needs. He also knew that the StaxUp testing items did not directly match his state standards and pacing guide, even though district and state leaders had assured him the StaxUp system would, in fact, prepare his students for the state exam, which was what he was trying to accomplish. The gap seemed evident to him, but he couldn't always see the tests to better align his instruction, so he would have to operate on the expertise of others and a little blind faith. This just *had* to work!

Finally, he recognized a potential challenge in his model in that all groups—even the students who scored proficient after each assessment—were always going to be engaged in intervention work rather than extension work. However, he reasoned, there was always room to improve, and no one could ever really be *done* learning, so he didn't believe his last concern was really much of an issue. The students themselves were adaptive, and a little repetition never hurt anyone.

By March, right before the state exam, Mr. Stifton was nervous. It seemed the class as a whole hadn't made dramatic gains in their weekly testing results. In truth, the students seemed entirely bored and maybe even a little frustrated with his well-orchestrated design. It seemed his students had fallen into a rut, demonstrating very little movement from one group to the next, and they began to accept their personal proficiency levels as reflections of permanent realities. Worse, though, he had overheard students begin labeling the various groupings. At least, he thought, they had a lot of experience taking computer-based tests at this point. Hopefully, *that* would work in their favor. Mr. Stifton crossed his fingers and hoped for good results at the end of the school year.

In truth, he was beginning to feel exhausted; even he was tiring of creating all the extra materials. He decided that he'd quit doing the intervention and grouping work after the state exam as a bit of a reward for his students and a reprieve for himself. After all, he now had some catching up to do in his curriculum because of all the time he had spent on test prep work.

The school year couldn't end fast enough. He just hoped it was all worth it in the end.

Reflection

Mr. Stifton was working hard to be instructionally responsive to his students, but his students did not seem to appreciate or benefit from his efforts. What went wrong? What would Mr. Stifton need to have done to be more responsive? Should being more responsive require so much extra effort on a teacher's part? What alternatives could Mr. Stifton have considered?

Part 2: Celebrations and Considerations

Mr. Stifton was deeply immersed in test prep, a strategy in which significant amounts of instructional time are set aside to prepare students for upcoming important exams, like state tests or national exams. Test prep became a widely accepted practice as test-based accountability efforts at state, provincial, and national levels began shaming or, worse, penalizing school systems that weren't meeting established metrics.

The notion of test preparation is not inherently wrong. For example, Mr. Stifton's efforts to support students in being successful on an assessment meant to measure the very things students must master is the exact purpose of quality instruction. Yet, this practice goes sideways when students are led to believe they are busy prepping for a test rather than preparing for life. Worse, the practice goes off the rails of schooling when test prep hijacks instructional efforts to prepare students for mastery on a given set of standards or expectations. In Mr. Stifton's case, he had no control over the assessment design for the StaxUp system, little understanding of what would actually be on each upcoming assessment, and great suspicions that the assessment itself didn't actually align with the standards his students had to master. As a result, he reallocated precious instructional time to address test readiness.

Poor test preparation strategies fall into three categories: (1) reallocation between subjects, (2) reallocation within a subject, and (3) coaching (not quality, process-oriented coaching but rather directive, deliberate efforts to advise on what content to provide and how to best provide it in order to earn high marks; Koretz, 2017). Fortunately, Mr. Stifton was engaged in the least troublesome of the three poor strategies: reallocation *within* the subject. At least he was sticking with mathematics during mathematics time and reading during reading time and not sacrificing other invaluable time like recess or subjects like art, physical education, and science. Still, in his use of reallocation within the mathematics and reading content areas, Mr. Stifton was surrendering the vital opportunity to address his standards through core instruction. With focused core instruction, Mr. Stifton could have specifically addressed his standard expectations, isolated gaps in understanding, empowered his learners to analyze errors and evaluate quality, activated the learners as resources to one another, and integrated small but powerful targeted intervention moments based on common errors. Instead, he opted for significant blocks of activity-based time that, in the end, may not have positively influenced students' outcomes.

Mr. Stifton accepted and embraced the need to be data driven if he was going to alter his students' trajectory of success. He understood that the best way to meet this need was to look at current data with a high degree of frequency. Already taxed with so many things to accomplish in his comprehensive intervention plan, Mr. Stifton used the StaxUp system to make the data-management system more manageable; it was the only ready measure close to his daily lesson planning. On the surface, his plan stacked up to the general expectation of being data driven at the classroom level.

Unfortunately, Mr. Stifton's data plans needed more focus in what data he gathered, how he organized and interpreted the data, and how he could use the data to monitor the effectiveness of his interventions along the pathway to learning. Mr. Stifton used overall proficiency levels to inform which of his students needed additional support. However, simply looking at proficiency levels is taking too broad of a swipe at isolating areas requiring intervention support. For example, if three students score 80 percent proficient on the same exam, but the three students each made different types of errors on different test items that represent different standards and various levels of rigor, are they equally proficient solely because they have earned the same score? Absolutely not.

Using blanket proficiency scores hides many truths and includes both false positives and false negatives. For Mr. Stifton to have been truly effective, he would have needed to dive more deeply into strand data—data that are set up by the relevant standard or range of standards—so he could search for trends and anomalies within those strands that would have illuminated the areas he needed to target with his instruction.

Even then, looking at the proficiency level per strand is too broad. Are there some items that all students missed? If so, is remediation the issue, or is test quality the issue? On the items that many students answered incorrectly, what types of errors did they make? Did all students make the same errors? Ideally, interventions are targeted based on individual student needs. Imagine that the standard being assessed is arguing from evidence. The student who has incorrect or insufficient evidence requires different instructional responses than the student who has accurate and sufficient evidence but is disorganized, the student who is organized but illogical, and so on.

The blanket categories of proficiency scale scores hide the critical diagnostic information a teacher requires and also tend to cause a sense of helplessness among students, who, in turn, fall into the helpless stance of fixed mindsets. The "it is what it is" ideology behind a fixed mindset happens when students are unable to break apart a poor score to recognize successes (such as they have mastered three of the five targeted areas) and isolate gaps (such as they are making only a simple mistake in one targeted area, and a common and easily fixed type of error in the other targeted area). It turns out that both teachers and students have a better understanding of what to fix and how best to fix it when the available data are frequent, diagnostic, and iterative so that learners can readily identify areas for improvement, intervene appropriately, and monitor for improvement based on the intervention (Dimich et al., 2017; Hattie, 2012; White, 2022). Not only did Mr. Stifton categorize students into broad ranges for his interventions, but he offered no extension opportunities, thereby relegating all learners to relearn and eliminating a key motivational purpose for students to invest.

What if Mr. Stifton had directly incorporated test prep and intervention systems into his Tier 1, core instructional efforts? And what if he had invited students as key decision makers in the process, activating them as resources to one another in collaborative rather than competitive ways? Learners who qualify for extension activities have already certified their proficiency in an assessment-based experience. This means they have no major conceptual or reasoning errors or omissions in their work. The evidence they have generated indicates that they understand all the critical concepts and can engage in all the necessary skills at the appropriate proficiency levels. As such, they do not require an additional assessment experience. Their extension experiences can expand learning opportunities without requiring another level of certification.

Extension activities should deepen or broaden learning in a manner that the learners involved find desirable. If learners who qualify for extension simply earn more work, they may not strive for future opportunities. And if they simply advance in the curriculum at a faster pace, the chasm between the learners within the classroom widens, and the process turns into ability grouping rather than flexible grouping based on unit-by-unit evidence. It stands to reason that if students knew something rewarding and enjoyable awaited them on the other side of proficiency, they'd be far more motivated to pass a unit of instruction in their first attempt.

Erkens (2019) proposed the checklist in figure 6.1 to brainstorm options for extension activities or to review the quality of extension activity plans once they are completed. Teachers must design all extension opportunities to meet the required criteria if they are to deepen the current learning in motivating ways. The additional desirable criteria help educators consider more enticing options within the extension experiences.

Check all that apply.	Criteria for High-Quality Extensions
Required Criteria for Extensions	
	It links directly to the learning targets of the unit.
	It requires the learner to apply knowledge and skills from the unit.
	It inspires fun and creativity.
	It increases the level of challenge.
	It can be accomplished in the provided time frame.
Desirable Criteria for Enhancing Extension Designs	
	It is based in collaboration.
	It provides opportunities for learners to work with a wide variety of their peers over time.
	It invites multiple perspectives.
	It integrates multiple concepts within the discipline or becomes interdisciplinary.
	It involves a degree of student choice or authorship in the experience.
	It provides opportunities for open-ended, inquiry-based, or problem-based investigations.
	It generates authentic learning experiences.

Source: Erkens, 2019, p. 198.

Figure 6.1: *Checklist for extension activities.*

*Visit **go.SolutionTree.com/assessment** for a free reproducible version of this figure.*

Extension should be fun and engaging. It should invite joy and a sense of accomplishment for the learners involved. When learners truly enjoy the opportunity before them, they do not worry about how many points an activity will accumulate, especially if the work they produce will actually be employed or shared in some public way. Rather, they *invest*.

In sum, Mr. Stifton employed a highly recommended teach-assess-respond pattern, such as the one found in figure 6.2, that involved using data to inform his instruction.

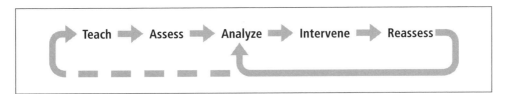

Figure 6.2: *The teach-assess-respond pattern.*

Unfortunately, Mr. Stifton did not incorporate five significant ingredients into his pattern: (1) teaching to the standards; (2) assessing what the standards required; (3) analyzing the data to impact core instruction; (4) intervening with extension and re-engagement activities for students who needed stretch and challenge and students who needed new ways to learn whatever they might be missing; and (5) *reassessing* outside of the StaxUp system to ensure his interventions were hitting the mark. (Of the five ingredients, this fifth ingredient is maybe the most important to include.) He needed information along the way to validate that his efforts were hitting his intended marks. Mr. Stifton was using hope as a strategy.

Part 3: Action to Take

To assess while teaching, teachers commonly employ strategic questions throughout the lesson. Teachers use questioning both to cause student thinking and to obtain information that assists instructional decision making, helping them know what to do next (Wiliam, 2018a). In-the-moment questions that are well placed and carefully worded can provide invaluable information to guide next instructional steps. A teacher could plan an in-the-moment question in advance in order to check for understanding of the important concepts (Erkens et al., 2018; Wiliam, 2018a). For example, when teaching students to retell, a teacher could plant a midlesson question to see whether students can find the middle part of the story. If most students identify the middle of the story as the beginning, then the teacher knows the learners are not yet recognizing all the parts and sequencing them appropriately.

An in-the-moment question might also emerge through class discussion and provide an opportunity to illuminate naive theories or misconceptions. For example, amid a history lesson, a teacher might note, "Hang on, everyone. I think something important just happened. Amir just stated that the colonies *first* declared independence from Britain on July 4, 1776, but Kiara countered him by saying that the colonies declared independence *earlier* than the actual signing of the document. Can both be right? If not, who's right, and how do we know? Let's work in teams to find text evidence to support or refute either claim."

As students respond to the well-thought-out question, "teachers must examine the evidence from the perspective of what it shows about student conceptions, misconceptions, skills, and knowledge. Sometimes teachers examine evidence on a moment-by-moment basis during the course of a lesson" (Heritage, Kim, Vendlinski, & Herman, 2008, p. 1). How a teacher interprets the evidence will inform the teacher's next steps. Misinterpreted evidence leads to poor instructional maneuvering by the teacher, leaving little opportunity to close the gaps emerging in student understanding. In this case, students miss what they need to be successful.

Practice work and test scores, albeit invaluable information, are insufficient indicators to support next steps in classroom instruction as it is evolving. If teachers base their decisions on post-instructional assessment findings (homework, quizzes, projects, and test scores), then they are not making different maneuvers during instruction. This is akin to curriculum coverage. It's nonresponsive and disrespectful to the students.

All assessment evidence should support next steps. Teachers can also use post-instructional assessment information to inform classroom groupings. However, if teachers use overall scores to plan intervention or extension group activities, their instructional maneuvers again miss the marks of precision and flexibility. Intervention efforts that are based on achievement levels (for example, students earning 60–70 percent on a test are placed in one group, and so on) combine students with mixed strengths and needs whose only common factor is the overall grade earned. Several students can earn the exact same mark or score on the same assessment and not have the same areas of concern requiring instructional modifications or intervention. Such general maneuvers are disconnected from both the learning targets and the specific common errors required to accurately address students' learning needs. Groupings based on overall scores not only miss the opportunity to make targeted instructional maneuvers but also shut down learning.

When students are grouped based on test scores or grades, they must navigate public embarrassment. Worse, when students do not know they are in a particular intervention group to deepen their understanding about a specific learning expectation, they begin to feel like they are being punished for not learning the general unit of study fast enough. In such a scenario, students can lose the desire to invest because it feels as if the education "game" is about good grades, and they sense they will always be in the losing category. Using overall scores to guide instruction can lead to student disengagement because it can feel like a low score is about one's self-worth, and it leaves students disempowered to make a difference in their reality.

On the other hand, if students get information about their strengths and growth areas, and the ensuing intervention or instructional time is focused on a specific learning expectation to help students learn more, then students gain confidence and can see their growth. This kind of experience in seeing and experiencing growth in the moment or the light bulb going off can boost confidence. When students feel more confident, they are going to invest more deeply. They are more likely to keep trying and come back ready for more.

Done well, instructional agility naturally leads to student investment because the real-time evidence teachers elicit and carefully examine clarifies next instructional maneuvers for both the teacher and the student. When the process is made transparent, students can articulate what they are learning and start to assess their own strengths, gaps, and next steps. In fact, the process of being instructionally agile is integral to learning. So teachers are best served if they intentionally model a variety of instructional options that students can use to learn concepts, and if they provide an array of plausible actions or responses to common errors and challenges that students are likely to discover throughout every unit of study. Learning to learn involves understanding instructional options so students can become self-sufficient in instruction.

It's a commonly understood value that education should produce lifelong learners. If learning is truly lifelong, then students grow into adults who can independently direct their own instruction. A key opportunity to reveal what it means to learn, unlearn, and relearn can happen during the intervention process—which all students require at some point in their learning careers. Students' ability to self-regulate means they can activate themselves as instructional resources during the learning process (Andrade, 2019; Brookhart, 2013a, 2017, 2020; Hillman & Stalets, 2021; Wiliam, 2018a). But it also means they can activate each other as resources during the learning process (Andrade, 2019; Wiliam, 2011).

Wiliam (2018a) asserts that directly teaching students to activate themselves and others as resources in the learning process *is* the work of formative assessment. Teachers would intentionally facilitate the development of such skills in their learners as they engaged in learning. Teachers engage students in critical conversations about learning, helping them consistently and accurately score their own and each other's work in a manner that mirrors the scoring their teachers would employ. Along the way, they teach students how to send and receive constructive feedback relative to the desired criteria for quality (Brookhart, 2017; Chappuis, 2015; Heritage, 2007; Hillman & Stalets, 2021). When students are capable of critiquing quality with accuracy, they are ideally positioned to make their own informed instructional maneuvers in response to their specific needs. In other words, students must also become instructionally agile.

Instructional practices that foster student investment involve offering students strategies for understanding and incorporating information, reflecting on progress, and intervening to ensure mastery. If students are to activate themselves as self-regulated learners, they must first acquire clarity on what's expected and then gain the skills to mobilize in informed ways. The following strategies—varied groupings, varied instructional strategies, conferencing and assessment conversations, empowered instructional decision making, instructional agility for learners, reassessment, extensions, and reflection and self-monitoring—can support teachers' instructional agility, and they can be modeled for and replicated by students as appropriate.

Varied Groupings

According to Erkens (2015a), classroom groupings should remain fluid, flexible, and purposeful. It's never appropriate to lock students into single-track groups for indefinite periods of time. Placing students into a low-performing group not only creates an intellectual scar and a sometimes-irreversible fixed mindset, but also denies those students access to on-grade-level material as well as the opportunity to watch learners at all levels of the learning spectrum productively struggle.

How and when to form groups depends on the work that teachers require of the groups. Putting students into various groupings throughout a course of study can prohibit the students' potential to develop fixed mindsets. It can also provide fresh perspectives on how to approach learning and empower learners to step into serving as resources to one another. Erkens (2015a) proposes teachers create ready labels and clear purposes for a variety of groupings that facilitate the rapid movements required for students to transition into different formations. Consider the following ABCs-of-grouping framework:

> **A = Assigned** (teacher discretion based on reteaching/intervention needs). These groups are determined *after* learners have been made aware of which learning targets they are going to be addressing through more focused efforts. It is a data-driven decision and the learners have their own data to support their various learning needs. In the A grouping, learners may be engaged in conducting error analysis, engaging in discussion, reviewing content or processes, engaging in extensions or enrichments, and so on.
>
> **B = Buddy** (student choice, but learners are encouraged to find different buddies throughout the term). On B days, learners are engaged in brainstorming, discussion, reflection activities, and so on. This is a generative

and play-based grouping when the stakes are low and fun or creativity are highly desired features of the activity.

C = Collaborative Project (teacher identification of 3–5 learners of mixed abilities in a group for 2–6 week collaborative projects). The letter C is on the board when collaboration is a focal point so learning activities will be very structured and ultimately assessed. The groupings are intentional and mixed abilities are involved. Social learning happens when the teacher outlines specific stretch activities that the team members do [scaffolded by learner readiness so that all can contribute to the outcome] in order to ensure success for [the team and the individuals on the team].

D = Design and Destination Work (teacher identification of 2–3 peers of like abilities to work together on feedback and goal-setting activities). Such groupings allow the teachers the opportunity to differentiate as they move in and among the various groupings. Learners work together to engage in practice, error analysis, peer review, reflection, goal setting, discussing concerns/needs, tracking progress against specific learning expectations, and so on.

E = Everyone (whole-group work for instruction, discussion, debate, setting criteria, collaborative scoring, error analysis, practicing feedback, and so on). When E is on the board, learners know that they will still have a high level of collaborative interaction as the teacher navigates whole-group discussion by using accountability strategies that keep everyone engaged in full participation. (Erkens, 2015a)

When learners know the letters in the grouping definitions, and the groupings of the day are posted at the front of the room, then students can help quickly move desks and resources to support rapid transitions.

It's equally important to help students understand the various groups' purposes and their roles within those groups. Ultimately, students need to understand when and with whom to group if they have questions about what they are learning or if they are struggling. Finding the right group to support personal learning is an ideal practice for a lifelong learner.

Varied Instructional Strategies

Teachers who are striving to be instructionally agile require a broad set of instructional tools to draw from when making alterations midstream. Teachers can increase the likelihood that students will invest in their learning when they find the sweet spot between an ideal instructional strategy and each student's individual preference on how best to learn something (Kise, 2021). It's important, then, that teachers and students maintain an open conversation, always noticing what's working and what's not while engaged in the instructional process.

One helpful option teachers can employ is to teach students a simple structure or framework for learning. The *5E model* (Duran & Duran, 2004), popularized as a model for engaging in scientific inquiry, is a helpful, easy model for students to employ in all subjects, not just science. The model itself drives learning deeper over time, and each of the five Es is fairly easy for students to grasp. The five Es, outlined as a generalizable learning process outside of scientific inquiry, are as follows (Duran & Duran, 2004).

1. **Engage:** Get connected to the topic by asking questions, making observations, and referencing prior knowledge.

2. **Explore:** Deepen the learning by seeking answers to questions, gathering additional information or data, and drawing conclusions.

3. **Explain:** Clarify understanding by putting concepts into personal frames of reference or sharing the learning with others.

4. **Elaborate:** Apply the learned concepts in situations with integrated curriculum such as project-based learning or challenge opportunities such as debates or Socratic forums.

5. **Evaluate:** Engage in self-assessments, reflection activities, or other such critiques so as to infuse judgment around the quality of what has been learned or how it has been learned.

Each phase of the five Es requires students to take their learning to a deeper and deeper cognitive level. Teaching students what the five Es are and providing them with the processes to engage in each E allows them to invest in their own desired future learning more successfully and independently.

Yet another option is to provide students with specific instructional strategies and to give those strategies names and protocols so that students know what the strategies are as well as how and when to use them. Many high-yield instructional strategies identified by Robert J. Marzano (2019) would be ideal to offer students. Strategies such as identifying similarities and differences; creating models, images, charts, graphs, and other nonlinguistic representations; generating and testing hypotheses; and summarizing and taking notes all provide students with memorable ways to grasp, organize, and make meaning around new concepts.

Finally, one more instructional option involves helping students understand how to write good questions to explore new ideas or challenge others' ideas. Sometimes, the question a student writes can illuminate their understanding as much as their answer to the question would. For example, when a student correctly answers a question of inference, a teacher then infers that the student understands the skill. But when the student develops a question of inference, it sheds additional light on how deep the student's understanding of inference might actually be. In classrooms where teachers provide sentence stems and frameworks for rigorous questioning, students are challenged to create their own meaningful questions worth exploring. In many cases, students use meaningful questions to challenge each other during the learning process, once again activating each other as resources to support their learning.

Conferencing and Assessment Conversations

Conferencing with students individually is a very powerful way to increase student investment (Cooper, 2022; Hillman & Stalets, 2021; White, 2022). One-on-one focused conversations in which the teacher is personalizing the feedback to a learner can directly influence the student's sense of possibility and personal awareness of direct needs. *Assessment conversations*:

> refer to these daily instructional dialogues that embed assessment into an activity already occurring in the classroom. . . . [They] permit teachers to gather information about the status of students' conceptions, mental models, strategies, language use, or communication skills to guide instruction. (Ruiz-Primo & Furtak, 2006, p. 207)

But it isn't a given that students automatically know how to have assessment conversations, especially those that involve their partnership in the protocols. Nor is it a given that teachers know how to co-construct metacognitive, rich conversations that lead to deep reflection. Educational consultant Katie White (2022) states:

> This willingness to co-construct [learning-rich environments that cultivate meta-learning skills and competence], while not always easy, is a necessary precursor to the kind of self-assessment that invites risk taking, supports decision making, and structures safe classroom spaces in which students can experience the consequences of their decisions to revise, relearn, and reimagine different outcomes. (p. 11)

Damian Cooper (2022), Garnet Hillman and Mandy Stalets (2021), and Katie White (2022) all note that assessment conversations should be planned, purposeful, and accessible to the learners, meaning the learners have a clear pathway and ready information of their own (test reflections; data trackers; feedback from the teacher, peers, or themselves; or their resulting goals and plans) for them to successfully engage in the conversation. Hillman and Stalets (2021) advise that teachers teach students *how* to prepare and that they themselves prepare by having the proper materials ready, planning for the appropriate guiding questions, and anticipating instructional responses for the learners based on their emerging needs.

When developing a robust conferencing system, it's important to take the long view, factoring in how to prepare students to develop the skills, gather the information needed, and build confidence in using scoring tools and providing self- and peer feedback (Hillman & Stalets, 2021; White, 2022). It's even important to consider where to begin and how much time to spend in each stage of independence—from teachers leading, to teachers partnering with students, to students taking some control while still partnering with teachers, to students leading (with peers and teachers).

Consider the following questions when designing a conferencing system.

- What are your criteria for the ideal assessment conversation? How will you weave those criteria into all your plans, protocols, and tools? How will you monitor your own effectiveness in meeting those quality criteria?

- What norms or expectations enable intellectual risk taking and protect students from experiencing blame or shame? When should those norms be taught, and how will they be reinforced? Would it be possible for students to begin holding each other accountable to the norms?

- When, where, and how will you find time for conferencing? How will you fit all the students into or rotate all the students through a conferencing schedule?

- What might you need to give up if you are creating space for these important conversations?

- What evidence or artifacts will be needed, and where will students record or store those materials? What templates or tools might students need to support their efforts?

- What strategies could be used to improve students' accuracy when self- or peer scoring with the attending tools (rubrics, scales, scoring guides, or checklists)?

- What responses can support students in continuing to learn the criteria or protocols when inaccuracies occur?

- What strategies can be used to support and engage shy learners, struggling learners, or learners with fragile egos?

- What will be the best way to help students accurately create their own meaningful, academic stretch goals?

- What systems will be needed to link the conferencing conversations so learning continues over time?

- Which growth-oriented assessment conversations will work best in small-group settings? Large-group settings? One-on-one settings?

- Where (or how) will you achieve privacy or maintain confidentiality within the classroom for those conversations?

- What self-habits or potentially over-supportive scaffolds might need to slip by the wayside when you genuinely partner with and eventually empower learners to run their own assessment conversations?

While the list of considerations might seem daunting at first, the resulting systems can become procedural to the degree that the teacher shifts from *creating* the systems to instead *leaning* on the systems to free up time for planning the right conversations.

It also helps when students can lean into familiar systems with consistency. There are a plethora of options available (see Cooper, 2022; Hillman & Stalets, 2021; and White, 2022, for many ideas). One such protocol, the compact conferencing protocol (Erkens et al., 2019), is patterned on Chappuis's (2015) three-minute conference and is intended to guide learners through the three questions of student engagement: (1) Where am I now? (2) Where am I going? and (3) How do I close the gap? The protocol, available in two parts as the reproducibles "Compact Conferencing Protocol Instructions" (page 173) and "Compact Conferencing Planning and Reflection Form" (page 175), covers both the planning and reflecting components, but teachers and students could isolate single parts to activate as needed.

No matter the section of the protocol that is activated (planning or reflecting), using a timer and training learners to limit their conversation to four minutes maximum will be helpful. In this way, teachers can schedule a few conferencing sessions per week. Also, students can use the exact same protocol in four-minute increments at the same time as the teacher is engaged in a conference with someone else, so it helps when everyone can hear the timer at the four-minute mark.

Teachers can also hold brief drop-by conferences (one minute or less) as a check-in at students' desks (see the reproducible "Drop-By Protocol" on page 178). When using this protocol, teachers can randomly select a handful of students to visit for a minute or less at any point in the class period. In such a brief exchange, it's important that students always know (1) they must have data or artifacts to back their answers, (2) they must be able to justify their thinking regarding those materials, and (3) they must be ready to consider next steps. The drop-by protocol can be powerful when students know what to expect in advance and the ensuing conversation is brief, immediate, and focused.

Once students learn the three conferencing expectations and are familiar with the drop-by protocol, teachers can engage students in peer conferences, creating the opportunity for a steady diet of feedback in the classroom. Of course, at the highest level of learner investment, the students themselves would orchestrate their own assessment conversations, calling to their desk peers and teachers to offer feedback or answer questions. For that to happen, classrooms would need a culture of safety, the shared expectation that students learn best when they activate themselves and each other as resources, and the time and resources necessary to support such fluid drop-by moments. It would be important for teachers to understand and to deliberately create a culture wherein students feel safe to activate each other as resources. The popular notion that collaboration could potentially lead to cheating would have to give way to the belief that collaboration is required to support deep learning for all.

Empowered Instructional Decision Making

No learner in the K–12 school system already has a PhD. So, all learners always need a next step, whether that next step involves seeking feedback, revising, intervening on their own behalf, or extending their own understanding with extended learning options. The biblical expression, "Physician, heal thyself" (Luke 4:23; King James Bible, n.d.), applies here as educators ask learners to attend to their own needs in a focused, honest, and productive manner. The challenge of empowering learners to engage in their own instructional decision making is threefold.

1. To inspire the motivation required for students to self-start and finish the task at hand

2. To teach learners how to accurately identify what they need next

3. To provide learners with the knowledge, skills, and resources necessary to address what comes next

To begin, learners must be motivated to engage in the work. Many schools and classrooms still struggle to figure out how to motivate their learners. Like many experts in the field of psychology, psychologist Johnmarshall Reeve (2018) defines *motivation* as "*wanting* . . . a condition inside us that desires a change" (p. 2). There are mixed theories on whether extrinsic rewards motivate students. Author Daniel H. Pink's (2009) findings indicate that reinforcement systems undermine intrinsic motivation; any activity of substance such as learning (which is ideally intrinsic) must be based on supporting a student to be autonomous, achieve mastery, and embrace purpose. However, professors W. David Pierce and Carl D. Cheney (2017) suggest that reward systems (which are extrinsic) can, in fact, generate favorable effects on student motivation. The challenge for educators striving to increase student motivation is that there isn't one right answer—and, even if a reward system works, reinforcement can eventually "[interfere] with problem solving because it [produces] stereotyped response patterns" (Pierce & Cheney, 2017, p. 119). This notion is common sense for teachers whose daily experience indicates grades motivate some learners but not others.

So, what's an educator to do when a generic approach won't motivate all learners, and motivation is the *root* to students' investing in their own learning? Behavioral science (motivating others) is complex, and there are many factors to consider, but educators can use the following three options to try to move away from extrinsic rewards and into intrinsic motivation.

Strategy 1: Engage With Relevance

Make the assessments themselves into highly relevant and engaging options (Erkens et al., 2019; White, 2019). It helps when the assessments are authentic and the products actually extend beyond the classroom, so learners are engaged in the process for more than simply achieving a score. Figure 6.3 highlights some options.

Subject	Traditional Approach	Authentic Approach
English Language Arts	Create a Venn diagram showing the differences between cats and dogs.	Use the specifics on your comparison of two pets to explain which pet would be the better option to have in your specific home environment and why.
Mathematics	Find the solutions to the mean, median, mode, and range problems that have been provided.	Gather data for a week on the number of times and ways you use a cell phone to support your learning. Then use the measures of central tendency and the range to create a data-rich argument on whether you should be able to use a cell phone to support your learning in school.
Social Studies	Name three factors that defined the Age of Exploration.	Use text evidence linking the factors that defined the Age of Exploration from the 1400s to the 1600s to defend or refute the argument that you are in the Digital Age of Exploration in the 2020s.
Science	Fill in the graphic organizer naming the sources of renewable and nonrenewable energy.	Once you have identified the most common sources of renewable and nonrenewable energy on our campus, pitch a plan to the principal for how our school's energy use could be more eco-friendly.

Figure 6.3: Options for making assessments more relevant.

Just as adults want their work to be meaningful, so do learners of all ages. When learners feel like their work adds value to a broader audience or fulfills a broader purpose, they are more likely to be motivated to complete it.

Strategy 2: Track Individual Learning Data and Assess With Purpose

Allow learners to use their own data to make informed decisions about what they need and don't need (Erkens, 2013; White, 2019). The assignment of practice work must specifically meet the needs of the individual learners. Making learners continually engage in the exact same assignment, when some might not need more of that specific practice and others might need even more practice than what's on that assignment, is a sure way to disengage learners. It's logical to ask students to gather and track their achievement data for a personal purpose and benefit, rather than to make them engage in the process for the sake of fulfilling another class exercise.

Students of all ages can track their own learning data. In kindergarten, learners can color in bar graphs to show how many numbers or letters they know. Or they can color in the evidence of their ability to skip-count, as indicated in the three data-tracking tables of figure 6.4.

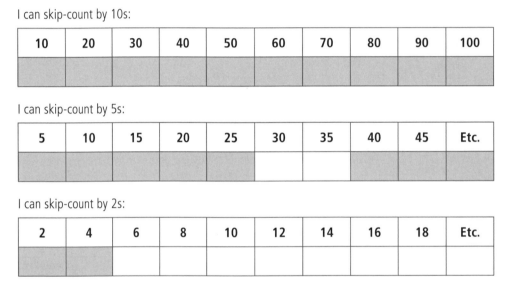

I can skip-count by 10s:

10	20	30	40	50	60	70	80	90	100

I can skip-count by 5s:

5	10	15	20	25	30	35	40	45	Etc.

I can skip-count by 2s:

2	4	6	8	10	12	14	16	18	Etc.

Figure 6.4: Kindergarten data-tracking tables for skip-counting.

When a kindergarten learner sees that she can successfully skip-count by tens, she can ask to bypass the additional practice work with tens and move to practicing skip-counting by twos, where she visibly needs more practice. Tracking data should be meaningful for the learners so they feel as if they have autonomy over their next steps. Learners need to confirm the data with teacher scoring or input, however, and not leave the data a matter of personal opinion.

Differentiated practice work may seem overwhelming or even chaotic for educators to consider. If educators plan a number of assessments or assignments around single learning targets or skills, differentiating practice work could easily be a matter of letting students opt out of the ones they have *proven* they no longer need. And learners can help teachers find additional practice work options that they would find meaningful when they recognize the need for additional practice.

Helping students accurately monitor their data and empowering them to make data-based decisions moves them along in understanding how to individually determine what they need next. Goal setting, then, helps students commit to what comes next.

Strategy 3: Set Personal Academic Goals

Setting meaningful, personal academic goals launches a student's ability and motivation to self-regulate. Andrade (2019) states, "Self-regulated learning occurs when learners set goals and then monitor and manage their thoughts, feelings, and actions to reach those goals." Though it is the launch, it can't come first in the process. As suggested by way of noting the previous strategies, students must first understand how to determine what they need next, and they must be able to use their own data to make a reasonable and personal stretch goal.

Goal setting is about both visualizing and *wanting* that plausible outcome. Hattie (2009) states, "Goals have a self-energizing effect if they are appropriately challenging for the student, as they can motivate students to exert effort in line with the difficulty or demands of the goal" (p. 164). When learners embrace a purpose and a direction through a clear, articulated goal, they are more likely to be successful in their learning endeavors and inspired to continue the learning as desired.

But not all goals meet the metric of being so inspirational or meaningful. Goals fall flat in the classroom if they can be categorized in any of the following ways.

- They are predetermined and pre-scripted by the teachers for student adoption.
- They merely outline tasks to be accomplished.
- They focus on low-level cognitive tasks such as rote memorization or simpler skills.
- They are formed by simply dropping key words into a preformed template.
- They are formed too early in the learning, before the students have time to grasp the essence of what is required.
- They set the bar too high without creating the relevance or inspiration necessary to capture the students' attention and commitment.
- They are not personalized in a manner that drives the students to focus specifically on their immediate needs while accomplishing the learning.
- There are too many of them to allow for the attention and commitment required.

Setting goals in the classroom is not as easy as filling in a simple template might suggest. Teachers must finesse the process to be individualized and timed appropriately while simultaneously making the process visible and manageable for all learners.

Goals must be data based and data driven. Too many times, students enter a new and possibly unfamiliar unit of learning and are asked to set goals with a very limited understanding of the content at hand. In such cases, goals become broad, catchall sweeps (for example, "Learn everything about the topic at hand") or a checklist of requirements that have no meaning or value to the student at that moment. The most personally meaningful goals are based on the context of background knowledge and evidence of what is understood and what is not yet understood. It's best, then, if goals are established *after* initial learning has been offered and early data have revealed the knowledge and skills worth targeting to improve.

In addition to being specific to the student needs, learning goals must be challenging. Easy goals seldom feel valuable, and they do little to inspire commitment or activate persistence (Sadler, 1989). Sadler (1989) defines hard goals as "being specific and clear rather than general or vague, harder and challenging rather than simple or easy, and closer to the upper limit of an individual's capacity to perform than to the current level of performance" (p. 129). Adding further clarity, Hattie (2009) cites research that notes:

> It is not the specificity of the goals but the difficulty that is crucial to success. There is a direct linear relationship between the degree of goal difficulty and performance. . . . The performances of the students who have the most challenging goals are over 250 percent higher than the performances of the subjects within the easiest goals. (p. 164)

When designed well, challenge goals can direct the student's attention to a clear picture of the learning demands *and* inspire action. Challenging goals that have no relevance quickly disintegrate into abandoned wishes. It might not seem easy, but creating a sense of relevance is required in the goal-setting phase, especially with challenge goals.

Goal statements that are created to address relevance, challenge, and specific needs tend to naturally follow the SMART goal framework (Conzemuis & O'Neill, 2014), as these statements already integrate so many components of SMART goals. While many different interpretations of the SMART acronym exist, one variation stands above the rest for ease of student understanding and use (ASVAB Career Exploration Program, n.d.).

- S = strategic (Challenge is required.)
- M = measurable (The goal can be tracked, preferably using multiple equitable data points from classroom assessments so growth can be monitored over time.)
- A = attainable (Even though there is a stretch, the student believes the goal can be reached with or without support.)
- R = relevant (The goal is based on current data that highlight specific needs.)
- T = time bound (There is a firm end point against which success can be measured.)

Students can create SMART goals for a unit, a course, or an entire year of study. Consider the examples of student-created SMART goals that follow.

- I will be reading on grade level (level M books) by the end of second grade.
- By the end of the geology unit, I will be able to provide sufficient, relevant evidence with 100 percent accuracy about how the solid parts of the earth are always changing.
- I will be able to use the quadratic formula with 95 percent accuracy by the end of the quarter.
- By the end of the term, I will be able to deconstruct a counterargument so I can win my argument in a debate.

As challenging or time consuming as it might seem, engaging students in setting academic goals is absolutely worth the effort for teachers. Research in the area of educational goal setting suggests students with goals tend to live up to the challenging expectations that they establish for themselves and that others hold for them (Frey, Hattie, & Fisher, 2018). Frey, Hattie, and Fisher (2018) note, "When teachers and students have goals for learning, the impact is positive with an effect size of 0.56" (p. 18), making goal setting a powerful strategy for increasing student achievement.

Inspiring motivation through creating relevant assessments, engaging learners in monitoring their own progress, and having learners set their own goals is the foundation of learners' ability to become instructionally agile in addressing their own needs.

Instructional Agility for Learners

At the highest level of student investment, learners become their own best teachers. They learn to tap into their own interests and strengths when approaching complex tasks. They learn to seek new strategies to support their continued learning in challenging situations, and they learn to self-assess with honesty and accuracy so they can determine if they need to intervene on their own behalf or extend learning by deepening their understanding and skill levels.

The word *intervention* can sometimes signal that something is wrong with the *learner*. It's important to set the appropriate tone so students neither adopt the experience as a personal flaw nor view the experience as a punishment. Rather, students should clearly know that intervention is designed (first by teachers and hopefully eventually by themselves) to help them accelerate their learning of an essential learning target or standard. More powerful than waiting for a teacher to fix them, the learners' belief in themselves, their understanding of the power of effort, their purposeful goals, and their ability to access the appropriate resources will determine whether they close their own gaps in understanding.

This is not to suggest that teacher-led opportunities to re-engage students in learning are less powerful. Indeed, direct, targeted instruction is necessary to challenge learners and ensure they are still focused on the standards and operating at the appropriate level of rigor and proficiency (Fisher, Frey, & Hattie, 2016; Hattie, 2009). Rather, it is to suggest that intervention efforts work *best* when the learners invest in closing their own gaps.

To help students understand how to intervene on their own behalf, teachers can engage the class in tracking the most common types of mistakes that might happen with a given learning target and then identifying possible strategies learners could use to avoid the errors. It's helpful to keep an anchor chart for *each* learning target during a unit of study that documents the potential errors and the best instructional fixes to address the errors. Figure 6.5 provides a sample anchor chart.

Another supportive strategy is to help the entire class keep track of the things they have successfully used in the past to learn something hard. A learning strategy list would work as an anchor chart as well. Figure 6.6 (page 162) outlines a potential list that students might generate as a class following a highly successful learning experience.

Intervention work should be done in partnership. Both students and teachers need to engage in addressing gaps in understanding. If a teacher's first round of quality instruction did not suffice to close all of a learner's gaps, then self-learning or packet-guided learning will be insufficient. The system works best if teachers design targeted and engaging interventions that offer *different* ways of learning the same content (not louder and slower versions of the original instruction) that are required for any student who needs them. Students can enter these intervention time slots with a note card that clarifies their specific learning target to address, the types of errors they made with that target, and their personal learning goal to address that target. From there, students can engage in additional independent practice (choice is powerful at this point), and they can use their accurate and thorough practice results as their qualifying ticket to reassess.

Reassessment

Once intervention has occurred, there must be the opportunity to reassess. Assessment is the means by which teachers and their learners gather proof that the learning has been mastered, so reassessment is a critical step to follow the intervention process. Without it, neither teacher nor learner will have proof that the intervention worked and the gaps have been closed. Reassessment cannot be a choice. As such, time for reassessment must be built into the unit of study of the school's pyramid of interventions.

Learning Target: When reading, I draw conclusions. This means I use both implied and stated evidence in and around the text and then form a reasonable judgment or decision about the meaning of the text.

Common Errors	Ways to Fix Errors
Restating the exact text	**Check:** Do any of your words show up exactly in the text? In the same sequence? That's a red flag that you have restated what the text said. **Idea:** Put the text away and use your own words to write one or two sentences to a friend saying what you think the text meant. Read your sentences to a friend to see if your friend agrees.
Using faulty or inappropriate evidence	**Check:** Is the evidence you provided actually found in the text? Is it relevant to the main idea of the passage? Is it relevant to your conclusion? **Idea:** If possible, use a highlighter to highlight the things that support the author's main message. If you can't use a highlighter, then write the details down on a piece of paper. Check with a friend to see if the text evidence you highlighted is relevant. Check also to see if you have enough evidence (more than one or two details) to support that message. Now, draw your conclusion by looking at the evidence you have highlighted.
Using accurate but insufficient evidence	**Check:** How many pieces of evidence were you using when you drew your conclusion? Count them. Are there more than one or two? Does the evidence you picked cover every part of the conclusion you drew? **Idea:** Write your conclusion at the top of a blank piece of paper. Put a number above each important word in your conclusion that would require evidence to support it. Then, list each piece of evidence below it on its own line. Does each number in your conclusion have enough evidence on the lines below to prove it true?
Using faulty reasoning	**Check:** Does the opinion, argument, or justification in your conclusion make sense to someone else? **Idea:** Write your claim on a piece of paper. Ask a friend to help you answer the following questions. • Is it accurate? • Does it make sense? • Is it comprehensive? • Is it reasonable? • Would someone else be able to find fault in it?

Figure 6.5: Sample anchor chart.

Things that work for us when learning:
- Taking notes on one side of the page and putting images that represent the notes on the other side of the page
- Putting ideas into graphic organizers that show relationships
- Using study buddies
- Using flash cards by myself or with a friend
- Recording voice notes on my phone and playing my own notes back to me
- Asking an adult or a friend to clarify something
- Writing down all my questions and looking up my own answers to my questions

Figure 6.6: *Sample list of successful strategies.*

There are a few guidelines to support student investment in the reassessment process.

- Only assess on the specific learning targets that students are yet to master. Making students take the entire assessment over again is unnecessary to prove their initial gaps are closed, and it's frustrating and cumbersome for the learners.

- Use different questions or tasks than the initial set. A learner could default to recall if the questions or tasks are the exact same.

- Engage the student in addressing the entirety of the target that students studied during the intervention. Simply using a replacement item for one or two questions from the original test will not provide sufficient evidence that the student has mastered the target.

- Keep the questions or tasks at the same level of rigor. Reassessment is not intended to punish a learner (too hard) or soft-pedal the learning (too easy).

- Do not let students just fix the wrong answers on the initial test and turn it back in for an improved score. Answers at this point could be based on seeing or hearing other students' answers. In addition, teachers often turn to this strategy after they have distributed the test and before students return it, which completely eliminates the necessary intervention period altogether.

- Do not let students reassess if they did not do some of their own additional work to qualify to retake the necessary parts of the assessment. In the absence of this condition, schools become testing factories, handing out multiple versions of the test until students eventually decide to take the testing opportunity seriously.

- Allow students full credit for attaining the required learning. If full credit is not granted, learners will not take reassessment seriously, and teachers will not be able to point to evidence that they did, in fact, help all their learners to high levels of achievement.

Reassessment is a necessary part of the intervention system, but it should not be cumbersome or painful for the teacher or the learner.

Extensions

In the same way, students who have mastered standards must not sense they have arrived. There is always room to grow, and extensions signal to students that learning is the goal and that with more time, even deeper learning will occur.

Typically, students will naturally extend their learning in areas that inspire or intrigue them, and that kind of extension happens outside of class and possibly for an extended period of time beyond the initial lessons. Students will not extend their learning within a unit of study if they are not given time to do so. A powerful strategy for driving students to *want* to extend their learning is to design an intriguing, collaborative, and fun learning opportunity for the end of the unit and then pitch the idea at the beginning of the unit as a reward for passing the assessment. A teacher might say, for example, "If you master this unit on information literacy, then you will get to be part of the team that develops a *Schoolhouse Rock!*–like video about fake news. If your video is a good one, we'll show it during a morning meeting" (or on the TVs in the cafeteria, in the hallways during passing time, and so on). Another option is to pique students' intrigue about a phenomenon related to the learning targets at hand and invite them to gather information the class has not yet explored.

Students should always have "What comes next?" as a pertinent question when learning. The trick is to keep students motivated and focused as they navigate their own way to success.

Reflection and Self-Monitoring

Learning to learn means students learn as much about who they are as people as they do about strategies to support their continued learning. Andrade (2019) notes that self-assessment and self-monitoring can be done with *or* without academic expectations. In other words, such metacognitive activities often illuminate more than just academic understanding, even though that is the ultimate goal.

A goal that is not acquired is a wish. The follow-through from students' goal setting comes in their ability to monitor their success along the way to meeting their goal. Monitoring learning is critical at this juncture. In fact, Andrade (2019) states, "Monitoring and self-assessing processes are practically synonymous with self-regulated learning." This dynamic interplay of using assessment information to guide instructional maneuvers on behalf of the learner is where true student investment comes into play.

Self-monitoring looks markedly like the data-tracking activities already explored, along with the learner's own reflective comments about what's working and what's not working. Learners keep these comments within the gathered evidence and notes about what to try next in the progression to mastery. There are many variations of reflection forms students can use, but these forms don't have to be complicated. At the end of the day, the most important questions are the following questions of self-regulation outlined by Chappuis (2015). The subquestions provide a host of options for students to ponder. Simply planting one question at the right time and place can be enough to move a learner forward in meaningful ways.

- Where am I going?
  - Do I know my learning targets? Do I have the necessary knowledge and skills to meet those expectations?
  - Do I understand the criteria for quality against which my work will be judged?
- Where am I now?
  - Is my work accurate? Thorough?
  - Do my data highlight what I have learned as well as what I still need to learn?
  - What specific types of errors am I making? Can I explain why I am making them? Is there a pattern I should watch out for?
  - Do my artifacts meet the highest degree of quality?
  - Can I accurately score my own or my peers' work using the success criteria or the scoring tools that have been provided?
- What can I do to close my gap (between where I am and where I need to be)?
  - What strategies have I tried that have worked?
  - What strategies have I tried that have been unsuccessful?
  - What keeps me going?
  - What shuts me down?
  - What resources are available to me?
  - What new strategies might I try?
  - Can I track my progress over time?

- Do I need to reset my goal? My strategies?
- What practice work can I do to help me?
- What evidence will I need in order to prove to myself that I have mastered the learning targets?

For students to self-monitor, they must be granted the time to reflect and the option to revise and improve their learning. Such work is intentional, and students should be taught the skills needed to self-monitor, stay on task, focus on what is most important, and let go of what doesn't serve them or bring them closer to achieving their goals. This type of work requires a significant amount of persistence over time from both teachers and students.

Part 4: A Learning Continuum for Implementation

Like assessment purpose (see chapter 2, page 37), the tenet of instructional agility centers the ideas of how learners use their assessment information to answer three important questions: (1) Where am I going? (2) Where am I now? and (3) How do I close the gap so I can move forward? (Chappuis, 2015). Unlike assessment purpose, instructional agility spotlights the process of making strategic instructional moves to close the gaps. The idea is to be metacognitive about the instruction so that students aren't merely receiving intervention about content; rather, they are learning the maneuvers that will empower them to close future gaps in their understanding.

When students are clear about how they learn best and what instructional strategies help them the most, the likelihood that they will invest in and improve their knowledge and skill increases. Clearly, this type of engagement is the ultimate form of self-directed learning. The most powerful instruction exposes students to the content in palatable ways; allows them to clarify their interests, strengths, and challenges within the content; and then facilitates their ability to own and self-direct their next steps with effective strategies for learning.

Like all the preceding continuums, the continuum in figure 6.7 (page 166) begins with teacher-directed practices, which move to student-directed practices in the context of teacher-centered facilitation. Also, it is important to note that this continuum, like the preceding ones, is not a unidirectional process. It is a synergistic, evolving process that must move back and forth regarding who owns the direction. Teachers always base such decisions on what the learner most needs or can handle at the time. If learners find the content too challenging, then it's a great time for the teacher to take control and provide instruction, whereas if learners understand the basis of the content, then it's the ideal time for the teacher to pass the baton of control to the learners. Both teachers and students must remain attentive, noticing the impact of any given move on the learning experience.

	Teacher Directed	Teacher Centered	Learner Centered	Learner Directed
Our school, teams, and teachers are intentionally instructionally agile to ensure students recognize their strengths and grow in achievement and confidence.	• Teachers notice where students are strong in their learning and where they need work. • Teachers plan instruction based on what they notice.	• Teachers notice where students are strong and where they need work in learning the essential standards and learning goals. • Learners engage in interventions and extensions based on teachers' interpreting assessment evidence and planning instruction. • Once this differentiated response occurs, students reassess to gather more recent evidence of where they are in understanding or achieving the essential standards and competencies. • Along the way, students reflect in general on their progress and on their time on task and behaviors that lead to productive learning opportunities.	• Students engage in interventions and extensions to help guide their next steps in learning. Teachers guide this process and ensure that students are making progress by monitoring ongoing assessment evidence (including conversations and dialogue). • Student reflections are consistent so that students clearly know the impact of intervention and extension on their learning. • Teachers guide students to reflect and self-monitor their progress, providing instruction on how to reflect and monitor their learning. • Students learn how to learn as a result of this focused instruction and practice in reflection and self-monitoring.	• Students are clear about what they are learning in interventions and extensions. They clearly articulate their learning and can effectively choose interventions and extensions that meet their needs. • Students practice self-reflection and can articulate where their strengths are and where they need to work more given the assessment evidence they have gathered. • Interventions and extensions are seen as part of the lesson flow and focused on learning. All students are able to activate skills and resources to address what comes next in their own learning. • Students consistently reflect and get feedback and instruction on how to reflect and notice learning in their own work. • Reassessment is a natural part of the process when students need additional time. However, reassessment is not nearly as needed, as students are reflecting along the way and being graded in the moment they are ready.

Figure 6.7: Continuum for nurturing student investment through instructional agility.

Part 5: Tips for Moving Forward

Instruction and assessment are two sides of the same coin. Instruction *is* intervention, and intervention must be data driven (as revealed through assessment) if it is to be targeted and successful. Anything less is merely curriculum coverage. It is a mistake to enter instructional efforts without a clear picture of the evidence that will be needed along the way and a plan for how to best interact with the emerging (and anticipated) evidence.

Many teachers wish to be agile. What's ideal is the ability to be precise yet flexible to the degree that students get what they need quickly. But when teachers own the entire process, their desired image as the modern instructional superhero can crumble before their very eyes. It is a mistake to keep instructional efforts a secret. When the entire classroom can activate the class's members as instructional resources, then *everyone* can succeed as instructional superheroes.

Because teachers naturally teach and assess every day, they can easily streamline manageable assessment and instructional processes, such as the following, and integrate the processes into lessons so as to build student investment through the learning journey.

- **Assess for action:** Simply *doing* assessment is not good enough; *using* assessment is the goal. Before students can invest in their learning, teachers need to design assessments that are usable (Erkens et al., 2017). That means assessments are designed with action in mind. When using selected response, ensure that each incorrect response represents a plausible misunderstanding; when using constructed response, be sure the prompt is specific enough to target aspects of misunderstanding or illogic. Assessments *for* learning need to be used *for* learning so the identified interventions align with each learner's needs. As teachers build the habit of assessment design in service of instructional agility, they will then be able to help their students learn to use assessment evidence for themselves.

- **Extend for depth and breadth:** Many times, assessment reveals that learning is on track or advanced. Being instructionally agile means teachers are ready to extend students by nurturing their curiosity, their talents, or their passions (Erkens et al., 2018). Learning is never truly final, so if there is time—possibly while interventions are being implemented for students who need more—students who have mastered standards can explore to greater depths of knowledge. The teacher can initiate or prescribe this. Though students should be in agreement that extension is desirable, teachers create the opportunities.

- **Differentiate for learning:** Mr. Stifton had the right idea, but he suffered from poor execution by using scores to determine the intervention stations. Scores are insufficient, as they rarely (if ever) reveal the type of error a student makes, and the type of error is what determines the intervention. Effective differentiation is specific; the stations were too generic. While it's possible to haphazardly have a positive impact with generic stations, intentionality and specificity make interventions efficient and effective. The good news is that several students often have the same intervention needs, so the group-based approach is usually still valid; however, teachers should determine that only after the assessment evidence is revealed.

- **Develop student self-monitoring skills:** The end goal of student investment is students accurately monitoring their own learning. This won't happen overnight. As students continue to learn to self-assess and monitor their learning trajectory, they will become better able to independently know where they are, what's next, and how to get there. Teachers must teach a process, allow students to practice, verify that students are on point, and then slowly release them to increasing levels of independence.

- **Make self-reflection habitual:** Being instructionally agile can also come after the fact. Once students have completed a demonstration of learning, they can take inventory of where they are and where to go next. The key is to be specific about the reflection. The self-reflection could focus on the learning; students might be asked to consider strengths, areas in need of strengthening, what they might do differently should they have another opportunity, or what they would repeat next time. The self-reflection could also be metacognitive, where students reflect on themselves as learners, what they learned about themselves as learners, or how they overcame obstacles and *stuck* moments; what others should notice about them could also be a focal point. The most effective reflection questions are specific and cause students to think deeply about their learning or themselves.

- **Reassess strategically:** Reassessment, if it is to be productive, cannot be an exercise in guessing differently the next day; it has to be predicated on a learning-focused endeavor. Each subsequent assessment should come as a result of more learning, where both the student and the teacher *know* that more learning has been achieved. Reassessment—the reverification of learning—is critical since what students are learning is important, and the verification of that learning is what ultimately leads to more accurate reporting.

Reassessment does take time, so it is incumbent on teachers to create routines that make it the most productive experience possible.

- **Infuse student agency:** Despite the existence of curricular standards, not everything is non-negotiable; student agency can be infused into the negotiable aspects of the standards. If the content is non-negotiable, then agency can come via the process of learning or how students demonstrate their learning. If the process of learning (for example, writing) is non-negotiable, then agency through the content and demonstration is possible; non-negotiable demonstrations of learning, of course, allow for agency through content and process. If even two aspects are non-negotiable, teachers can still infuse agency. The key is not to force it.

Part 6: Questions to Guide Your Conversations With Students

Instructional agility is rooted in noticing how students are coming along in learning. Students' words, actions, nonverbal cues, and emotions, along with the work they produce, are pieces of evidence that give teachers opportunities to make inferences and moves to deepen student learning and correct misunderstandings. These instructional agility moves, when effective, build students' confidence as they feel they can ask questions, gain clarity, and see possibility in the steps they are taking. These kinds of interactions with teachers build trust, especially when teachers exercise profound patience and relentlessly persist in figuring out what students' strengths are and where students need to go next. This instructional agility practice is also highlighted when teachers prompt students to reflect on their own learning and explicitly see what is helping them learn, where their strengths are, and where they need to go next (or what they need to do next or learn next). The following prompts are designed to facilitate conversations and actions teachers and students can take to create the conditions for student investment when being instructionally agile. (Visit **go.SolutionTree.com/assessment** for reproducible versions of these questions.)

Questions to elicit conversation on confidence include the following.

- How confident are you that you know how you learn best?

- How confident are you that you know what to do when you get stuck?

- What steps do you take to build your level of confidence?

Questions to elicit conversation on overcoming challenges include the following.

- What kinds of conversations with your teachers and with your peers help you the most?

- What are the potential traps that might get in the way of your learning? How will you deal with those traps when they emerge?
- What helps you recognize what you are strong in and where you need work?

Questions to elicit conversation on trying again include the following.

- What motivates you to try again?
- What inhibits your efforts to try again?
- What is the purpose of reassessment?
- Is there ever a time when you should not reassess? Explain.

Questions to elicit conversation on self-monitoring include the following.

- How important is it to be able to self-monitor your learning?
- How do you know you are on track?
- What helps you keep focused, and what distracts you?
- What strategies or resources do you use to move yourself forward when you are unsure?

Part 7: Dangerous Detours and Seductive Shortcuts

Often, teachers feel as if they are not allowed to be agile because of strict requirements with pacing guides, mandated assessments, and curriculum-based expectations, to name just a few of the many demands placed on them. At some point, it almost feels as if attempts to be instructionally agile would be considered creative disobedience or flat-out noncompliance. And in truth, it *is* easier to simply follow along. For that reason, the pathway to instructional agility is brimming with dangerous detours and seductive shortcuts.

- **Seeing *formative* as a noun:** The quick fix is to simply *do* formative assessment without any subsequent action, treating the existence of formative assessment as some sort of checklist. The promise of formative assessment is to increase achievement, but that increase doesn't come from the procedure; rather, it comes from the student's acting on what's next in a purposeful and specific way.
- **Extending through *more*:** Extension is about deeper, more sophisticated opportunities, not volume. Teachers need to be careful they don't reward an efficient rise to proficiency with a

disproportionate amount of more difficult work, especially if the students have no agency behind the extension.

- **Doing ironclad preplanning:** While locking in preplanned core instruction and differentiated responses for those students needing intervention might be more *efficient*, it might not be more effective. It is credible to anticipate learning needs in advance of a lesson or unit of study; in fact, it's highly recommended when considering assessment architecture. The trick is to avoid developing ironclad plans or even resources. Instructional agility is most effective when it is an authentic response. A better approach is to map the assessment blueprint but then use evidence that is intentionally sought during the formative phases to make targeted refinements based on emerging student needs. Remember, plan with precision while being ready to respond with agility.

- **Reflecting vaguely:** Student reflection and metacognitive opportunities are not as effective as specific questions that require learners to take a deeper look at themselves and their learning. Students can't reasonably reflect on everything simultaneously; focus their attention on different aspects so, in the collective, they get a broad understanding of themselves. Open-ended questions like, "What are you thinking?" or "Now reflect on your learning," may be effective for the most advanced learners, but the prompts are too vague for most.

- **Only reflecting:** Reflection is less helpful if students are passive recipients of the first two parts of the learning cycle (before and during); it's not something that can simply be turned on. Students' active involvement in the before (for example, goal setting) and during (for example, self-monitoring) primes the pump for meaningful reflection by allowing students to gather real-time evidence along the way.

- **Engaging in try-it-again reassessment:** What seems like a shortcut can quite quickly become an overload of preparation without any payoff. Like most things, *doing* reassessment is not enough; reassessment needs to give students an authentic opportunity to demonstrate their increased proficiency. Constantly duplicating assessments while expecting different results is one version of the definition of insanity. Quality, not quantity, must shape the reassessment experience as students invest in reaching higher levels of learning.

- **Self-grading:** Another apparent shortcut is having students self-grade. First, grades are not informative in terms of what's next for the learner to keep growing. Second, it is the teacher's job to be the final arbiter of achievement. Of course, having students hypothesize about their level for a particular assessment or their overall grade can be a useful exercise as long as teachers use their expertise to affirm what the students have posited. Identifying a level or grade may trigger some broad motivational increase (that is, "I need to do better"), but it's not enough to initiate an agile response to the student's current status.

Compact Conferencing Protocol Instructions

The compact conference steps involve *planning* (done by the student alone or by the student with teacher guidance in advance) and *reflecting* (a three- to four-minute conference, teacher to student or peer to peer). Instructions on how to complete these planning and reflecting pages are as follows.

Planning Page

1. Fill in the specific details required on the planning page, with teacher guidance as needed.

   - What is the purpose of the conference?
   - Who will be the reviewer (if not the teacher)?
   - What's the assignment?
   - What's the learning target?
   - What's the area of focus for the discussion (based on the quality criteria for the assignment that will be reviewed)?

2. Select the work to be reviewed. If the work is long, consider selecting a small portion for the review (for example, one minute of the presentation, one paragraph from the essay, and so on).

3. Make sure all parties know what's on the planning page in advance of the gathering and have a chance to read, watch, or listen to the selection that will be discussed.

4. Fill in the first few lines of the reflection page before the conference starts. (The student [creator or author] does this.)

Reflection Page

1. The student (creator or author) starts the conference by sharing what they wrote on the first few lines of the reflection page before the conference started.

2. The reviewer shares their feedback but lets the student be the one to write the feedback on the reflection page.

3. Together, the student and the reviewer co-create the next steps based on the purpose of the conference. Students need to consider both their own and the reviewer's feedback when thinking about next steps.

4. The teacher can help as needed, even after the conference has occurred, to focus the plan and ensure it can be implemented in the immediate future. Sometimes, peer-to-peer work can be too broad.

Jackpot! Nurturing Student Investment Through Assessment © 2023 Solution Tree Press
SolutionTree.com • Visit **go.SolutionTree.com/assessment** to download this free reproducible.

Notes for Teachers

It's helpful to set a timer so that each meeting sticks to the allotted three or four minutes. When the timer goes off, the conference is done.

Because teachers can't get to every student for each established conference day, consider having conferences with only three to five students in a given time slot.

While you are having conferences, students can also have peer conferences in the room, taking turns as the student and the reviewer.

Consider designating a consistent time frame (for example, "Feedback Fridays") so that you use the process often and all students can engage in conferences with the teacher over a period of time.

Compact Conference Planning and Reflection Form

Whenever possible and as appropriate, the owner of the form (the student) is the one who should fill in all the lines—including what the reviewer says.

Planning Page

Name: _____ Date: _____

Name of reviewer (if not the teacher): _____

Conference purpose (check one):

❑ Goal setting   ❑ Focused revision

❑ Feedback   ❑ Reflection

Assignment or project:

_____

_____

_____

_____

_____

Learning target:

_____

_____

_____

_____

_____

Focus area for discussion (tied to quality criteria for the learning target):

_____

_____

_____

_____

_____

page 1 of 3

Reflection Page

One minute for the student (creator or author) to share:

My strengths are:

_____

_____

_____

_____

_____

My opportunities to improve include:

_____

_____

_____

_____

_____

One minute for the reviewer (peer or teacher) to share (if possible, the creator or author should fill in all lines):

The creator or author's strengths are:

_____

_____

_____

_____

_____

The creator or author's opportunities to grow are:

_____

_____

_____

_____

_____

One to two minutes for the student and reviewer to identify next steps based on the conference purpose:

What comes next?

- If the conference was for goal setting, what's the new goal?
- If it was for focused revision, what revisions will be made?
- If it was for feedback gathering, what happens next?
- If it was for reflection, what was learned, and how will that impact future work?

_____

_____

_____

_____

_____

Drop-By Protocol

This protocol should take one minute or less for the actual assessment conversation.

1. Randomly select a few students to drop by and visit at their desk. Give the students five minutes' notice that you will be returning for a drop-by conversation. (One minute or less per student)

2. Let them know which data or artifacts you will want to review with them. A range of options to consider are as follows. (Part of the initial one minute)

    *   A data-tracking sheet

    *   A goal sheet

    *   A sample of completed work (a paragraph, a model, a data table, and so on)

    *   A draft of not-yet-submitted work

    *   The current practice work (In this case, randomly dot two or three completed items, and ask the students to recheck their answers before you return. Some of the dots might be placed next to correct answers and some next to incorrect answers. The students are tasked with determining which might be right or wrong.)

    *   One or two pieces of your feedback from prior assessments that they are working on improving

    *   One or two pieces of feedback they would assign themselves from prior assessments

    *   The assignment rubric or proficiency scale (In this case, have students see whether they can use their own artifacts to prove or disprove a level of quality on the assignment-scoring tools.)

3. Name your expectation for the conversation you are about to have. Consider the following options. (Part of the initial one minute)

    *   I will be checking for accuracy.

    *   I will be checking for understanding.

    *   I will be checking to see if we agree on your score(s).

    *   I will be checking in on your progress since our last visit (or on your stated goals). Please show and tell with the artifacts you have created.

4. Circle back to the students in the sequence in which you tagged them so everyone has equal preparation time. Your conversation should do three things: (a) focus on your stated expectation, (b) empower the student to do the thinking, and (c) conclude with an agreed-on action step that addresses the question, Where to now? (One minute per student)

EPILOGUE

The proverbial elephant in the room when it comes to student investment is grading and reporting. Nothing can nor will undercut all student investment efforts quite like traditional grading practices. Maximizing the effectiveness of student investment will ultimately mean having some tough conversations about the shifts that are needed to ensure grading and reporting systems don't become inhibitors to student investment.

Pulling the Plug on Traditional Grading

In all honesty, schools and districts for which traditional grading and reporting practices are the norm will have a much more difficult and rockier climb in developing student investment, with many possibilities for distraction. In so many ways, traditional grading runs counter to all that is plausible with student investment. Whether it's a percentage-based achievement scale, the accumulation of points, or the inclusion of non-achievement factors in grade determination, each subsequent traditional grading practice serves only to further the divide between what students have learned and what ultimately is reported (Guskey, 2015; Schimmer, 2016; Townsley & Wear, 2020). The percentage system, for example, asks teachers to distinguish between 101 levels of performance, which is something they simply can't do if the cognitive complexity of the assessment is far beyond simply counting correct versus incorrect answers. If teachers can't describe proficiency outside of point accumulation, how are students supposed to be able to do it? How can they invest in understanding the depth of their own learning if they are not provided with clarity (via teacher expectations or feedback) on what accuracy looks like beyond right and wrong answers?

The summative purpose of assessment is a real and important part of a balanced assessment system, so while student investment does not mean students give themselves grades unadjudicated by the teacher, it does mean students are authentically involved throughout the summative process. Having students assess their overall level of learning

179

allows them to see the big picture of their own learning; it allows them to examine the preponderance of their learning evidence to make a holistic judgment of quality. Counting points or chasing right and wrong answers scratches only the surface of the kind of depth of analysis student investment requires. To change the culture of grading from point accumulation to proficiency levels, teachers and administrators need to shift their collective mindset about what grades are and what they communicate; grades should reflect learning and not a commodity students acquire through any means.

Admittedly, shifting the culture of grading is not easy; however, starting with a standards-based mindset makes it easier (Schimmer, 2016). Student investment requires a clear focus on learning; traditional grading and reporting distracts teachers and students from that by allowing non-achievement factors to influence grading and reporting decisions. To begin the conversation—if it has not already started in your context—teachers, schools, or districts can focus on the following three grading fundamentals to ensure a foundation that seamlessly fits with student investment.

First, *no student should be able to directly behave their way up or down the achievement scale*. Behavioral transgressions require behavioral feedback and responses. The key word here is *directly*. Obviously, a student sent home on a suspension is away from school; being away from school means they're not learning the same as if they were in attendance. Do not address behavior issues related to compliance or timeliness of work completion by reducing points on achievement assessments. These behaviors need to be reported and addressed separately from achievement.

Second, *a student's grade should never be dependent on who their teacher is*. If grades are to reflect learning, and that learning is in relation to the curricular standards that are universally implemented within a school or district, then a student's grade should reflect the degree to which the student has met the standards regardless of who their teacher is. In other words, two teachers teaching the same grade-level subject must determine achievement in a similar or like-minded fashion. If not, there is a strong possibility they will compromise inter-rater reliability, which results in meaningless grades or at least grades that can't be relied on for clear information about achievement.

Finally, *a student's grade should never be dependent on their relative standing in the class*. Simply, the normative-type process of comparing students to establish a distribution of grades is antiquated and is antithetical to a criterion-referenced or standards-based system. How a student's demonstration of learning compares to another student's is irrelevant; how the student work compares to the criteria is what matters. If comparisons and distribution systems are the norm, then students and teachers can never know for certain what an exemplary level of learning looks like.

There are, of course, many more details and context-based idiosyncrasies to consider. However, teachers, schools, and districts who initiate reflection on grading practices through the lens of these three fundamentals will begin to reshape the collective grading mindset to one more aligned and conducive to creating a culture of student investment.

Attributing Success

The links between sustained student investment and social psychologist Bernard Weiner's (1979) now-classic attribution theory are obvious. Attribution is about *causality*—the reason why something happened. Not only is it important that students experience investment in their learning that is worth it in terms of their success, but it is also critical that they attribute that success to their efforts and they have the bulk of the control over their achievement. Engineering student investment can lead to a point where students experience increased motivation because they consistently see their efforts pay off.

Weiner (1979) characterizes three important aspects of causality: (1) locus, (2) stability, and (3) controllability. *Locus* refers to whether the source of causality is internal or external; do students see the causality of their successes (or lack thereof) as being within or without them? *Stability* quite literally refers to whether the conditions are stable or unstable; can students depend on, predict, or rely on the conditions for success? *Controllability* refers to whether the conditions are controlled or uncontrolled; do students see the conditions for success as something they can control within themselves, or are the conditions out of their hands?

The first two dimensions of causality—locus and stability—are particularly important for student investment. So much of the school experience is uncontrollable even for individual teachers, schools, and districts, never mind students, that a focus on locus and stability is wise. While engineering student investment, direct students' attention to the fact that their success causality is internal and stable; that they can disproportionately influence their own success; and that their influence is predictable over time. With all of that, controllability, at least on a smaller scale, can be part of the attribution conversation and experience in the sense that if students authentically believe the locus of causality is predominantly internal, then teachers can direct student attention to the fact that only an internal locus is controllable. The bottom line is to ensure that students don't attribute their success to luck or the teacher's doing.

The art and finesse of causation is going to come when students are not successful. One can imagine a scenario where a teacher relentlessly associates achievement results with an internal and stable causation only to have students associate their lack of success with a lack of inherent ability rather than with causations within their control. If teachers fail to examine such presuppositions or to clarify the connection between achievement and effort, then they put struggling students in danger of erroneously thinking that they are incapable of ever succeeding. This is where the merging of Weiner's (1979) attribution theory and Dweck's (2016) growth mindset would be most beneficial. Helping students connect the ideas that their success is controlled by internal and stable causes (attribution theory) and that intelligence is malleable (growth mindset) underpins a teacher's success in getting students to invest in their own learning. Balancing the two theories may not always be easy, but it is nonetheless important for creating an atmosphere of hope and efficacy. Help students see that their current status is only a starting point and that their sustained effort toward reaching success is what will get them there. Effort is not a consolation prize in the sense of "Well, at least you tried"; rather, focused and purposeful effort is how students will cultivate their abilities in any learning.

Internal, stable, and controllable causality may not always mean immediate success. When students experience initial setbacks and negatively unexpected results, it is critical that teachers emphasize the growth mindset approach to learning. A teacher might say, "Just because you weren't successful today doesn't mean you can't be successful next time. And here's the good news: you (internal) can keep working (stable) toward proficiency, and I'm here to help you!" Initial setbacks must be married to a clear pathway of recovery that eventually leads to success. This way, students see setbacks not as definitive declarations of their ability but as additional opportunities to recognize what's next and then take the necessary action to get there; after all, causality is internal and stable.

Driving Student Investment With Assessment

Assessment is the engine that drives student investment. The symbiotic relationship between the self-regulation of learning and assessment reveals that using assessment to drive student investment would be the thoughtful approach; purposeful work toward student investment would also lead to improved achievement as measured by assessments. Critical to this is the reimagining of assessment's role in learning by resisting the narrow, regressive view of *assessment as test* or *as standardized*. That reimagining, of course, is not new, but it may be new to particular cohorts, groups of stakeholders, parents, students, and even some faculty.

The six tenets of assessment are not hierarchical or separate silos; they are interdependent and cyclical. This means that student investment as one tenet is dependent on the other five and, therefore, can be addressed throughout the assessment cycle. Opportunities to immerse students as real decision makers throughout the learning process (and therefore the assessment process) are readily available. Again, this is not a zero-sum game whereby teachers lose control as students expand their agency;

teacher expertise and partnership are still necessary and critical. The six tenets provide a structured framework to purposefully approach student investment at the beginning (purpose; architecture), in the middle (interpretation; instructional agility), and at the end (communication of results) of the learning cycle.

Although doing so at various speeds, schools and districts throughout the United States and Canada (and around the world) are continuing to pursue the infusion of 21st century critical competencies as key learning outcomes for their learners. Now more than ever, it is essential that students actively participate in their own growth and development since self-regulation is a key competency (Battelle for Kids, 2019; Erkens et al., 2019). Students cannot simultaneously be passive recipients of their educational experience and develop as critical, collaborative, and creative thinkers. The *who*, *what*, *where*, and *when* of learning can be searched and sourced; the *how* and *why* require thinking deeply and wrestling with several plausible responses and decisions that all have consequences. Student investment is the only way to maximize the development and impact of critical competencies.

Student investment is the endgame. Teachers develop their own assessment literacy not so they can become experts in and of themselves; they do it so they can use their expertise in assessment practices to create the conditions necessary for students to invest in their own learning. Teacher expertise is why and how students will efficiently and effectively become self-assessors and self-regulate their growth and development. The teacher's role is to establish, enable, and empower a path toward student investment; it is to create a metacognitive culture of learning to guide students toward future decisions and goals. Being aware of *how* they learn will serve to solidify students' view of what's next and the pathway to growth and proficiency. By accentuating strengths and navigating hurdles along the way, students will develop the agency and the academic stamina needed to personalize their journeys toward deep, meaningful learning as engaged citizens.

REFERENCES AND RESOURCES

Alcala, L. [Andy Midwinter]. (2015, March 14). *My favorite no* [Video file]. Accessed at www.youtube.com/watch?v=srJWx7P6uLE on April 11, 2022.

Allal, L. (2010). Assessment and the regulation of learning. In P. Peterson, E. Baker, & B. McGaw (Eds.), *International encyclopedia of education* (Vol. 3, pp. 348–352). Oxford, UK: Elsevier.

Anderson, M. (2016). *Learning to choose, choosing to learn: The key to student motivation and achievement*. Alexandria, VA: Association for Supervision and Curriculum Development.

Anderson, M., & Jiang, J. (2018, May 31). *Teens, social media and technology 2018*. Washington, DC: Pew Research Center. Accessed at www.pewresearch.org/internet/2018/05/31 /teens-social-media-technology-2018/ on February 22, 2022.

Andrade, H. L. (2013). Classroom assessment in the context of learning theory and research. In J. H. McMillan (Ed.), *SAGE handbook of research on classroom assessment* (pp. 17–34). Thousand Oaks, CA: SAGE.

Andrade, H. L. (2019, August 27). A critical review of research on student self-assessment. *Frontiers in Education*. Accessed at www.frontiersin.org/articles/10.3389/feduc.2019 .00087/full#B6 on March 15, 2022.

Andrade, H. L., & Brookhart, S. M. (2016). The role of classroom assessment in supporting self-regulated learning. In D. Laveault & L. Allal (Eds.), *Assessment for learning: Meeting the challenge of implementation* (pp. 293–309). New York: Springer International.

Andrade, H. L., & Brown, G. T. L. (2016). Student self-assessment in the classroom. In G. T. L. Brown & L. R. Harris (Eds.), *Handbook of human and social conditions in assessment* (pp. 319–334). New York: Routledge.

Andrade, H. L., & Heritage, M. (2017). *Using formative assessment to enhance learning, achievement, and academic self-regulation*. New York: Routledge.

ASVAB Career Exploration Program. (n.d.). *S.M.A.R.T. goal setting for students*. Accessed at www.asvabprogram.com/media-center-article/65 on February 2, 2022.

Ayers, W. (2001). *To teach: The journey of a teacher* (2nd ed.). New York: Teachers College Press.

Battelle for Kids. (2019). *Partnership for 21st Century Learning: A network of Battelle for Kids.* Accessed at www.battelleforkids.org/networks/p21 on April 2, 2022.

Belgrad, S. F. (2013). Portfolios and e-portfolios: Student reflection, self-assessment, and goal setting in the learning process. In J. H. McMillan (Ed.), *SAGE handbook of research on classroom assessment* (pp. 331–346). Thousand Oaks, CA: SAGE.

Black, P. (2013). Formative and summative aspects of assessment: Theoretical and research foundations in the context of pedagogy. In J. H. McMillan (Ed.), *SAGE handbook of research on classroom assessment* (pp. 167–178). Thousand Oaks, CA: SAGE.

Black, P., Harrison, C., Lee, C., Marshall, B., & Wiliam, D. (2004). Working inside the black box: Assessment for learning in the classroom. *Phi Delta Kappan, 86*(1), 8–21.

Black, P., & Wiliam, D. (1998). Inside the black box: Raising standards through classroom assessment. *Phi Delta Kappan, 80*(2), 144, 146–148.

Boekaerts, M. (2006). Self-regulation and effort investment. In K. A. Renninger & I. E. Sigel (Eds.), *Handbook of child psychology: Volume four—Child psychology in practice* (6th ed., pp. 345–377). New York: Wiley.

Briggs, D. C., & Furtak, E. M. (2020). Learning progressions and embedded assessment. In S. M. Brookhart & J. H. McMillan (Eds.), *Classroom assessment and educational measurement* (pp. 146–169). New York: Routledge.

Brookhart, S. M. (2011). Educational assessment knowledge and skills for teachers. *Educational Measurement: Issues and Practice, 30*(1), 3–12.

Brookhart, S. M. (2013a). Classroom assessment in the context of motivation theory and research. In J. H. McMillan (Ed.), *SAGE handbook of research on classroom assessment* (pp. 35–54). Thousand Oaks, CA: SAGE.

Brookhart, S. M. (2013b). Grading. In J. H. McMillan (Ed.), *SAGE handbook of research on classroom assessment* (pp. 257–272). Thousand Oaks, CA: SAGE.

Brookhart, S. M. (2017). *How to give effective feedback to your students* (2nd ed.). Alexandria, VA: Association for Supervision and Curriculum Development.

Brookhart, S. M. (2020). Feedback and measurement. In S. M. Brookhart & J. H. McMillan (Eds.), *Classroom assessment and educational measurement* (pp. 63–78). New York: Routledge.

Brown, G. T. L., & Harris, L. R. (2013). Student self-assessment. In J. H. McMillan (Ed.), *SAGE handbook of research on classroom assessment* (pp. 367–394). Thousand Oaks, CA: SAGE.

Cash, R. M. (2016). *Self-regulation in the classroom: Helping students learn how to learn.* Minneapolis, MN: Free Spirit.

Chappuis, J. (2012). "How am I doing?" *Educational Leadership, 70*(1), 36–40.

Chappuis, J. (2015). *Seven strategies of assessment for learning* (2nd ed.). Portland, OR: Pearson Assessment Training Institute.

Chappuis, J., & Stiggins, R. (2020). *Classroom assessment for student learning: Doing it right—Using it well* (3rd ed.). New York: Pearson.

Conley, D. T. (2018). *The promise and practice of next generation assessment.* Cambridge, MA: Harvard Education Press.

Conzemius, A. E., & O'Neill, J. (2014). *The handbook for SMART school teams: Revitalizing best practices for collaboration* (2nd ed.). Bloomington, IN: Solution Tree Press.

Cooper, D. (2022). *Rebooting assessment: A practical guide for balancing conversations, performances, and products.* Bloomington, IN: Solution Tree Press.

Corcoran, T., Mosher, F. A., & Rogat, A. (2009, May). *Learning progressions in science: An evidence-based approach to reform* (CPRE Research Report RR-63). Philadelphia: Consortium for Policy Research in Education.

Cowie, B. (2005a). Student commentary on classroom assessment in science: A sociocultural interpretation. *International Journal of Science Education, 27*(2), 199–214.

Cowie, B. (2005b). Pupil commentary on assessment for learning. *The Curriculum Journal, 6*(2), 137–151.

Dabrowski, J., & Marshall, T. R. (2018, November). *Motivation and engagement in student assignments: The role of choice and relevancy.* Washington, DC: The Education Trust.

Darling-Hammond, L., Herman, J., Pellegrino, J., Abedi, J., Aber, J. L., Baker, E., et al. (2013, June). *Criteria for higher-quality assessment.* Stanford, CA: Stanford Center for Opportunity Policy in Education.

Davies, A. (2007). Involving students in the classroom assessment process. In D. Reeves (Ed.), *Ahead of the curve: The power of assessment to transform teaching and learning* (pp. 31–57). Bloomington, IN: Solution Tree Press.

Deci, E. L., Koestner, R., & Ryan, R. M. (1999). A meta-analytic review of experiments examining the effects of extrinsic rewards on intrinsic motivation. *Psychological Bulletin, 125*(6), 627–668.

Deci, E. L., & Ryan, R. M. (1985). *Intrinsic motivation and self-determination in human behavior.* New York: Plenum.

Deci, E. L., & Ryan, R. M. (2000). The "what" and "why" of goal pursuits: Human needs and the self-determination of behavior. *Psychological Inquiry, 11*(4), 227–268.

Deming, W. E. (1986). *Out of the crisis.* Cambridge, MA: MIT Press.

Deming, W. E. (1993). *The new economics for industry, government, education.* Cambridge, MA: MIT Press.

Dimich, N. (2015). *Design in five: Essential phases to create engaging assessment practice.* Bloomington, IN: Solution Tree Press.

Donohoo, J. (2017). *Collective efficacy: How educators' beliefs impact student learning.* Thousand Oaks, CA: Corwin.

Duckworth, A. (2016). *Grit: The power of passion and persistence.* New York: Scribner.

DuFour, R. (2015). *In praise of American educators: And how they can become even better.* Bloomington, IN: Solution Tree Press.

DuFour, R., DuFour, R., Eaker, R., Many, T. W., & Mattos, M. (2016). *Learning by doing: A handbook for Professional Learning Communities at Work* (3rd ed.). Bloomington, IN: Solution Tree Press.

Duran, L. B., & Duran, E. (2004). The 5E instructional model: A learning cycle approach for inquiry-based science teaching. *Science Education Review, 3*(2), 49–58.

Dweck, C. S. (2000). *Self-theories: Their role in motivation, personality, and development.* Philadelphia: Psychology Press.

Dweck, C. S. (2006). *Mindset: The new psychology of success.* New York: Random House.

Dweck, C. S. (2007). The perils and promises of praise. *Educational Leadership, 65*(2), 34–39.

Dweck, C. S. (2013). *Self-theories: Their role in motivation, personality, and development* (2nd ed.). New York: Routledge.

Dweck, C. S. (2016). *Mindset: The new psychology of success* (Updated ed.). New York: Random House.

Education Northwest. (2021, January). *6+1 trait writing resources.* Accessed at https://educationnorthwest.org/traits/61-trait-writing-resources on March 1, 2022.

Erkens, C. (2013, October 21). *Data notebooks* [Blog post]. Accessed at www.anamcaraconsulting.com/wordpress/2013/10/21/data-notebooks/ on March 2, 2022.

Erkens, C. (2015a, April 21). *Groupings for collaborative learning* [Blog post]. Accessed at www.solutiontree.com/blog/groupings-for-collaborative-learning on February 11, 2022.

Erkens, C. (2015b, July 16). *On target with learning targets* [Blog post]. Accessed at https://allthingsassessment.info/2015/07/16/on-target-with-learning-targets on February 11, 2022.

Erkens, C. (2016). *Collaborative common assessments: Teamwork. Instruction. Results.* Bloomington, IN: Solution Tree Press.

Erkens, C. (2019). *The handbook for collaborative common assessments: Tools for design, delivery, and data analysis.* Bloomington, IN: Solution Tree Press.

Erkens, C., Schimmer, T., & Dimich, N. (2017). *Essential assessment: Six tenets for bringing hope, efficacy, and achievement to the classroom.* Bloomington, IN: Solution Tree Press.

Erkens, C., Schimmer, T., & Dimich, N. (2018). *Instructional agility: Responding to assessment with real-time decisions.* Bloomington, IN: Solution Tree Press.

Erkens, C., Schimmer, T., & Dimich, N. (2019). *Growing tomorrow's citizens in today's classrooms: Assessing seven critical competencies.* Bloomington, IN: Solution Tree Press.

Fisher, D., Frey, N., & Hattie, J. (2016). *Visible learning for literacy, grades K–12: Implementing the practices that work best to accelerate student learning.* Thousand Oaks, CA: SAGE.

Frey, N., Hattie, J., & Fisher, D. (2018). *Developing assessment-capable visible learners, grades K–12: Maximizing skill, will, and thrill.* Thousand Oaks, CA: Corwin.

Friesen, S., & Scott, D. (2013, June). *Inquiry-based learning: A review of the research literature.* Edmonton, Alberta, Canada: Alberta Ministry of Education.

Gay, G. (2018). *Culturally responsive teaching: Theory, research, and practice* (3rd ed.). New York: Teachers College Press.

Gregory, K., Cameron, C., & Davies, A. (1997). *Setting and using criteria.* Courtenay, British Columbia, Canada: Connections.

Gross-Loh, C. (2016, December 16). How praise became a consolation prize. *The Atlantic.* Accessed at https://theatlantic.com/education/archive/2016/12/how-praise-became-a-consolation-prize/510845 on September 1, 2017.

Guskey, T. R. (2015). *On your mark: Challenging the conventions of grading and reporting.* Bloomington, IN: Solution Tree Press.

Guskey, T. R. (2018). Feedback, correctives, and the use of pre-assessments. In A. A. Lipnevich & J. K. Smith (Eds.), *The Cambridge handbook of instructional feedback* (pp. 432–450). New York: Cambridge University Press.

Guskey, T. R., & McTighe, J. (2016). Pre-assessment: Promises and cautions. *Educational Leadership, 73*(7), 38–43.

Hargreaves, A., & Fullan, M. (2012). *Professional capital: Transforming teaching in every school.* New York: Teachers College Press.

Harris, L. R., & Brown, G. T. L. (2018). *Using self-assessment to improve learning.* New York: Routledge.

Hattie, J. (2009). *Visible learning: A synthesis of over 800 meta-analyses relating to achievement.* New York: Routledge.

Hattie, J. (2012). *Visible learning for teachers: Maximizing impact on learning.* New York: Routledge.

Hattie, J., Fisher, D., & Frey, N. (2016, April 1). *Do they hear you?* [Blog post]. Accessed at www.ascd.org/el/articles/do-they-hear-you on March 9, 2019.

Hattie, J., & Timperley, H. (2007). The power of feedback. *Review of Educational Research, 77*(1), 81–112.

Hattie, J., & Yates, G. C. R. (2014). *Visible learning and the science of how we learn.* New York: Routledge.

Heritage, M. (2007). Formative assessment: What do teachers need to know and do? *Phi Delta Kappan, 89*(2), 140–145.

Heritage, M. (2013). Gathering evidence of student understanding. In J. H. McMillan (Ed.), *SAGE handbook of research on classroom assessment* (pp. 179–196). Thousand Oaks, CA: SAGE.

Heritage, M., Kim, J., Vendlinski, T. P., & Herman, J. L. (2008, August). *From evidence to action: A seamless process in formative assessment?* (CRESST Report 741). Los Angeles: National Center for Research on Evaluation, Standards, and Student Testing.

Hillman, G., & Stalets, M. (2019). *Coaching your classroom: How to deliver actionable feedback to students.* Bloomington, IN: Solution Tree Press.

Hillman, G., & Stalets, M. (2021). *Assessment as a catalyst for learning: Creating a responsive and fluid process to inspire all students.* Bloomington, IN: Solution Tree Press.

Jackson, Y. (2011). *The pedagogy of confidence: Inspiring high intellectual performance in urban schools.* New York: Teachers College Press.

Jang, H., Reeve, J., & Deci, E. L. (2010). Engaging students in learning activities: It is not autonomy support or structure but autonomy support and structure. *Journal of Educational Psychology, 102*(3), 588–600.

Jenkins, L. (2011). System problem or people problem? *The Systems Thinker, 22*(9), 11–12. Accessed at http://bibsrv.udem.edu.mx:8080/publications/Systems_Thinker_vol_18-/Vol.%2022%20No.%209,%20nov.%202011.pdf on February 16, 2022.

Jordan, P. W., & Miller, R. (2017, September). *Who's in: Chronic absenteeism under the Every Student Succeeds Act.* Washington, DC: FutureEd. Accessed at www.future-ed.org/whos-in-chronic-absenteeism-under-the-every-student-succeeds-act/ on February 2, 2022.

Jung, L. A. (2017). In providing supports for students, language matters. *Educational Leadership, 74*(7), 42–45.

Kane, M. T., & Wools, S. (2020). Perspectives on the validity of classroom assessments. In S. M. Brookhart & J. H. McMillan (Eds.), *Classroom assessment and educational measurement* (pp. 11–26). New York: Routledge.

Kanter, R. M. (2004). *Confidence: How winning streaks and losing streaks begin and end.* New York: Crown Business.

Katz, J. (2012). *Teaching to diversity: The three-block model of Universal Design for Learning.* Winnipeg, Manitoba, Canada: Portage & Main Press.

King James Bible. (n.d.). *King James Bible Online.* Accessed at www.kingjamesbibleonline.org/Luke-Chapter-4/#23 on April 2, 2022. (Original work published 1769)

Kise, J. A. G. (2021). *Doable differentiation: Twelve strategies to meet the needs of all learners.* Bloomington, IN: Solution Tree Press.

Klinger, D. A., McDivitt, P. J., Howard, B. B., Muñoz, M. A., Rogers, W. T., & Wylie, E. C. (2015). *Classroom assessment standards for preK–12 teachers.* Kalamazoo, MI: Joint Committee on Standards for Educational Evaluation.

Kluger, A. N., & DeNisi, A. (1996). The effects of feedback interventions on performance: A historical review, a meta-analysis, and a preliminary feedback intervention theory. *Psychological Bulletin, 119*(2), 254–284.

Koretz, D. M. (2017). *The testing charade: Pretending to make schools better.* Chicago: University of Chicago Press.

Lane, S. (2010). *Performance assessment: The state of the art.* Stanford, CA: Stanford Center for Opportunity Policy in Education.

Lane, S. (2013). Performance assessment. In J. H. McMillan (Ed.), *SAGE handbook of research on classroom assessment* (pp. 313–330). Thousand Oaks, CA: SAGE.

Latham, G. P., & Locke, E. A. (2006). Enhancing the benefits and overcoming the pitfalls of goal setting. *Organizational Dynamics, 35*(4), 332–340.

Lopez, S. J. (2013). How can schools foster hope? Making hope happen in the classroom. *Phi Delta Kappan, 95*(2), 19–22.

Lopez, S. J. (2014). *Making hope happen: Create the future you want for yourself and others.* New York: Atria.

Louisiana Department of Education. (2019). *Louisiana student standards: Grade 6 social studies—Year-long overview.* Baton Rouge, LA: Author. Accessed at www.louisianabelieves.com/docs/default-source/scope-and-sequence/updated-social-studies-sample-scope-and-sequence-grade-6.pdf?sfvrsn=97478f1f_15 on April 2, 2022.

Love, B. L. (2019, February 12). "Grit is in our DNA": Why teaching grit is inherently anti-Black. *Education Week.* Accessed at https://edweek.org/leadership/opinion-grit-is-in-our-dna-why-teaching-grit-is-inherently-anti-black/2019/02 on April 1, 2021.

Marzano, R. J. (1998). *A theory-based meta-analysis of research on instruction.* Aurora, CO: Mid-Continent Regional Educational Laboratory.

Marzano, R. J. (2019). *The handbook for the new art and science of teaching.* Bloomington, IN: Solution Tree Press.

Marzano, R. J., Pickering, D. J., & Pollock, J. E. (2001). *Classroom instruction that works: Research-based strategies for increasing student achievement.* Alexandria, VA: Association for Supervision and Curriculum Development.

McMillan, J. H. (2013). Why we need research on classroom assessment. In J. H. McMillan (Ed.), *SAGE handbook of research on classroom assessment* (pp. 3–16). Thousand Oaks, CA: SAGE.

McMillan, J. H. (2020). Discussion of part 1: Assessment information in context. In S. M. Brookhart & J. H. McMillan (Eds.), *Classroom assessment and educational measurement* (pp. 79–94). New York: Routledge.

Meyer, A., Rose, D. H., & Gordon, D. (2014). *Universal Design for Learning: Theory and practice.* Wakefield, MA: CAST Professional.

National Governors Association Center for Best Practices & Council of Chief State School Officers. (2010). *Common Core State Standards for English language arts and literacy in history/social studies, science, and technical subjects.* Washington, DC: Authors. Accessed at www.corestandards.org/assets/CCSSI_ELA%20Standards.pdf on December 1, 2021.

Nelson, L. L. (2021). *Design and deliver: Planning and teaching using Universal Design for Learning* (2nd ed.). Baltimore: Brookes.

NGSS Lead States. (2013). *Next Generation Science Standards: For states, by states.* Washington, DC: The National Academies Press.

Nikolaidis, A. C. (2018). Interpretation and student agency. *Philosophical Studies in Education, 49,* 34–46.

Novak, K. (2016). *UDL now! A teacher's guide to applying Universal Design for Learning in today's classrooms* (Rev. & expanded ed.). Wakefield, MA: CAST Professional.

Pandey, A., Nanda, G. K., & Ranjan, V. (2011). Effectiveness of inquiry training model over conventional teaching method on academic achievement of science students in India. *Journal of Innovative Research in Education, 1*(1), 7–20.

Pierce, W. D., & Cheney, C. D. (2017). *Behavior analysis and learning: A biobehavioral approach* (6th ed.). New York: Routledge.

Pink, D. H. (2009). *Drive: The surprising truth about what motivates us.* New York: Riverhead Books.

Pintrich, P. R., & Zusho, A. (2002). The development of academic self-regulation: The role of cognitive and motivational factors. In A. Wigfield & J. S. Eccles (Eds.), *Development of achievement motivation* (pp. 249–284). San Diego, CA: Academic Press.

Reeve, J. (2018). *Understanding motivation and emotion* (7th ed.). Hoboken, NJ: Wiley.

Reibel, A. R., & Twadell, E. (Eds.). (2019). *Proficiency-based grading in the content areas: Insights and key questions for secondary schools.* Bloomington, IN: Solution Tree Press.

Richardson, W. (2019). Sparking student agency with technology. *Educational Leadership, 76*(5), 12–18.

Rohn, J. (2015, August 23). *Rohn: There's no telling what you can do when you get inspired* [Blog post]. Accessed at https://success.com/rohn-theres-no-telling-what-you-can-do -when-you-get-inspired on January 6, 2020.

Ross, J. A., & Starling, M. (2008). Self-assessment in a technology-supported environment: The case of grade 9 geography. *Assessment in Education: Principles, Policy and Practice, 15*(2), 183–199.

Ruiz-Primo, M. A., & Furtak, E. M. (2006). Informal formative assessment and scientific inquiry: Exploring teachers' practices and student learning. *Educational Assessment, 11*(3 & 4), 205–235.

Ruiz-Primo, M. A., & Li, M. (2013). Examining formative feedback in the classroom context: New research perspectives. In J. H. McMillan (Ed.), *SAGE handbook of research on classroom assessment* (pp. 215–232). Thousand Oaks, CA: SAGE.

Ryan, R. M., & Deci, E. L. (2000a). Intrinsic and extrinsic motivations: Classic definitions and new directions. *Contemporary Educational Psychology, 25*(1), 54–67.

Ryan, R. M., & Deci, E. L. (2000b). Self-determination theory and the facilitation of intrinsic motivation, social development, and well-being. *American Psychologist, 55*(1), 68–78.

Sadler, D. R. (1989). Formative assessment and the design of instructional systems. *Instructional Science, 18*(2), 119–144.

Schimmer, T. (2016). *Grading from the inside out: Bringing accuracy to student assessment through a standards-based mindset.* Bloomington, IN: Solution Tree Press.

Schimmer, T., Hillman, G., & Stalets, M. (2018). *Standards-based learning in action: Moving from theory to practice.* Bloomington, IN: Solution Tree Press.

Schneider, M. C., Egan, K. L., & Julian, M. W. (2013). Classroom assessment in the context of high-stakes testing. In J. H. McMillan (Ed.), *SAGE handbook of research on classroom assessment* (pp. 55–70). Thousand Oaks, CA: SAGE.

Schumpeter, J. (2011, April 16). Fail often, fail well. *The Economist.* Accessed at https:// economist.com/business/2011/04/14/fail-often-fail-well on October 17, 2013.

Schunk, D. H. (2003). Self-efficacy for reading and writing: Influence of modeling, goal setting, and self-evaluation. *Reading and Writing Quarterly, 19*(2), 159–172.

Self-esteem. (n.d.). In *Merriam-Webster's online dictionary*. Accessed at www.merriam-webster .com/dictionary/self-esteem on April 6, 2022.

Senge, P., Cambron-McCabe, N., Lucas, T., Smith, B., Dutton, J., & Kleiner, A. (2012). *Schools that learn: A fifth discipline fieldbook for educators, parents, and everyone who cares about education* (Updated and revised ed.). New York: Crown Business.

Shepard, L. A. (2013). Foreword. In J. H. McMillan (Ed.), *SAGE handbook of research on classroom assessment* (pp. xix–xxii). Thousand Oaks, CA: SAGE.

Shepard, L. A., Daro, P., & Stancavage, F. B. (2013, August). *The relevance of learning progressions for NAEP*. Washington, DC: American Institutes for Research.

Shepard, L. A., Penuel, W. R., & Pellegrino, J. W. (2018). Using learning and motivation theories to coherently link formative assessment, grading practices, and large-scale assessment. *Educational Measurement: Issues and Practice, 37*(1), 21–34.

Stiggins, R. (2008). Correcting "errors of measurement" that sabotage student learning. In C. A. Dwyer (Ed.), *The future of assessment: Shaping teaching and learning* (pp. 229–244). Mahwah, NJ: Erlbaum.

Stiggins, R. (2014). *Revolutionize assessment: Empower students, inspire learning*. Thousand Oaks, CA: Corwin.

Stiggins, R. (2018). The emotional dynamics of feedback from the student's point of view. In A. A. Lipnevich & J. K. Smith (Eds.), *The Cambridge handbook of instructional feedback* (pp. 519–530). New York: Cambridge University Press.

Stroh, D. P. (2015). *Systems thinking for social change: A practical guide to solving complex problems, avoiding unintended consequences, and achieving lasting results*. White River Junction, VT: Chelsea Green.

Stuart, T. S., Heckmann, S., Mattos, M., & Buffum, A. (2018). *Personalized learning in a PLC at Work: Student agency through the four critical questions*. Bloomington, IN: Solution Tree Press.

Thompson, M., & Wiliam, D. (2008). Tight but loose: A conceptual framework for scaling up school reforms. In E. C. Wylie (Ed.), *Tight but loose: Scaling up teacher professional development in diverse contexts* (pp. 1–44). Princeton, NJ: Educational Testing Service.

Tishman, S., & Clapp, E. P. (2017). Building students' sense of agency. *Educational Leadership, 75*(2), 58–62.

Townsley, M., & Wear, N. L. (2020). *Making grades matter: Standards-based grading in a secondary PLC at Work*. Bloomington, IN: Solution Tree Press.

Tyler, R. W. (1950). *Basic principles of curriculum and instruction*. Chicago: University of Chicago Press.

Usher, A., & Kober, N. (2012). *Student motivation: An overlooked piece of school reform— Summary*. Washington, DC: Center on Education Policy.

Webb, N. L. (2002, April). *Assessment literacy in a standards-based education setting* (WCER Working Paper No. 2002-4). Madison, WI: Wisconsin Center for Education Research.

Weiner, B. (1979). A theory of motivation for some classroom experiences. *Journal of Educational Psychology, 71*(1), 3–25.

White, K. (2019). *Unlocked: Assessment as the key to everyday creativity in the classroom.* Bloomington, IN: Solution Tree Press.

White, K. (2022). *Student self-assessment: Data notebooks, portfolios, and other tools to advance learning.* Bloomington, IN: Solution Tree Press.

Wiliam, D. (2011). *Embedded formative assessment.* Bloomington, IN: Solution Tree Press.

Wiliam, D. (2013). Feedback and instructional correctives. In J. H. McMillan (Ed.), *SAGE handbook of research on classroom assessment* (pp. 197–214). Thousand Oaks, CA: SAGE.

Wiliam, D. (2018a). *Embedded formative assessment* (2nd ed.). Bloomington, IN: Solution Tree Press.

Wiliam, D. (2018b). Feedback: At the heart of—but definitely not all of—formative assessment. In A. A. Lipnevich & J. K. Smith (Eds.), *The Cambridge handbook of instructional feedback* (pp. 3–28). New York: Cambridge University Press.

Wiliam, D., & Thompson, M. (2008). Integrating assessment with learning: What will it take to make it work? In C. A. Dwyer (Ed.), *The future of assessment: Shaping teaching and learning* (pp. 53–82). Mahwah, NJ: Erlbaum.

Willis, J., & Adie, L. (2016, April). *Developing teacher formative assessment practices through professional dialogue: Case studies of practice from Queensland, Australia* [Conference presentation]. American Educational Research Association annual meeting, Washington, DC.

Wilson, D., & Sperber, D. (2006). Relevance theory. In L. R. Horn & G. Ward (Eds.), *The handbook of pragmatics* (pp. 607–632). Malden, MA: Blackwell.

Wylie, E. C., & Lyon, C. J. (2020). The role of technology-enhanced self- and peer assessment in formative assessment. In S. M. Brookhart & J. H. McMillan (Eds.), *Classroom assessment and educational measurement* (pp. 170–191). New York: Routledge.

Yacek, D. W., & Jonas, M. E. (2019). The problem of student disengagement: Struggle, escapism and Nietzsche's birth of tragedy. *Philosophical Inquiry in Education, 26*(1), 64–87.

Zimmerman, B. J. (2002). Becoming a self-regulated learner: An overview. *Theory Into Practice, 41*(2), 64–70.

Zimmerman, B. J. (2011). Motivational sources and outcomes of self-regulated learning and performance. In B. J. Zimmerman & D. H. Schunk (Eds.), *Handbook of self-regulation of learning and performance* (pp. 49–64). New York: Routledge.

Zimmerman, B. J., & Schunk, D. H. (2011). Self-regulated learning and performance: An introduction and an overview. In B. J. Zimmerman & D. H. Schunk (Eds.), *Handbook of self-regulation of learning and performance* (pp. 1–12). New York: Routledge.

Zumbrunn, S., Tadlock, J., & Roberts, E. D. (2011, January). *Encouraging self-regulated learning in the classroom: A review of the literature.* Richmond, VA: Metropolitan Educational Research Consortium.

INDEX

Essential Assessment
Cassandra Erkens, Tom Schimmer, and Nicole Dimich
Discover how to use the power of assessment to instill hope, efficacy, and achievement in your students. Explore six essential tenets of assessment that will help deepen your understanding of assessment to not only meet standards but also enhance students' academic success.
BKF752

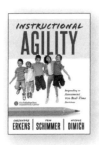

Instructional Agility
Cassandra Erkens, Tom Schimmer, and Nicole Dimich Vagle
This highly practical resource empowers readers to become instructionally agile—moving seamlessly among instruction, formative assessment, and feedback—to enhance student engagement, proficiency, and ownership of learning.
Each chapter concludes with reflection questions that assist readers in determining next steps.
BKF764

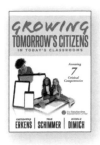

Growing Tomorrow's Citizens in Today's Classrooms
Cassandra Erkens, Tom Schimmer, and Nicole Dimich Vagle
For students to succeed in today's ever-changing world, they must acquire unique knowledge and skills. Practical and research-based, this resource will help educators design assessment and instruction to ensure students master critical competencies, including collaboration, critical thinking, creative thinking, communication, digital citizenship, and more.
BKF765

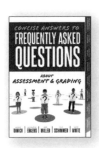

Concise Answers to Frequently Asked Questions about Assessment and Grading
Nicole Dimich, Cassandra Erkens, Jadi Miller,
Tom Schimmer, and Katie White
Get answers to your most challenging questions about implementing effective assessment and grading practices. Each chapter contains answers to dozens of questions covering key tenets of assessment and grading, making it easy to build strong practices quickly.
BKG051

Solution Tree | Press

a division of
Solution Tree

Visit SolutionTree.com or call 800.733.6786 to order.